The International Impact
of the Boer War

Edited by Keith Wilson

© Keith Wilson and contributors, 2001

This book is copyright under the Berne Convention.
No reproduction without permission.
All rights reserved.

First published in 2001 by Acumen

Acumen Publishing Limited
15A Lewins Yard
East Street
Chesham HP5 1HQ
www.acumenpublishing.co.uk

ISBN: 1-902683-18-8 (hardcover)
ISBN: 1-902683-19-6 (paperback)

British Library Cataloguing-in-Publication Data
A catalogue record for this book is available from the British Library.

Index by Indexing Specialists, Brighton.
Designed and typeset by Kate Williams, Abergavenny.
Printed and bound by Biddles Ltd., Guildford and King's Lynn.

Undergraduate Lending Library

WITHDRAWN

Contents

Notes on the Contributors

Martin Bossenbroek teaches Dutch history at Leiden University. He has published widely on Dutch colonial, social, and political history, including *Holland op zijn breedst: Indië en Zuid-Afrika in de Nederlandse cultuur omstreeks 1900*. Since 1998 he has been coordinating a project on the return and relief of Second World War victims in the Netherlands.

F. Roy Bridge is Emeritus Professor of Diplomatic History at the University of Leeds. His books include *Great Britain and Austria-Hungary, 1906–14*, *From Sadowa to Sarajevo: the Foreign Policy of Austria-Hungary, 1866–1914* and *The Habsburg Monarchy among the Great Powers, 1814–1918*.

Fernando Dores Costa is the author of *Portugal e a guerra Anglo-Boer 1899–1902* and other works in Portuguese military history.

Gilles Ferragu is on the staff of the Ecole Française de Rome. He is the author of *Camille Barrère: ambassadeur de France, et le rapprochement franco-italien de 1898 à 1914*.

Sandra Ferreira is completing a PhD at the School of Oriental and African Studies at the University of London. She was born in Beira, Mozambique and went to school in South Africa and Portugal.

Peter Henshaw, is a member of the Department of History, Queen's University, Kingston, Canada. His current projects include a book on John Buchan as Governor-General of Canada, and *Britain and South Africa, 1900–94* (with Ronald Hyam).

Martin Kröger published *Le bâton égyptien: Die Rolle der "ägyptischen Frage" in der deutschen Aussenpolitik von 1875/6 bis zur "Entente Cordiale"* in 1991. Between 1990 and 1995 he was a member of the Internationale Historikerkommission zur Herausgabe der "Akten zur deutschen Auswärtigen Politik 1918–45". Most recently, he has published *Vermiedene Kriege: Deeskalation von Konflikten der Grossmächte zwischen Krimkrieg und Erstem Weltkrieg* (with Jost Dülffer and Rolf Harald Wippich).

Pedro Lains is Research Fellow at the Instituto de Ciencias Sociais, University of Lisbon, and Visiting Professor at the Universidade de Evora. He is the author of *A economia portuguesa no seculo XIX*.

Wolfgang J. Mommsen has been Director of the German Historical Institute, London (1977–85) and Professor of Modern and Contemporary History at the University of Düsseldorf. His many publications include *Theories of Imperialism*, and *Bismarck, Europe and Africa: The Berlin Africa Conference, 1884–1885 and the Onset of Partition* (co-editor).

Derek Spring was formerly Senior Lecturer in Russian and East European History at the University of Nottingham. He has published widely on Russian foreign policy before 1914 and has edited and contributed to *Propaganda, Politics and Film, 1918–45*, *The Impact of Gorbachev* and *Stalinism and Soviet Cinema*.

William N. Tilchin teaches international history at Boston University. He is the author of *Theodore Roosevelt and the British Empire* and many historical essays.

Pascal Venier is Lecturer in French History and Politics at the University of Salford. He is the author of *Lyautey avant Lyautey* and is currently working on a monograph on Delcassé and Franco-British relations between 1898 and 1904.

Keith Wilson is Reader in International History at the University of Leeds. He is the author of *The Policy of the Entente*, *Empire and Continent*, *Channel Tunnel Visions, 1850–1945*, and has edited *Decisions for War, 1914* and *Forging the Collective Memory: Governments and International Historians Through Two World Wars*.

Feroz Yasamee is a senior lecturer in the Department of Middle Eastern Studies at the University of Manchester. He is the author of *Ottoman Diplomacy: Abdulhamid II and the Great Powers, 1878–1888*.

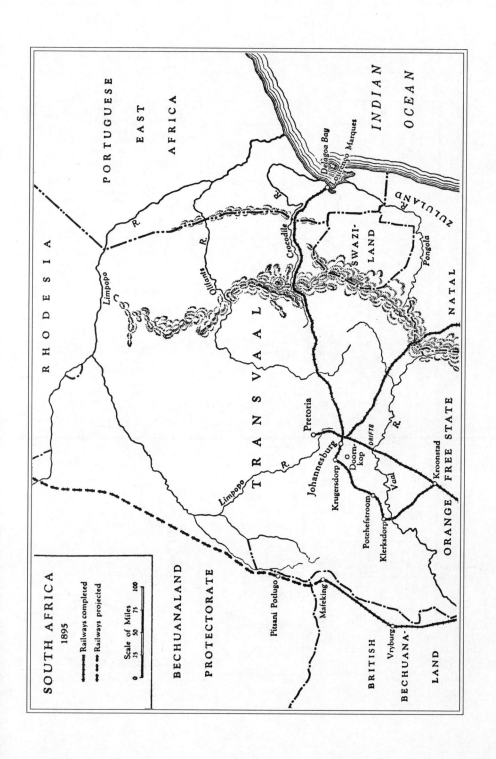

SOUTH AFRICA
1895

Railways completed
Railways projected

Scale of Miles
0   25   50   75   100

PORTUGUESE   EAST   AFRICA

INDIAN   OCEAN

Delagoa Bay
Lourenço Marques

RHODESIA

SWAZI-LAND

ZULULAND

NATAL

Limpopo
R.
Olifants
R.
Crocodile R.
Pongola

T R A N S V A A L

Pretoria
Johannesburg
Krugersdorp
Doornkop
Potchefstroom
Klerksdorp
DRIFTS
Vaal
R.
Kroonstad

ORANGE   FREE   STATE

Limpopo
R.

BECHUANALAND   PROTECTORATE

Pitsani Potlugo
Mafeking
Vryburg

BRITISH
BECHUANA-LAND

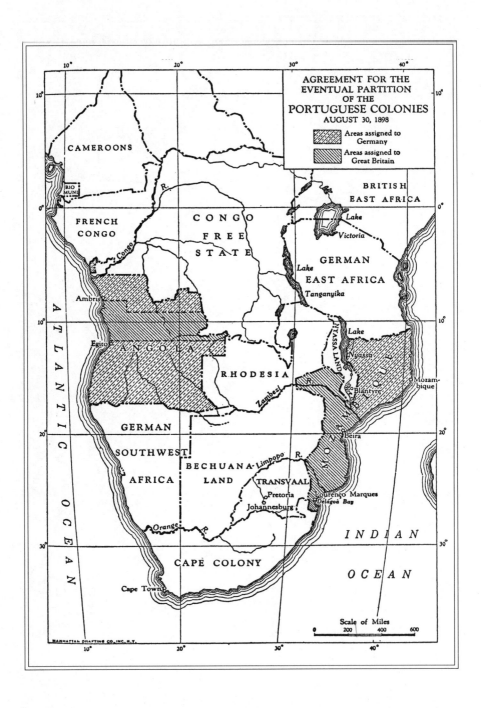

AGREEMENT FOR THE
EVENTUAL PARTITION
OF THE
PORTUGUESE COLONIES
AUGUST 30, 1898

Areas assigned to
Germany

Areas assigned to
Great Britain

CAMEROONS

RIO MUNI

FRENCH
CONGO

CONGO
FREE
STATE

BRITISH
EAST AFRICA

Lake
Victoria

Lake

GERMAN
EAST AFRICA

Tanganyika

Ambris

ANGOLA

Egito

RHODESIA

Zambezi

NYASSA LAND

Lake
Nyassa

Blantyre

Mozam-
bique

GERMAN

SOUTHWEST

AFRICA

BECHUANA-
LAND

Limpopo R.

TRANSVAAL

Pretoria

Johannesburg

Orange R.

Beira

Lourenço Marques
Delagoa Bay

A T L A N T I C
O C E A N

I N D I A N

O C E A N

CAPE COLONY

Cape Town

Scale of Miles

0   200   400   600

MANHATTAN DRAFTING CO., INC., N.Y.

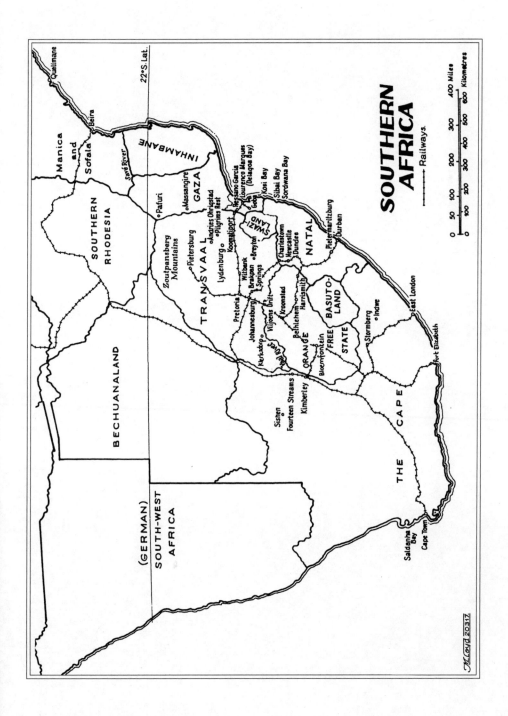

SOUTHERN
AFRICA

→ Railways.

0   50 100   200   300   400 Miles
0   100 200   300 400 500 600 Kilometres

THE CAPE

BECHUANALAND

(GERMAN) SOUTH-WEST AFRICA

SOUTHERN RHODESIA

Manica and Sofala

Savé River

22°S. Lat.

Quelimane

Beira

INHAMBANE

GAZA

Paturi

Massangire

TRANSVAAL

Zoutpansberg Mountains

Pietersburg

Andries Ohrigstad
Pilgrims Rest

Lydenburg

Koomatipoort

Messano Garcia
Lourenço Marques
(Delagoa Bay)
Goba

Kosi Bay
Sibai Bay
Sordwana Bay

SWAZI-LAND

Witbank
Brakpan
Springs

Pretoria

Johannesburg

Kerkdorp

Charlestown
Newcastle
Dundee

Viljoens Drift

Kroonstad

Bethlehem

Harrismith

BASUTO-LAND

NATAL

Pietermaritzburg

Durban

Stormberg

Indwe

East London

Bloemfontein

ORANGE FREE STATE

Kimberley

Fourteen Streams

Sishen

Saldanha Bay

Cape Town

Port Elizabeth

J.F.Loyd 20317

Introduction

Wolfgang J. Mommsen

The Boer War was in many ways the climax of the age of high imperialism.
Numerous factors contributed to it: the material interests of the capitalists on
the Rand, who believed that their interests were best served by a modern
South African state under British rule; the "men on the spot", notably Cecil
Rhodes and Sir Alfred Milner, with their ambitious plans for a future British
Empire that would become a sort of worldwide super-state transcending the
old-fashioned system of reluctant rule by Downing Street assisted by a not
always well informed Colonial Office; the expansionist ambitions of a few
determined imperialists like Joseph Chamberlain; and the concerns of statesmen and the military about the security of the Empire and the status of Britain
within the international system.

Throughout the world the public showed great sympathy with the Boers
and anglophobia reached new heights. The governments of the major powers,
however, took a different line; here real politics dominated and diplomatic
considerations took precedence. It would appear that the other powers were
entangled in imperialist ventures of their own and for this reason were not
inclined to antagonize Britain on account of the fate of the Boers, even though
the latter enjoyed a great deal of support among the public, and although it
was not in doubt that this was an unjust war brought about by the British
despite the fact that military operations had been commenced by the
Transvaal. All the same, the Boer War had considerable repercussions in the
international arena. It affected, however indirectly, the alliance systems and
the international balance of power in many ways, with far-reaching consequences. This is the theme of the collection of essays assembled in this
volume.

The interplay of local and international causes of the Boer War is assessed
by Peter Henshaw in an exemplary manner. He emphasizes the general
considerations that motivated the British government to opt for a radical

solution of the South African problem, in particular the notion that the British Empire must maintain its hegemonial status at the Cape, a status that seemed to be threatened by the rise of the Transvaal into a major power in the region. Given that, due to the rapidly changing economic conditions there, all the other territories in South Africa were gravitating towards the rapidly growing economic centre of the Rand, it was envisaged that sooner rather than later the region would be dominated by the Boer republics. The prospect of a future United States of South Africa under Boer rule worried the decision-makers in London and elsewhere a great deal, and in this context the conventional strategic argument that the Cape shipping route must remain firmly under British control played an important role. This was the reason why the Boer Republic had to be brought under British rule. The Uitlanders issue as such played a secondary role. Even the industrialists of the Rand considered this an issue that could be solved in negotiation with the Transvaal government without recourse to war. Rather, it served as a tool to bring matters to a head and force President Kruger into war.

The British government, moreover, was afraid that if the Boers got their way, other European powers might try to acquire a foothold in South Africa as well as themselves, either by territorial gain or by establishing coaling stations in the region, which might develop into naval stations that could threaten Britih hegemony at the Cape. They were concerned that their European rivals harboured plans for economic expansion in this region, which a South African Federation of States under Boer dominance would greatly encourage. These fears applied in the first place to Imperial Germany, but in some ways also to France, still seen as a major rival to British imperial power. Ambitions of territorial gain, however, did not play a significant role in the considerations of the decision-makers in London. They were not on the agenda of Lord Salisbury at all. With the exception of Joseph Chamberlain, the British were loath to further increase imperial burdens, whether in South Africa or elsewhere. The predicaments of British imperial policy at the turn of the century were already substantial, as Keith Wilson describes in his contribution to this volume. The race for a foothold in China had commenced with Germany's seizure of Kiao-Chow in 1897, followed by the Russian occupation of Port Arthur. A dispute over Samoa between Britain, Germany and the US remained unresolved. The position of Britain in the Persian Gulf and Afghanistan was threatened by further Russian encroachments. There was even the fear that Russia might increase its potential threat to the British Raj in India. These concerns were substantial enough to induce the policy-makers in London to consider seriously a change in the overall direction of British foreign policy and to look out for possible allies instead of maintaining "splendid isolation".

Since 1895 the South African question had been at the forefront of British imperial policy, because of the machinations of the "men on the spot", who were not inclined to compromise, as Gladstone had done after Majuba Hill in 1881. London's concerns about the possible threat to British paramountcy in South Africa posed by the ascendancy of the Transvaal probably would not have led to war without the activities of the British High Commissioner, Milner, who persistently worked for a radical solution. The Uitlander issue was pursued by him with the utmost vigour, not because it was all that important (the number of English-speaking Uitlanders in the Transvaal was much smaller than was claimed at the time, and for the most part the industrialists were not very concerned about it) but because it could be used as a tool to push the Transvaal government into war. Milner, for one, and Rhodes, for another, were convinced that British imperial interests could be secured only by the ending of the sovereignty of the Boer republics, although this could be achieved only by war. Even Joseph Chamberlain, who in principle stood for the maintenance of British paramountcy at the Cape at all costs, advised Milner in July 1899 to take a less rigid stance on the issue of enfranchising the Uitlanders.

On the other hand, it cannot be doubted that Chamberlain, although not the British government in its entirety, had long envisaged a war in order to subdue the Boer republics. There can be no doubt that the rapprochement with Germany that was advocated by Chamberlain was, at least in part, intended to get the potentially most dangerous adversary in the European arena out of the way in case a conflict arose in South Africa. It may well be doubted that Chamberlain was in earnest when he suggested that the three Teutonic peoples – the British, the Germans and the Americans – were destined to become joint rulers over the indigenous peoples of the world. In German historiography the myth has long been spread that Germany was in a position to forge a German–British alliance, which would have solved the problems of German world politics once and for all.

Actually, neither the British, not even Chamberlain, nor the Germans, were prepared to go that far. Prince Bülow and his advisers believed that Germany must not tie itself either to Britain or to Russia. They preferred to retain the advantages of a "free hand", given their expectation that Anglo–Russian antagonism would dominate European politics for a long time to come. Moreover, Bülow did not relish becoming the "junior partner" of the British in imperial politics, for this would not square with Germany's international status as one of the Great Powers in the European system of states. Nor did British statesmen believe that a formal alliance with Germany would deliver the desired goods, as Germany, with its long Eastern frontier, was permanently exposed to Russian pressure. The risk of becoming embroiled in a conflict between Tsarist Russia and the Central Powers, in which conflict the British had no direct stake, was much too high. However, this did not preclude a substantial re-alignment of German and British policies concerning concrete issues that would reduce existing tensions and open up the way for future cooperation.

From the German point of view an agreement on the Portuguese colonies in Africa, solicited by the British government in 1898, was an important step in the right direction; for it improved the chances of dividing up the Portuguese colonies in Africa in the foreseeable future, on the assumption that sooner or later the Portuguese would have to give up their colonial possessions due to financial difficulties. It was the predicament of German "world politics", which Bülow proclaimed with great fervour, that at that time it consisted of little more than a bundle of hollow propaganda phrases. As yet, Bülow had nothing concrete to display: the German share of Samoa was in dispute; the commercial value of Kiao-Chow was doubtful; and no other overseas colonial opportunities were in sight. For an agreement that delivered the prospect of a substantial share of the Portuguese colonies, Bülow was prepared to persuade William II to abandon the Boer republics, whose independence the emperor had been considering helping to maintain by force of arms as recently as 1895–96. Portuguese colonies would round off the scattered German possessions in Central Africa in a satisfactory way. The secret agreement concerning the Portuguese colonies in Africa was a typical imperialist treaty that, although couched in pragmatic terms and using peaceful language, in fact rested on the assumption that, sooner or later, there would arise an opportunity to implement this claim to colonial territory by diplomatic means, but, if needs be, by recourse to force as well. By participating in a loan to Portugal, guaranteed by taxes and duties of her colonies, a formal claim could be made for an eventual territorial takeover.

The British government, however, devised ways and means to make sure that such a situation would not arise. In 1899 the seventeenth-century British guarantee of Portuguese possesions was formally renewed. Although in formal terms this did not conflict with the Anglo–German agreement, it ensured that the Anglo–German agreement would not be implemented. The conclusion of the so-called Treaty of Windsor was a piece of shrewd statesmanship on the part of the British, but one must add that, in a way, it was forced on them by the Portuguese, whose cooperation during the Boer War was even more important than the connivance of the Germans. All the same, the primary objective of the Anglo–German treaty of 1898 was achieved, namely the deflection of German colonial expansion away from the southern regions of Mozambique and especially from Delagoa Bay. What is more, the Germans formally undertook not to interfere in South African affairs if conflict with the Boer republics arose again. For the moment it mattered little that the Germans were, from the beginning, deprived of ever realizing their part of this mutually acquisitive bargain!

No more than the British did the German government seriously consider the rapprochement reached by the Anglo–German treaty of 1898 to be of a lasting nature. The ambitious naval construction programme of Tirpitz was launched at almost the same time. Ostensibly the strong navy to be built within the next two decades was merely to protect German commerce on the high seas. In fact, it was directed against Britain, which as a result of the potential threat of a strong German battle fleet in the North Sea would be

4

forced in the future to give proper consideration to German colonial demands. Even worse, after the commencement of the Boer War the German authorities were primarily interested in exploiting anti-British emotions among the public in order to get the Navy Bills accepted by a Reichstag that initially had been unwilling to grant the enormous sums necessary for this venture, and this for many years to come. "Friendship with the British" was therefore not the tune that the government was inclined to play *vis-à-vis* German public opinion. Moreover, Bülow found it difficult to sell the official policy line on South African affairs, a line that demanded absolute neutrality, to a German public infatuated with sympathies for the Boers. His ambivalent statements did not make him any friends, either at home or in Britain. One thing is certain: there was little love lost between the Germans and the British in spite of the 1898 treaty, a settlement of the Samoan dispute hastily agreed upon, and a treaty of October 1900 on Chinese matters, which, in the end, satisfied neither party. Agreements that both partners enter into with reservations, and, in the case of the British, with a good deal of duplicity, are rarely a secure basis for establishing lasting friendly relations.

Even so, the Anglo–German rapprochement was enough to become a worrying issue for other powers, notably Russia. As Derek Spring demonstrates in his contribution, the Russian suggestion that, possibly, the other European powers ought jointly to intervene in the conflict and enforce a speedy ending of the war, thus securing the independence of the Boer republics, was in the first place a *ballon d'essai* in order to find out more about the state of Anglo–German relations. It was not a serious venture, all the less so as Muraviev had made it a condition that Germany should take the lead in this matter, which, in the circumstances, the Germans could not possibly do without losing face. The precondition for a joint intervention by the powers, namely the formal recognition by France of the results of the Peace of Frankfurt (1871) was more than a little far-fetched.

In fact, most of the European powers did give some thought to the possibility that the predicament of the British in South Africa might be exploited in order to promote or secure imperialist designs of their own elsewhere. In the end, however, none of them actually did so, with the possible exception of Portugal. By observing benevolent neutrality bordering on active support of the British forces that were landed in and supplied through Delagoa Bay, Portugal forced the British government to guarantee the Portuguese colonial empire against any future encroachment by third parties. This would have infuriated the Germans had they known about it. The French foreign minister, Delcassé, made no real attempt to exploit the situation, even though revenge for Fashoda might have been on the cards. The Italian government, on the other hand, was concerned that the British would do badly in their campaign against the Boer republics, and feared that this would encourage the French to make expansionist moves in the Mahgreb, thus forestalling future Italian imperialist designs in that region. In the event, the Italians were all too happy to conclude with France an agreement that alleviated their fears. As far as the US was concerned, the British had taken steps at an early stage to accommodate American wishes in other overseas matters, including Samoa and the Philippines. In a way, the imperialist objectives of the Great Powers and their mutual treaty obligations were entangled with one another in such ways as to cancel each other out in this particular case. Hence, the British got away with what was, at bottom, an unjust war without any intervention by other powers, either during or after the end of the fighting.

European public opinion was, on the whole, solidly in favour of the Boers. This sympathy was to be found in many quarters, and it naturally fostered anti-English feelings. This was particularly the case in Germany, where a violent outburst of popular anglophobia was triggered off. General Colmar von der Goltz concluded from the evidence of the Boer War that a war between Germany and Britain was unavoidable. He preached to the German nationalist right that such a war was likely to be protracted, that it would be a war for existence for both nations, and that it could be won by Germany.

In the Netherlands, the ties of kinship with the Boers, however dated they really were, fostered the sympathy with their case even more strongly. There even developed a popular movement that dreamt of a revival of the historic Dutch dominance in South Africa. These romantic ideas were, however, not held universally; rather, support for the Boers was fragmented, at least when it came to deeds. These vague South African schemes were by no means in line with actual Dutch imperial policies, which counted in the eyes of the protestant middle classes far more than the prospects of a "Dutch Republic" in South Africa. The difficult situation that the Dutch faced in Indonesia, where they were involved in a protracted war with the Sultan of Aceh, banned any conflict with Britain on behalf of the Boers. Rather, it was advisable to seek a friendly understanding with the British, who had just established themselves in Borneo. Even in the Dutch case imperialist ambitions worked in favour of the official Dutch policy of strict neutrality during the Boer War.

Nowhere did the popular sympathy with the struggle of the Boers for independence influence substantially the attitudes of the European powers. In all cases, including that of the US, it was thought sensible to avoid any active conflict with the British. Perhaps most outspoken in this respect was Austria-Hungary. The Austrian establishment was united on this point, whatever the public might say, and Emperor Francis Joseph condemned the obstinacy of the Boers in the strongest terms. The decisive motive was that the Austrians did not want to put at risk the however loose support of the British in their long-standing rivalry with Russia in the Balkans. Austrian public opinion was another matter. It was fortunate for the British that in Vienna foreign policy was still made exclusively by the emperor and the imperial government. Indeed, the leading statesmen there showed their disdain for public opinion and its support for the Boer cause. As Roy Bridge puts it aptly in his contribution to this volume, foreign policy was still being conducted by a small cosmopolitan elite "with a lofty disregard for the passions of the masses and the demands of press and public opinion". But this era was, as he points out, rapidly drawing to a close.

It soon turned out that public opinion could no longer be dismissed as marginal. The Germans had to realize this perhaps most directly. The pressure of the German public, which was deeply dissatisfied with the management of foreign affairs during the Boer War and its aftermath, undermined the public status of the imperial government as well as that of Chancellor Bülow. The flood-wave of an aggressive nationalism, which had evolved during these years, could never again be brought under control by the German government. This came to be a major factor that, in July 1914, pushed the German and Austro-Hungarian élites, against their own better judgement, over the brink of war.

Changes also took place in Britain, although perhaps in the opposite direction. The protest movement against the conduct of the Boer War, which emerged after 1901, eventually helped to produce a shift in the political climate. Chamberlain was driven into the political wilderness and the Liberal Campbell-Bannerman won a landslide victory in the General Election of 1906 on an essentially anti-imperialist programme. Moreover, the South African Federation created in 1906 eventually drifted out of the control of Whitehall. In the very long run, the struggle for the maintenance of British paramountcy in South Africa by crushing the Boer republics proved fruitless. The contributions to this volume demonstrate, however, that the international system was deeply affected by the upheaval of the Boer War, in multifarious ways. Although on the surface of things all seemed much as it had been before, the long-term repercussions were momentous.

CHAPTER ONE

The Origins of the Boer War[1]

The Periphery, the Centre and the "Man on the Spot"

Peter Henshaw

After the passage of a century and the appearance of countless publications on the Boer War, there remain the most profound differences of opinion about the war's origins. Many of the more recent accounts have emphasized Britain's economic interests in the southern African periphery – principally in the production and supply of gold – and the consequent necessity of removing the administratively backward and economically obstructionist regime of Paul Kruger in Pretoria.[2] Other accounts have stressed the concerns of British government decision-makers at the imperial centre – concerns about British power and prestige, about the necessity of maintaining British paramountcy in southern Africa, and about safeguarding the strategically vital Cape route.[3] Further divisions exist between those accounts that stress the broader structural forces at play and those that give a central role to key individuals such as Sir Alfred Milner (Britain's High Commissioner and regional proconsul for southern Africa) or Joseph Chamberlain (the colonial secretary in London).[4] This chapter will attempt to explain the war's origins through an analysis combining the broader economically driven developments in southern Africa, the geopolitical concerns of decision-makers in London and the influence of Milner as the key "man on the spot" and intermediary between the periphery and the centre.[5]

This explanation will be based on a model of imperial expansion first proposed by Ronald Hyam.[6] Hyam's model presumes that an event such as the Boer War cannot be explained except in terms of the *interaction* between the colonial periphery and the imperial centre, interaction in which the influence of the British government's proconsular "man on the spot" might be crucial. Developments within southern Africa could not by themselves be decisive. Nor could actions solely by decision-makers in London or solely by the British High Commissioner. The model further presumes that economic forces and motives had their greatest influence on developments in the periphery, while decisions at the centre were determined by geopolitical calculations relating to Britain's power and prestige in relation to other states. Finally, Hyam's model indicates how individual human agency could shape the course of events; how the action of a man such as Milner operating at the point of "proconsular interlock" could have disproportionate significance.

The "two-level"-"proconsular interlock" model will be used to tie together several arguments about the origins of the Boer War. The first is that the gold mining industry of the Transvaal – the private and public wealth that it created, and the pressures for economic and political change that it stimulated – produced some of the key local pressures for a showdown with the Kruger regime in the 1890s. Some mining capitalists, concerned about the declining profitability of their investments, saw their salvation in a radical transformation of the Transvaal state, a transformation that would clear the way for cost-reducing reforms. Some even saw that this could best be achieved by promoting the cause of Uitlander rights (i.e. the rights of foreign white settlers in the Transvaal). This would produce a Transvaal dominated by British settlers rather than Boers; a territory more likely to form part of a larger British dominion of South Africa; a state better adapted to meet the long-term needs of the mining industry. The second argument is that the activities of this gold mining industry also intensified the pressures felt by decision-makers in London to assert British paramountcy in southern Africa; but that these pressures at the centre were quite different in nature and character from the ones shaping developments at the periphery. The chief fear of the British government in London was that the wealth of the mines would not only enable the Transvaal to assert its independence from Britain, but it would also enable the Transvaal to dominate the region economically and, eventually, politically. This threatened British ascendancy in the Cape Colony and Natal, damaging enough in terms of London's strategic preoccupation with the protection of the Cape sea route to India and the East. No less importantly and more immediately, though, a strong Transvaal aspiring for independence was a source of grave uncertainty and weakness in Britain's dealings with its European rivals, particularly Germany but also France and Russia. For the British government, then, the political and economic transformation of the Transvaal was less important as an end in itself than as a *means* of removing this weakness and uncertainty. Indeed, once it became apparent that the Transvaal could use the Delagoa Bay route through Portuguese East Africa to escape from dependence on British ports and railways, it was clear to Milner and the Colonial Office that early intervention on the issue of British settler rights was the only effective means of asserting control over the Transvaal. The third argument is that the interests of the British government and of the mining capitalists, while generally quite different or even conflicting, coincided on the issue of the political transformation of the Transvaal. Both came to see that this could best be brought about through Uitlander enfranchisement. Both were encouraged to adopt this view by Milner, who, through his influence at the point of interlock between the centre and the periphery, was able to build up the Uitlander issue and shape events in a way that made war almost inevitable.

I

Although debate persists, most historians would now agree that by the mid-1890s the main source of local pressure for a radical transformation of the Transvaal state came from those mining capitalists who were concerned about the profitability of their long-range mining programmes.[7] These mining capitalists were particularly anxious about the extra and, in their view, unnecessary costs their operations had to bear because of the inadequate supply and control of cheap labour; because the granting of monopolies for the supply and manufacture of such vital inputs as dynamite significantly raised their price; and because tariffs, customs duties and railway rates further increased costs of production either directly or indirectly through the higher local cost of living. Such concerns are generally seen as the principal cause of the Jameson raid – the attempt, led by the mine magnate Cecil Rhodes and tacitly supported by Chamberlain, to overthrow the Kruger regime through the combination of an armed incursion and an Uitlander rebellion on the Rand.[8]

The failure of the raid in December 1895, and the subsequent steps taken by the Transvaal government to address the grievances of the mine owners and the Uitlanders, may have induced some mining capitalists to work with the Kruger regime rather than to seeks its overthrow; but for the remainder of the 1890s some powerful mining interests continued to agitate for more radical change there. For many mining capitalists the key thing was that the Transvaal should "modernize" to the benefit of the mining industry. How that modernization came about, and whether a modernized Transvaal should be inside or outside the British Empire, were entirely secondary. Some mining capitalists would conclude, however, that their interests might be better served by a united British South Africa. The most important of these were associated with the Wernher-Beit & Eckstein group and its allies.[9] By the late 1890s they were particularly powerful by virtue of their extensive control of the English-language press in southern Africa. Moreover, it now seems evident that this group remained seriously concerned about the long-term profitability of their operations in the absence of a major political transformation of the region. They were worried not only about the additional costs arising out of the Transvaal's protectionist and monopolistic policies, but also about the general inefficiency of the Transvaal state, the unpredictability of its politics and policies and the threat of arbitrarily high and ruinous new taxes.[10] "There is no law and no appeal against any decision" in the Transvaal, complained one capitalist in November 1898.[11] And, no less importantly, they remained concerned about the supply and control of cheap labour and looked to a united, reformed and British South Africa to provide the state structures in which in their operations might prosper.[12]

This was the context in which some mining interests pressed the case for Uitlander rights in 1898 and 1899, seeing it as the best way of securing the political and economic transformation they desired. Isolation from the Uitlander cause was seen as a real danger. It would play into the hands of the Kruger regime, which was seeking to promote division between Uitlander mines workers and the capitalists. It would also antagonize Milner, who was so evidently trying to promote Uitlander rights. As one capitalist noted, Transvaal

> legislators and other big officials . . . are determined to make as much as they can and squeeze the industry to the utmost. Hence this official campaign carried on by official organs against capitalists. They do all they can to get the poorer classes up in arms against capital.[13]

In the view of the Wernher-Beit & Eckstein group, the safest course was to support the Uitlander cause in the hope that a new regime would soon emerge in the Transvaal, a regime that would be sympathetic to the British connection and, more importantly, to mining interests as well.[14]

A further force for political change and regional integration in southern Africa was exerted by the requirements of railway finance. The governments of the Cape Colony, Natal, the Orange Free State and the Transvaal were all heavily dependent on the revenues generated either directly or indirectly by the railways. Customs duties, transit duties and railway receipts were closely interlinked and were the mainstays of government revenue in the region. A large proportion of the Cape Colony and Natal's government debt arose from capital expenditure on government-owned railways. These had been built principally to link their ports with mineral producing areas of the interior.[15] The Delagoa Bay route – on which neither the port nor the railway was British controlled – was the shortest link between the Rand and the sea. If properly developed and managed it promised to become the cheapest and most heavily used route. These facts were perfectly apparent at the time, not only to governments in southern Africa but also to decision-makers in London. The latter saw that the Transvaal's largely independent access to the sea through Delagoa Bay gave the Kruger regime an increasing degree of leverage in dealing with other governments in the region, leverage that might lead to political domination. Lord Selborne, the junior minister at the Colonial Office, outlined the problem for Lord Salisbury, the prime minister and foreign secretary. If the Delagoa Bay railway were operated by Transvaal or other hostile interests, they could reduce the governments of the Cape and Natal:

to the verge of bankruptcy, so dependent are they upon their railway revenue. It needs no words to prove what a powerful use could be made of this instrument in squeezing the British South African Colonies into joining a United South African Republic.[16]

It was partly because of the unifying forces of railway geography and finance that the Colonial Office believed that southern Africa would either unite "into a confederacy on the model of the Dominion of Canada and under the British flag" or "inevitably amalgamate itself into a United States of South Africa".[17] Another economic force encouraging the political unification of southern Africa was the wealth generated by, and the population attracted to the Transvaal's gold mining industry. As Selborne noted in 1896:

> South African politics must revolve around the Transvaal, which will be the only possible market for the agricultural produce or the manufactures of Cape Colony and Natal. The commercial attraction of the Transvaal will be so great that a Union of the South African states with it will be absolutely necessary for their prosperous existence. The only question in my mind is whether that Union will be inside or outside the British Empire.[18]

Within southern Africa, powerful economic forces were not only pushing for a radical transformation of the Transvaal state. They were also tending to draw the region together under the leadership of the local economic power-house: the Transvaal. As far as the British government was concerned, the crucial question was whether the Transvaal's transformation and the region's integration would weaken or strengthen Britain's power and prestige locally and in the wider world.

II

Whatever the methods and motives of individuals and groups seeking to influence British policy in southern Africa, government decision-makers in London conceived and justified their southern African polices in terms of national power and prestige. Power in this context meant armed and economic strength in relation to other states. This of course had geographical and territorial dimensions to the extent that political control of key parts of the globe conferred strategic advantage. Strategy in the official British parlance of the day related to more than just the projection of, or defence against, armed force. It also related to a mercantilist concern to protect the sea-borne trade on which Britain and the empire depended for their material strength. Prestige related to the perceptions of both Britain's power and its willingness to defend its interests. It was "power based on reputation" or the "shadow cast by power".[19]

During the 1890s, decision-makers in London became increasingly concerned about the impact of southern African developments on Britain's power and prestige, not only within southern Africa but also in the European and wider international context. The most threatening of these developments arose from the Transvaal growing ever stronger on the back of the mining industry and ever more anxious to assert its independence from Britain. So long as Britain's control over the region was in doubt, Britain's European rivals could be expected to exploit this uncertainty to Britain's international disadvantage. Indeed, it was the wider international implications of this uncertainty that explain why Salisbury and the Foreign Office were so anxious to force a showdown with the Transvaal on the question of British paramountcy.[20] From London's perspective, the threat posed to British power and prestige by an independent Transvaal could best be removed by forcing Pretoria to accept Britain's supremacy in principle and to implement the political reforms that would ensure Britain's predominance in practice.

The pivotal point in any consideration of British power in southern Africa was the strategic significance of the Cape route. The importance of this route had diminished little, if at all, after the opening of the Suez Canal in 1869. The Admiralty intelligence department was clear about this in an 1897 report: "It is impossible to over-estimate the strategical value of the Cape. In the probable event of the interruption in time of war of the Suez canal route to the East, the Cape would at once become the most important coaling station of the Empire". This report also reiterated the accepted wisdom of the 1882 Royal Commission on Defence that the defence of the Cape route was "essential to the retention by Great Britain of her possessions in India, Mauritius, Ceylon and even Australasia".[21] The Cape route's defence had three main dimensions: first, the protection of the Royal Navy's main dock-yard and repair facility at Simon's Town on the Cape peninsula; secondly, the protection of the other key British coaling stations in the region – St Helena, Cape Town, Durban and Mauritius; and, thirdly, the prevention of rival powers' gaining a controlling influence at other ports in the region, ports from which they might threaten British maritime traffic.

By the 1890s, the chief local problem associated with maintaining control of Simon's Town and the other ports in British southern Africa was to ensure that the internally self-governing colonies of the Cape and Natal remained firmly within the British Empire. Some decision-makers in London sought to hedge Britain's strategic bets by proceeding on the assumption that in the final resort Britain would always be able to hang on to Simon's Town, even if the rest of southern Africa were lost. In fact, it was with such an eventuality in mind that in 1897 the Salisbury Cabinet agreed that the expensive new dockyard proposed for the Cape should be built at Simon's Town rather than Cape Town. The alternative view, though, had been stated clearly by Lord

Kimberley in 1881 (a statement published in his memoirs in 1898): "It is an entire delusion to imagine that we could hold Cape Town, abandoning the rest. If we allow our supremacy in South Africa to be taken from us, we shall be ousted before long from that country altogether".[22] The War Office also assumed that it was "impossible, for obvious political reasons, to create a Gibraltar out of the Cape Peninsula, and that the permanent retention of this peninsula . . . is dependent upon the maintenance of British ascendancy in all South African Colonies".[23] But, whatever was thought in London about possible futures in southern Africa, it seems clear that most senior British decision-makers believed that strategically valuable coaling stations, anchorages and dockyards in southern Africa could best be safeguarded by the establishment of a large united British dominion there.

In addition to the strategic dangers of a gradual drift of the Cape and Natal towards the Transvaal and away from the British Empire, there was the more immediate threat that the Transvaal would seek to assert its regional predominance by force of arms. The Transvaal's purchase of huge quantities of arms and ammunition in the 1890s was thought to have completely altered the local strategic situation. In 1896 one Colonial Office official noted that "it is now quite clear that the Boers have arms and ammunition enough to shoot down all the armies of Europe".[24] In 1898 Major Edward Altham, Britain's senior military intelligence officer in South Africa, warned that the scale of the Transvaal's military preparations pointed:

> to the existence of a definite policy which will build up a Dutch Oligarchy in South Africa strong enough to shake off English suzerainty when favourable opportunity offers, and, perhaps, even to carry out the larger dream of a great Dutch independent State reaching from the Zambezi down to the Hottentots Holland Mountains, and with Delagoa Bay as its sea port.[25]

Field Marshal Lord Wolseley, the commander-in-chief of the British Army, concurred: "sooner or later we shall have a violent explosion" in South Africa. "Were we now or at any time in the near future to have any serious trouble with a foreign power, that explosion would take place at once".[26] European tensions thus intersected with and exacerbated the Transvaal armed threat. Great Power rivalries thereby served to increase the British government's determination to assert its ascendancy in southern Africa.

The chief threats posed to the Cape route by rival European powers were all linked to the problem of Britain's uncertain paramountcy in southern Africa. The Cape route could never be secure so long as the Transvaal sought to assert its independence from Britain. This was true whether the Transvaal acted alone or as the leading influence in a United States of South Africa outside the British Empire. In 1896 Selborne recorded that:

So long as the British South African Colonies have not united with the Transvaal into a British Dominion . . . France and Germany will . . . strive only to disintegrate British influence and Empire in South Africa by playing off the different South African states against each other and by helping the Transvaal in its game of attracting British Colonies away from the British Empire.[27]

Should a United States of South Africa be established, France would seek to strengthen its strategic position in Madagascar where its naval base at Diego Suarez had been "established avowedly as the head-quarters of offence against our commerce passing round the Cape for India".[28] Moreover, "The next day after the United States of South Africa had declared her independence Germany would walk into Walfisch Bay", the Cape-controlled port on the coast of German South-West Africa.[29] Hence, even if a United States of South Africa could be induced to keep rival powers out of its own ports and to allow Britain to retain Simon's Town, it was likely that the loss of British paramountcy would allow rival European powers to gain bases in neighbouring territories from which to threaten the Cape route.

There was a further strategic threat associated with Britain's lack of control over the Transvaal. This was that a rival power might gain a commercial foothold in Portugal's southern African empire and turn this to strategic advantage. Typical of such anxieties was a report by Britain's chief representative in Pretoria in 1897 about the development of a German trading concession at Delagoa Bay to serve a proposed new line of Transvaal steamers. This development might include a coaling station

> under the management of German officers, which might serve in case of need as a naval station; and, as these commercial vessels will be manned by able-bodied German seamen, up to the standard of the Imperial Navy, Germany would thus secure a footing in peace or war in Lourenço Marques.[30]

The Anglo-German Convention of August 1898 was intended to reduce such German threats in southern Africa, but, to the horror of the Colonial Office (which was shut out of the British negotiations with Germany), the convention not only permitted the development of port facilities at Delagoa Bay by a German company, but it also renounced Britain's previous right of veto over such developments.[31] The strategic threat posed by German or French commercial developments in Portuguese territory would, though, be much reduced if the Transvaal no longer sought to encourage such schemes as a way of reducing its dependence on British controlled railways and ports.

The strategic significance of southern Africa, and of the Cape route more generally, was not confined to matters of naval warfare and military transport routes. It also related to trade protection. This fact is crucial to understanding British policy debates in the 1890s, although it has typically been over-looked or misunderstood by historians. The link between strategy and trade could not have been more apparent than in the Admiralty report[32] that formed the basis of the great naval works programme of the 1890s – a programme that included the allocation in 1899 of £2.5m for the construc-tion of a "first-class dock" at Simon's Town.[33] This report noted that through the East Indies, Cape and China Stations "lie the great trade routes to the East, whether the Suez canal be blocked or not, and the importance of protecting them will be vital".[34] This point was repeated in Cabinet memoranda in 1896, 1898 and 1899.[35] It was also made in the House of Commons by Austen Chamberlain, a junior Admiralty minister, in his defence of the Naval Works Bill: "The importance of the Cape is patent to everyone. It is a great calling place for our trade in time of peace, and a much larger volume of trade would, probably, pass there in war time".[36] Even the Admiralty's own assessments of the strategic value of ports were based in considerable measure on the amount of trade that passed through them.[37] To some extent this reflected nothing more than a recognition of the fairly obvious point that Britain's wealth and power were more heavily dependent on sea-borne trade than those of its great rivals. It also reflected a recognition that national commercial interests were often in this period the basis on which Great Powers made political or terri-torial claims in areas controlled by weaker states. It should therefore come as no surprise that the British government so concerned itself with questions of trade and commercial concessions in this period, and particularly with the threats posed by rival powers to British trade and commerce.

In southern Africa this concern centred on the efforts being made by Ameri-can, French and, above all, German enterprises to secure larger shares of the region's trade and commerce. Colonial and Foreign Office representatives in southern Africa, the Board of Trade and the inter-departmental Commercial Intelligence Committee in London all paid close attention to such matters in the 1890s. And they gave special attention to reports that Germany and France might be using subsidized shipping rates, preferential customs and railway rates, or monopolistic concessions to secure a larger share of the Transvaal trade.[38] Whatever the private calculations of the German government in this period,[39] there continued to be concerns in Whitehall after the signing of the 1898 Anglo-German Convention that German and Transvaal interests would conspire to increase the German economic stake in southern Africa at Britain's expense.[40] And there were fears of similar conspiracies involving France.[41] But however worrying these developments may have been economically, it seems that the principal concern at the senior decision-making level in London was that they all increased the possibility that the Transvaal would succeed in asserting its independence and in becoming the leader of a United States of South Africa.

The British government's concerns about the mining industry and gold sales seem to have been based on similar anxieties about the future of British paramountcy in southern Africa and about the interference by rival powers in free British trade. This may certainly be inferred from a Colonial Office note written in December 1898. Henry Lambert noted that the Transvaal's restrictive economic policies, particularly the granting of monopolies to non-British firms, would cripple the territory in the long run; the immediate result was "loss to the mining industry run mainly by English capital and the deanglicising of the country by emigration of the English, Australians etc. who cannot get work".[42] If the British Uitlander population declined sufficiently, the British government would lose what seemed to be its best means of asserting control there: to insist that Pretoria grant full political rights to British subjects in the Transvaal, something that would (it was assumed) lead to the establishment of a pro-British government in Pretoria. If senior political decision-makers in London were anxious about the production and sale of Transvaal gold itself (and there is still no direct evidence from the late 1890s to demonstrate the existence of such anxieties) it seems likely that they would have had no more than a general concern to ensure that rival European powers did not conspire with the Transvaal to take control of the gold trade away from Britain. There is certainly no reason to suppose that anyone in the Salisbury Cabinet had a clear understanding of Transvaal gold's specific significance for the London gold market or for the Bank of England's management of sterling as an international currency.[43] Such concerns as were expressed by British officials focused on the problem of how gold was shipped from southern Africa and to which destinations. Close attention was paid to the redirection of gold away from British ships departing from Cape Town, to be carried instead by German and French ships sailing from Delagoa Bay.[44] But the concern seems have been as much about the fact that Britain's European rivals were taking control of this trade as about the fact that less Transvaal gold was flowing directly to London.

In the 1890s senior British decision-makers were beset by fears about southern African threats to British power and prestige, threats that arose from the weakness and uncertainty of Britain's position there. The first threat was that most of southern Africa would gradually fall under the control of an independent and anti-British Transvaal. This would not only endanger British control of strategically vital ports in the Cape Colony and Natal, but it would also provide an opportunity for Britain's European rivals to gain a foothold in other ports in the region – most dangerously Delagoa Bay and Walfisch Bay – from which to challenge British control of the Cape route. The second threat was that the Transvaal would assert its independence and regional predominance by force of arms the moment that Britain became engaged in a serious military confrontation with another Great Power. The third was that Britain's European rivals would continually conspire with the Transvaal to undermine British influence in the region, seeking wherever possible either to challenge Britain's local economic and strategic dominance or to exploit Britain's weakness in southern Africa for geopolitical gain elsewhere in the world – as indeed was the German goal in the negotiation of the 1898 Anglo-German Convention.[45] The obvious, and perhaps the only way to defuse these threats was to make clear both to the Transvaal and to rival powers that Britain was the paramount power. To impose order on the region the British government wished ultimately to unite the Boer republics with the British colonies there. The precursor to that was the establishment of a pro-British regime in Pretoria. And, as it turned out, the most effective way of doing all that in the local, British and international political circumstances of the late 1890s was to insist that Pretoria recognize the political rights of British Uitlanders. This recognition would, it was thought, transform the Transvaal and the region to the great benefit of Britain's power and prestige, locally and around the world.

III

While economic conditions within southern Africa, and concerns in London about British power and prestige, generated converging pressures for a rapid transformation of the Transvaal state and for the political unification of rival colonies in the region, war might not have broken out in 1899 without the intervention of Milner, Britain's determined and influential proconsul. He successfully linked and harnessed the local and metropolitan pressures for change in the Transvaal. He did so by building up the Uitlander issue as the one that could best serve the often divergent interests of the British government and the mining capitalists. And he was able to exert a crucial influence over the course and timing of events by virtue of his position as the "man on the spot" controlling the lines of communication between the imperial centre and the southern African periphery.[46]

Milner himself recognized clearly what was at stake in southern Africa; at stake economically for the mines and geopolitically for Britain and its empire. From his contacts with mining capitalists he knew all about the problems the mines faced as a result of Kruger's policies. But he was also an imperial visionary who saw the importance for the empire as a whole of a strong, united and *British* South Africa. And he was a realist in international affairs, who believed that Britain needed a united empire in order to stand up to its Great Power rivals. Much of the world was watching British policy in southern Africa. A failure to defend British interests, or the rights of British subjects there, was bound to undermine Britain's prestige in the eyes of many. Furthermore, he hoped that South Africa was going "not only to federate itself as a free nation like Canada and Australia, but to be one of the means of federating the Empire".[47]

Milner saw the crucial importance of the Uitlander issue as a means of linking the demands of the mining capitalists for an economic transformation of the Transvaal and the desire of the British government to assert Britain's supremacy in the region. The Uitlander issue was, in itself, of no great moment to either group. For the capitalists, Uitlander rights were a means to an end, an end that might be secured through an accommodation with the Kruger regime rather than through its replacement by an Uitlander-dominated one. By 1899, though, some key mining capitalists (particularly those associated with the Wernher-Beit & Eckstein group and its allies) had become convinced they must support the South African League campaign for Uitlander rights, "otherwise we should have everyone against us".[48] Such capitalists feared the consequences of political isolation either from white mine workers or from the British government as represented locally by Milner. By then the Kruger regime was seen by some mining capitalists as being too untrustworthy, corrupt and inefficient to establish a political and economic framework in which the mines could prosper in the long term. The High Commissioner and his local agents, for their part, worked hard to established close links with the South African League and with some of the leading mining capitalists themselves.[49] Through these links Milner and the High Commission encouraged the leaders of the South African League, certain key capitalists and the newspapers they controlled to take a strong stand on the Uitlander issue as the best way of securing the desired transformation of the Transvaal.[50] By May 1899, one associate of the Werner-Beit & Eckstein group insisted that "England is our only possible security and Milner the only possible intermediary".[51]

In London senior British policy-makers did not hold either the Uitlanders or the capitalists in high regard. Selborne thought that the Kruger regime could have been forced to change by 1897 "had not the pre-eminent Uitlanders been generally so worthless and contemptible".[52] Milner, too, had his doubts about the Uitlanders. But he saw the importance of building up their cause as a way of persuading the British government to take a strong stand against the Transvaal and, in effect, to force it into a united British South Africa. As Milner noted in January 1899, Chamberlain's support for this aggressive policy

> depends on the amount of external pressure and excitement corresponding to our prodding of him from within. If only the Uitlanders stand firm on the formula of 'no rest without reform' . . . we shall do the trick yet . . . And by the soul of St Jingo they get a fair bucking up from us all one way and another".[53]

Despite Milner's best efforts – through his heated despatches to London and through his influence over press coverage of the issue – some British ministers continued to the end to doubt the wisdom of forcing a showdown with the Transvaal on the issue of Uitlander political rights. The prime minister himself wanted "to get away from the franchise issue, which will be troublesome in debate".[54] Salisbury saw, however, that Milner had effectively forced the British government to confront the Transvaal on this issue:

> We have to act upon a moral field prepared for us by him and his jingo supporters. And therefore I see before us the necessity for considerable military effort – and all for people whom we despise, and for territory which will bring no profit and no power to England.[55]

Moreover, as Sir Michael Hicks Beach (the Chancellor of the Exchequer) saw, "equality of the white races in the Transvaal would really secure all we can desire, viz. British predominance".[56]

The Uitlander franchise was the issue that Milner could use most readily "to work up to a crisis".[57] It was on this issue that he was able to take a stand and terminate the Bloemfontein Conference with Kruger in June 1899. The rapid breakdown of these talks annoyed senior decision-makers in London who were less willing than Milner to push the Transvaal to the brink of war at this time. Joseph Chamberlain had wanted Milner to be "restrained rather than encouraged at the moment".[58] Milner intervened again in July 1899 to urge a stiffer British line on the franchise question, just when tensions between London and Pretoria seemed to be easing.[59] Milner himself had no doubts about the part he had played prior to the outbreak of war. He had, he admitted in 1900, "been largely instrumental in bringing about a big war".[60]

IV

In October 1899 the Transvaal government declared war on Britain and, along with its Orange Free State ally, launched an invasion of Natal and the Cape. For Pretoria it was a fight for freedom and independence. To have met all of Britain's demands, demands backed locally by the mining capitalists and the South African League, was to concede political control of the Transvaal. And this the Kruger regime steadfastly refused to do.

Capital's demands for improved returns on southern African investments was an undeniably powerful force for political change in the region. But it did not, by itself, draw Britain into war with the Transvaal. Few mining capitalists were so desperate for a transformation of the Transvaal state that they wished to see a war to bring it about. Many capitalists preferred to seek improved economic conditions through more gradual reforms. Moreover, the unification of the Cape and Natal with the Boer republics and the amalgamation of their railways, may have been financially desirable to these British colonial governments and to the holders of their debt, but it was not necessarily to the advantage of capital invested in the Rand. More desirable from the latter's perspective was that the shorter, and potentially cheaper, Delagoa Bay should predominate – something that might bankrupt the Cape and Natal and place them at the Transvaal's economic mercy. But, under the influence of Milner and the British government, and fearful of an alliance between working class Uitlanders and the Kruger regime, some key mining capitalists gave their support to the Uitlander and British imperial cause in the belief that this was the best way to secure what they desired.

Some mining capitalists, like some British government decision-makers, were anxious for change in the Transvaal, although neither group was as anxious as Milner. He saw, more clearly than most, that time was on the side of the Kruger regime, particularly after it had become apparent that there would be no "second Rand" in Rhodesia and that Britain would be unable to get control of Delagoa Bay: "if we are not to fight and are yet not to be worsted, one of two things must happen. Either Rhodesia must develop *very* rapidly, or we must get Delagoa Bay".[61] By late 1898 it was obvious to Milner that neither of these things was possible and that war might be the only way to assert control over the Transvaal. The alternative was to allow it to grow in strength and independence, gradually drawing the rest of the region under its political sway; this in no small measure because of the inescapable logic of railway geography and finance. Milner, though, had a key role in building up the Uitlander issue as one that could link and serve the interests of both mining capitalists and the British government. In doing this, and in exercising, at the point of "proconsular interlock", a critical degree of control over the course and timing of events, Milner helped to create a situation in which war was almost inevitable.

Although the Boer republics took the initiative in declaring war on Britain, the British government had nevertheless been well prepared to fight in principle, even if not in effective military practice. It fought neither to transform the Transvaal nor unite southern Africa for the benefit of the mining capitalists; nor, in truth, to defend the rights of British subjects there. It fought because it seemed to be the best way to place southern Africa – and all that was at stake there for Britain's power and prestige – more firmly under British control. Indeed, it was feared in London that unless Britain asserted its paramountcy, southern Africa would remain a source of grave international uncertainty and growing strategic weakness. The Transvaal's position would have become inexorably stronger with its growing wealth, its increasingly free access to the sea through Delagoa Bay, and with its shared interest with European powers in frustrating Britain's regional ambitions. Unless Britain intervened it seemed clear that the Transvaal would eventually become the centre of a United States of South Africa outside the British Empire. It even seemed likely that the Transvaal would seek to assert its independence and regional predominance by force of arms as soon as Britain went to war with another Great Power. Moreover, Britain's European rivals seemed more than likely to take advantage of any British weakness in southern Africa to gain advantages for themselves at Britain's expense in this region, in Europe or elsewhere in the world. As Joseph Chamberlain put it so succinctly to his Cabinet colleagues in September 1899, "What is now at stake is the position of Great Britain in South Africa and with it the estimate of our power and influence in our colonies and throughout the world".[62]

Notes

1. This chapter is based on research undertaken while I was a Caird Research fellow at the National Maritime Museum, Greenwich. I would like to thank the Museum for allowing me to digress from my forthcoming book on the history of Simon's Town and the Royal Navy in South Africa, 1890 to 1957.
2. See, for example, S. Marks and S. Trapido, "Lord Milner and the South African State Reconsidered", in *Imperialism, the State and the Third World*, M. Twaddle (ed.), 80–94 (London, 1992); S. Marks and S. Trapido, "Lord Milner and the South African State", *History Workshop* 8, 50–802 (1979); P. J. Cain and A. G. Hopkins, *British Imperialism: Innovation and Expansion, 1688–1914* (London, 1993), pp. 369–81; and R. Ally, *Gold and Empire: The Bank of England and South Africa's Gold Producers 1886–1926* (Johannesburg, 1994).
3. I. R. Smith, *The Origins of the South African War, 1899–1902* (London, 1996); A. N. Porter, *Origins of the South African War: Joseph Chamberlain and the Diplomacy of Imperialism, 1895–99* (Manchester, 1980); J. S. Marais, *The Fall of Kruger's Republic* (Oxford, 1961); A. N. Porter, "The South African War (1899–1902): Context and Motive Reconsidered", *Journal of African History* 31(1), 43–5 (1990); I. R. Smith, "The Origins of the South African War (1899–1902): A Re-Appraisal", *South African Historical Journal* 22, 24–60 (1990); and N.G. Garson, "British Imperialism and the Coming of the Anglo-Boer War", *South African Journal of Economics* 30, 140–53 (1962).
4. Thomas Pakenham called the conflict "Milner's War" in *The Boer War* (Johannesburg, 1979). G. H. L. le May did likewise in *British Supremacy in South Africa 1899–1907* (Oxford, 1965). D. M. Schreuder called it Chamberlain's war in *The Scramble for Southern Africa* (Cambridge, 1980), p. 53.
5. An explanation of the war in terms of the intersection between local economic pressures and the strategic preoccupations of the metropolis has been provided by R. Robinson and J. Gallagher, *Africa and the Victorians: the Official Mind of Imperialism* (London, 1961), Ch. 14. Two of the best recent discussions of metropolitan and local pressures for war are found in B. Nasson, *The South African War 1899–1902* (London, 1999), pp. 15–45, and I. Phimister, "Unscrambling the Scramble for Southern Africa: the Jameson Raid and the South African War Revisited", *South African Historical Journal* 28, 203–20 (1993).
6. See R. Hyam, *Britain's Imperial Century: A Study of Empire and Expansion*, 1st edn (London, 1976), pp. 373–5; and R. Hyam, *Britain's Imperial Century: A Study of Empire and Expansion*, 2nd edn (London, 1993), pp. 285–90. See also R. Hyam, "The Primacy of Geopolitics: The Dynamics of British Imperial Policy, 1763–1963", *Journal of Imperial and Commonwealth History* 27(2), 27–52 (1999).
7. Phimister, "Unscrambling the Scramble for Southern Africa", p. 215. R. Mendelsohn, "Blainey and the Jameson Raid: The Debate Renewed", *Journal of Southern African Studies* 6(2), 170 (1980).
8. I. R. Smith, "Joseph Chamberlain and the Jameson Raid", in *The Jameson Raid: A Centennial Retrospective,* J. Carruthers (ed.) (Houghton, 1996), p. 99; and I. R. Smith "Thirty Years' Debate on the Economic Origins of the Raid", in *The Jameson Raid,* J. Carruthers (ed.), pp. 55–87.
9. This was the London partnership of Wernher, Beit and Co., and their Johannesburg subsidiary H. Eckstein and Co. See A. Jeeves, "Hobson's *The War in South Africa*: A Reassessment", paper presented at the "Rethinking the South African War 1899–1902" conference, Pretoria, 1998.

10. Jeeves, "Hobson's *The War in South Africa*", p. 9.
11. G. Rouliot to J. Wernher 19 November 1898, quoted in A. Jeeves, "The Rand Capitalists and Transvaal Politics, 1892–1899" (unpublished PhD thesis, Queen's University, 1971), p. 326.
12. Jeeves, "Hobson's *The War in South Africa*", pp. 6–10.
13. G. Rouliot to J. Wernher 19 November 1898, quoted in Jeeves, "Rand Capitalists and Transvaal Politics", p. 327.
14. A. Jeeves, "Rand Capitalists and the Coming of the South African War, 1896–1899", *Historical Papers*, 61–83 (1973).
15. By the late 1890s, railway revenues had become of dominant importance for the Cape and Natal, with the Cape earning three-quarters of its railway profits in 1897 from through-traffic to the Transvaal; J. van der Poel, *Railway and Customs Policies in South Africa 1885–1910* (London, 1933), pp. 46, 98.
16. D. G. Boyce, *The Crisis of British Power: the Imperial and Naval Papers of the Second Earl of Selborne, 1895–1910* (London, 1990), pp. 36–7 (memorandum by Lord Selborne, 26 March 1896).
17. Boyce, *Crisis of British Power*, pp. 36–7 (memorandum by Lord Selborne, 26 March 1896).
18. Boyce, *Crisis of British Power*, p. 44 (Selborne to J. Chamberlain, 18 October 1896).
19. See Hyam, "Primacy of Geopolitics", p. 29.
20. A. Porter, "Lord Salisbury, Mr Chamberlain and South Africa, 1895–9", *Journal of Imperial and Commonwealth History* 1(1), 3–26 (1972).
21. PRO Admiralty [ADM hereafter] ADM 231/28, Intelligence Department (No. 494) *British Colonies*, 1897.
22. D. Schreuder, *Gladstone and Kruger: Liberal Government and Colonial "Home Rule" 1880–85* (Toronto, 1969), p. 15 (Kimberley to R. P. Selborne, 11 October 1881).
23. Schreuder, *Gladstone and Kruger*, p. 503 (War Office Memorandum, 1 October. 1884).
24. PRO Colonial Office [CO hereafter] CO 537/130, Note by E. Fairfield, 3 June 1896.
25. CO 537/134, E.A. Altham to Colonial Office, 17 March 1898.
26. PRO War Office [WO hereafter] WO 32/7844, Wolseley to permanent under-secretary, 20 April 1898.
27. Boyce, *Crisis of British Power*, p. 44 (Selborne to J. Chamberlain, 18 October 1896).
28. PRO Cabinet [CAB hereafter] CAB 37/50, 36, Cabinet memorandum by A. Chamberlain, 10 June 1899.
29. Boyce, *Crisis of British Power*, p. 35 (Selborne to Salisbury, 30 March 1896).
30. CO 537/131, C. Greene to Lord Rosmead, 11 February 1897.
31. P. Henshaw, "The 'Key to South Africa' in the 1890s: Delagoa Bay and the Origins of the South African War", *Journal of Southern African Studies* 24(3), 538–9 (1998).
32. CAB 37/41, 8, Memorandum by the Admiralty Hydrographer, 11 January 1896, forwarded to Cabinet by G. Goschen, 7 February 1896.
33. CAB 37/48, 36, Memorandum by A. Chamberlain on the Naval Works Bill, 10 June 1899.
34. CAB 37/41, 8, Memorandum by the Admiralty Hydrographer, 11 January 1896.
35. CAB 37/41, 8, 7 February 1896; CAB 37/48, 68, 22 August 1898; and CAB 37/50, 36, 6 June 1899.
36. *Hansard, Parliamentary Debates*, col. 278, 25 July 1899.
37. ADM 231/28, Intelligence Department (No. 494) *British Colonies*, 1897.
38. Henshaw, "Key to South Africa", pp. 532–3. Porter, "Lord Salisbury", p. 4.
39. M. Seligmann, *Rivalry in Southern Africa, 1893–99: The Transformation of German Colonial Policy* (London, 1998).
40. Henshaw, "Key to South Africa", pp. 538–9.
41. CO 417/271, notes by Selborne, 1 June, and J. Chamberlain, 2 June 1899.
42. CO 417/251, note by Lambert, 31 December 1898.
43. This assertion should not surprise historians. After all, few historians have ever demonstrated an effective understanding of gold's significance. Fewer still have agreed on the subject.
44. In August 1899 the British consul in Lourenço Marques reported that there was "every reason to believe that this trade" in gold through Delagoa Bay to Paris would increase "because of lower shipping costs", *Board of Trade Journal* 27(159), 472 (1899). See also the similar report from this source in *Board of Trade Journal* 26(150), 89 (1898).

45. Seligmann, *Rivalry in Southern Africa*, pp. 113–36.
46. J. Benyon, *Proconsul and Paramountcy in South Africa: The High Commission, British Supremacy and the Sub-Continent 1806–1910* (Pietermaritzburg, 1980), pp. 260–87.
47. Hyam, *Britain's Imperial Century*, 2nd edn, pp. 244–5.
48. Georges Rouliot (a partner in Ecksteins) to Julius Wernher, 9 January 1899, quoted in Jeeves, "Rand Capitalists and the Coming of the South African War", p. 75.
49. Benyon, *Proconsul and Paramountcy*, pp. 269–74.
50. Jeeves, "Rand Capitalists and the Coming of the South African War", pp. 61–83.
51. P. FitzPatrick to J. Wernher, 1 May 1899, quoted in Jeeves, "Rand Capitalists and Transvaal Politics", p. 327.
52. CO 537/129, Note by Selborne, 24 March 1897.
53. E. Stokes, "Milnerism", *Historical Journal* 5(1), 54 (1962) (Milner to G. Fiddes, 3 January 1899).
54. Quoted in E. Drus, "Select Documents from the Chamberlain papers Concerning Anglo-Transvaal Relations, 1896–1899", *Bulletin of the Institute of Historical Research* 27, 181 (1954) (Salisbury to J. Chamberlain, 18 September 1899).
55 Quoted in Drus, "Select Documents", p. 189 (Salisbury to Lord Lansdowne, 30 August 1899).
56. Quoted in Drus, "Select Documents", p. 187 (Hicks Beach to J. Chamberlain, 29 September 1899).
57. Milner quoted in Hyam, *Britain's Imperial Century*, 2nd edn, p. 244.
58. Porter, "Lord Salisbury", p. 17.
59. Benyon, *Proconsul and Paramountcy*, p. 276.
60. J. Benyon, "'Main Show or Side-Show'? Natal and the South African War", *Journal of Imperial and Commonwealth History* 27(1), 29 (1999) (Milner to Lord Roberts, 21 June 1900).
61. C. Headlam, *Milner Papers: South Africa 1897–99* (London, 1931), p. 267 (Milner to J. Chamberlain, 6 July 1898).
62. Quoted in Drus, "Select Documents", p. 187 (Chamberlain's memorandum to Cabinet, 6 September 1899).

CHAPTER TWO

Imperial Germany and the Boer War[1]
From Colonial Fantasies to the Reality of Anglo-German Estrangement

Martin Kröger

Heinrich von Treitschke belonged to those historians who feel at home on the slippery ground of current affairs. Where German colonial policy was concerned – especially that relating to Southern Africa – he committed himself very early on: what flourished there by way of culture, he averred, was German, "Teutonic", although he was prepared to include Dutch in this category. "Thus", he wrote in the autumn of 1884, "it would be no more than a natural turn of events if racially related Germany should some day in some manner become responsible for the protection of the Teutonic population of Southern Africa, inheriting the legacy of the British in a neglected colony".[2] Treitschke's dictum combined the three essential elements of German colonial propaganda: it was anti-British, its objective was (southern) Africa, and it was racialist.

Canvassing of the idea that Germany should acquire colonies had begun soon after the unification of Germany in 1871. It translated the desire to make externally evident Germany's recent gain in international importance into the then generally current political demand for territorial acquisitions. At the same time, the desire for colonies was a reflection of the prospective economic potential of the regions under consideration. Starting with Johann Jakob Sturz's concept of a "new India" in the southern part of the dark continent,[3] a lively propaganda campaign developed, targeted at the British Cape Colony and the Boer state of the Transvaal. The prime mover was Ernst von Weber, who had first-hand knowledge of southern Africa, where he owned a diamond mine. Weber's arguments were not, however, based on prospects of instant wealth in gold and precious stones; rather he hailed the climate and the terrain as favourable to agriculture: "What nation knows how to colonise through cultivation better than the German?"[4] Friedrich Fabri, probably the most influential of the colonial propagandists, was more sceptical, taking the view that the economic possibilities had been over-estimated:

"The Republic of the Transvaal . . . is poor in water and . . . only usable . . . as grazing-land". As a result, its capacity to absorb colonists was, according to Fabri, limited.[5] If the focus on Southern Africa derived from Sturz, it was Weber who contributed the idea of a "racial affinity" between Boer and German. From that point on it would no longer be possible to omit the racial factor from the discussion about colonies. In 1890 Julius Langbehn, normally hostile to everything that was modern, went so far as to assert, anonymously, that Boers and Prussians were "politically akin and culturally equal". "Only with equals," he added, "can one conclude lasting alliances".[6] That such policies were bound to lead to friction with Britain was obvious, but this did not trouble the colonial propagandists. The explorer Bernhard Schwarz proposed that British predominance in South Africa should be entirely demolished at once, and that in collaboration with the Boers a great German colonial empire, a "German India",[7] should be created. From Weber on, the publicists took it for granted that the Boers would even be glad to be thus "embraced". What were the political and economic grounds for such expectations of a German–Boer alliance?

True, the Boers, interested in having a counterweight to British predominance in the Cape region, had, as early as 1867, invited Prussia to recognize the Republic of the Transvaal and had wished to despatch a diplomatic representative to Berlin. A second *démarche* to the same end made in 1871 remained equally fruitless. Where German foreign policy was concerned, the Transvaal was a long way away, nor was the colonial periphery as yet exerting the influence it was later to have on the network of relationships between the European states. In addition, the exchange of goods between Germany and the Boer Republic was still minimal. The area only became significant once diamonds, and later gold, had been found there. The more the Republic's economic attraction grew, the greater became the German involvement in it. The major trading houses established themselves in Johannesburg, economic relations quickly grew closer, and the conclusion, on 22 January 1885, of a German–Boer treaty of friendship and trade bore witness to this development. At the same time, Germany was in the process of adopting an active colonial policy. Its twofold intrusion into the British sphere of interest, politically and territorially in south-west Africa and in the economic sense in the Transvaal and the Cape Colony itself, threw down the gauntlet before Britain, the then predominant power in the region.[8]

When the once agriculturally based Transvaal turned into a serious economic competitor with the Cape Colony, the Boer Republic sought to assert itself as an independent factor, free from Britain's clutches, and for this ambition President Kruger believed he had Germany's support.[9] British fears that, with Germany's influence thrown into the balance, the centre of gravity might shift from the Cape to the Transvaal, were by no means unfounded. Nowhere else outside Europe were German investors active on the same scale. The Boers made adroit use of the increase in independence from Britain gained in 1884. President Kruger's friendly feelings towards Germany were well known; it was no accident that Germans played an important role in the Boer Republic as economic and political advisers. The government of the Transvaal gave preference to German enterprises when allocating contracts. Between 1886 and 1896 the exchange of goods increased tenfold. At times German investors were responsible for 20 per cent of foreign capital investment.

While the Boers wished to reinforce their independence, London and the neighbouring Cape Colony desired, on the contrary, to restrict it. They demanded the franchise for foreigners settled in the Transvaal (Uitlanders), the great majority of whom were British. In 1894, in face of this transparent attempt to gain influence over Transvaal politics, Germany for the first time formulated clear demands. State Secretary Adolf Marschall von Bieberstein protested against the pressure being exerted on the Boer Republic and against attempts to undermine Portugal's sovereignty in east Africa. In London, Ambassador Paul von Hatzfeldt repeatedly warned that Germany would not tolerate an alteration of the status quo in the Transvaal or the annexation of Portuguese territory. He deployed the threat that German support in Egypt might be terminated, something that would have resulted in massive damage to British interests and that London was thus obliged to treat with appropriate seriousness.[10]

Neither the Boer Republic nor the old colonial power Portugal was prepared to surrender its rights unilaterally. As a result of the opening of the railway line between Pretoria and Lourenço Marques, on Delagoa Bay, in early 1895, the Transvaal now possessed its own link with the Indian Ocean and was no longer dependent on the British lines. At the same time, the already considerable tension between Berlin and London over the Transvaal and rights of intervention in Delagoa Bay escalated. A speech that President Kruger made on 27 January 1895, helped to exacerbate the situation. In connection with the birthday of Kaiser Wilhelm II, he compared the relationship between Germany and the Boer Republic with that between a parent and child. According to Kruger, Germany was showing a proper awareness of the Transvaal's impending attainment of adulthood, and, in contrast to Britain, was ensuring betimes that the young State had "a larger suit of clothes". *Vis-à-vis* the British ambassador to Berlin, Marschall yet again indulged in "a great show of friendship for the Transvaal Government".[11]

At the end of December 1895 the situation in southern Africa worsened. The Boer Republic had for some time been prepared for unrest, and had taken appropriate precautions, which duly brought about the failure of the Jameson Raid.[12] This attempted invasion stemmed in part from a sub-imperialism pursued by the Cape Colony under the leadership of Rhodes, entirely independently from London, although the destabilization of the Transvaal was wholly in accord with the British strategy of containment. However, matters threatened to get out of hand when Germany intervened by giving the Boers renewed assurances of friendship.[13]

London's sharp condemnation of the Jameson Raid appeared in essence to have dissipated German fears that Britain had instigated the invasion. It was due to the Kaiser that for a while the affair rumbled on: he wanted to signal to his colonial rival that there were limits to be observed in world politics. He couched his "reminder" in the form of a congratulatory telegram to Kruger, who, he said, had succeeded in "preserving his country's independence against external encroachment".[14] Germany's pro-Boer policy, culminating in this communication, and the British anger at and vehement criticism of this line of conduct, sprang from the general economic, political and colonial rivalry between Britain and Germany, which was merely venting itself in the Transvaal affair. As was quite clearly recognized in Berlin following the Jameson Raid and the Kruger telegram, the German side could have no interest in any lasting enmity over this question. Any renewed intensification of the differences between Britain and the Boers was expected to lead to war; in such a development, however great its sympathy for the Boers, Germany had no desire to become involved.

Wilhelm II, it is true, was still, as late as March 1897, clinging to a pro-Boer line. He wished to ensure that, in the event of war, Germany should have sufficient troops on the spot to be able to come to the aid of the Boers against Britain.[15] The Chancellor, Hohenlohe, however, managed to persuade the Kaiser to agree to a reduction in troop strength. Friedrich von Holstein, in particular, urged the Chancellor to dismiss any thought of a war on land: "The Kruger telegram has already done enough harm. We cannot go to war against [both] Britain and France".[16] To expose oneself to the enmity of Britain for the sake of the Boers seemed to Holstein a "luxury",[17] while he regarded German policy on South Africa as a "blind alley".[18] Since it is only an about turn that leads out of a cul-de-sac, Holstein sought to achieve nothing less than a complete departure from the previous German position on the Transvaal question. What he envisaged was a German foreign policy free from the constraints arising from the hostility between Britain and Russia, which he deemed to be insuperable. Differences with one of these two powers always pushed the Reich over to the other side, whereas real independence could only stem from good relationships with both sides. At the same time, he hoped to be able to obtain concessions "if we agree not to place any further obstacles in England's way in South Africa".[19] In this he evidently had the support of Marschall and Hatzfeldt.[20] Holstein expected to have less trouble with Britain than with the Kaiser, but he too would come to see "how greatly Germany's power would be increased if we, without sacrificing our good relations with Russia, were to restore our relations with England in such a way as to make it more feasible than it is at present to operate *à cheval* between Russia and England".[21]

Hatzfeldt failed to win over the British prime minister to Holstein's plan. The ambassador was soon obliged to admit that "The matter is, it seems to me, not yet sufficiently advanced for me to report upon it officially".[22] Yet the

German resolve to trade the Boers off against compensation remained firm. And in the spring of 1898 there was an historic moment when it seemed as if there might be an "about-turn in German-British relations".[23]

In 1897 it had still looked to Salisbury as if he would have no need of a German readiness to make concessions in order to reap the harvest of a policy of strength. The following year, however, Britain's goals in South Africa were nowhere near being achieved. Additional disquieting factors were, firstly, Russia's expansion in the Far East (Port Arthur was occupied in December 1897), secondly, the fact that France was steering a course toward confrontation in the upper Nile valley (the Fashoda crisis was already looming), and, thirdly, the underlining of Germany's claim to a global standing through the occupation of Kiao-Chow and the start of naval armament. It was in this context that the British Colonial Secretary, Joseph Chamberlain, conveyed to the German ambassador a "desire for a binding agreement between Britain and the Triple Alliance".[24]

In previous years, the British government had eluded all attempts to bind the United Kingdom down in one or other alliance. Above all, in view of the likely reaction of Russia, and, yet more important, France, any clear linkage with the Triple Alliance had been eschewed. The British had always put their faith in a carefully adjusted balance of power on the continent, with the empire remaining uncommitted. Chamberlain's alliance proposal signalled a willingness to abandon this policy of "splendid isolation", and with it (as a result of a possible commitment to the Triple Alliance) the policy of the balance of power. This represented an "almost sensational reversal of British policy".[25] Given the alternatives, the choice of a potential ally was no accident. In the light of the global cost-benefit analysis, the only suitable European power was Germany: in comparison with Russia and France, the clashes of interest were minor, and the Reich was seeking only small concessions in the colonial field.[26] But even before Salisbury had received an answer to his enquiry as to whether Germany's participation in closer relations, which he regarded as desirable, could be achieved at all,[27] the *Wilhelmstrasse* had made up its mind. The new state secretary at the Foreign Ministry, Bernhard von Bülow, did not wish to commit his country to Britain in the role of a "junior partner", and hence he rejected Chamberlain's offer.[28] The clash between the global policy that London already had in place and Germany's world policy, then in its dilettantish infancy, was an insuperable obstacle to far-reaching agreements. Negotiations were, however, brought about between Germany and Britain on "lesser matters" not adding up to an alliance.[29] The outcome was in the first place an agreement that defined the respective spheres of interest in southern Africa. After tough negotiations beginning in the middle of June 1898, the two powers agreed in a treaty, concluded on 30 August, that in the event of a division of the Portuguese possessions they would jointly resist any interference by third powers. Germany confined its African interests to those territories bordering on already existing colonies: the northern part of Mozambique and the southern portion of Angola. With southern Mozambique, Delagoa Bay, previously contested, fell within the British sphere of interest, which now wholly encircled the republic of the Transvaal. In that the treaty promised Germany future colonial gains – gains never in fact achieved in the desired manner – it excluded the Reich from southern Africa and particularly the Transvaal, thus appearing to do away with the long-standing German–British rivalry.[30] In British eyes this was the especial, if not the only, advantage that the agreement conferred. Chamberlain was aware that the treaty was limited in its effect: "Germany feels no particular gratitude to us". Yet, as he wrote to Balfour, they could now be sure "of Germany's abstention from further interference in Delagoa Bay and [the] Transvaal".[31] The British High Commissioner in the Cape Colony, Lord Milner, similarly emphasized that the treaty "formally and for ever eliminates Germany as a political influence in the Transvaal".[32]

Bülow, too, later viewed the agreement with Britain chiefly in the light of its implications for the Transvaal, of which "no mention was made". True, he said, "the Treaty deals purely with the possibility of alterations in Portugal's colonial possessions", yet it implied "a completely neutral attitude for Germany vis-à-vis the Anglo-Transvaal differences".[33] Even before the agreement had been concluded, Bülow had made it clear that he "would retain no sentimental feeling for the Boers", if in return for their "more or less covert abandonment", he could purchase an understanding with Britain and an "instantly recognisable and in some degree adequate recompense".[34] In the last analysis, this realism produced a policy realignment, away from the previous interference in favour of the Boers and towards a neutrality that, at the least, did not hamper British war-time actions during 1899.

The Kruger telegram at the beginning of 1896 was at once the symbol and high-water mark of German pro-Boer policy, but it also marked its turning point. The German consuls on the spot were for some time left in ignorance of the change in German policy in regard to the Transvaal. Yet the Boer government must have been given cause for thought when, as early as 1897, the negotiations conducted in Berlin by their State Secretary, Leyd, remained entirely fruitless in terms of intensifying their relations. All pressure for an active policy in favour of Pretoria was ignored by the Reich government. Bülow sharply dismissed rumours that the Transvaal's diplomatic representative for the whole of Europe was to be headquartered in Berlin. The German consul in Pretoria, Franz von Herff, was instructed to declare against such a secondment to Berlin "immediately, in the interests of the Transvaal".[35] At the same time the decision was made in the German Foreign Ministry to replace the strongly pro-Boer von Herff,[36] a measure that, although it was welcomed by Britain and its representatives on the spot, displeased both the Boer government and the German propagandists for the colonial cause. In the summer of 1898, Leyd, who had meanwhile been appointed envoy to Europe with his headquarters in Brussels, was for the space of several months denied the opportunity to present his credentials to Wilhelm II.[37]

While, over a period of two years, German policy was gradually and increasingly more clearly distancing itself from the Transvaal, the economic basis of German–Boer relations was also changing. German capital continued to be involved on a substantial scale in South African mining for precious metals and coal, cement works and the production of electricity. But after 1896 the exchange of goods – especially the supply from Germany of the potassium cyanide used in the extraction of gold, and of medicines and machinery, and from the Transvaal of wool, ore-slag and a modest amount of gold – began for the first time to decline.[38] Given the recession in South Africa, there was no likelihood of an upturn, the less so since the government of the Transvaal, partly in reaction to the German change of policy, was now placing its orders chiefly in France.[39]

One factor that had underlain Germany's original pro-Boer policy had been the colonial propaganda put out by individuals in collaboration with influential pressure groups. For this reason Holstein was justifiably nervous about the effect that groups such as the *Alldeutscher Verband* or the *Deutsche Kolonialgesellschaft* and their organs might have on public opinion and the Reichstag: "In the South African question we must take care that the phrase about our having left our racial brothers the Boers in the lurch does not become common coin".[40] When the new envoy, Leyd, took up his post in October 1898, he was even instructed to exert a calming influence on German pro-Boers.[41] It is true that pro-Boer propaganda remained a factor which German policy had to reckon with,[42] but it evidently did prove possible, when in the course of 1899 tensions rose, to persuade the press to confine itself to a measured commentary upon events. Chamberlain was "glad to see that the German press generally is taking a very moderate line and is on the whole not unfavourable".[43]

State Secretary Bülow demanded of the press that it hold:

> calm, sober and dispassionate language . . . It should everywhere be emphasised that when France, Russia, Italy and Austria have no intention of setting themselves at odds with Britain over South African questions, Germany on her own cannot press for advantage and engage herself there.[44]

Privately, he declared that the German attitude must be neutral, absolutely honourable and, compared with that of France, markedly friendly.[45] It was probably with these considerations in mind that the acting State Secretary, Eduard von Derenthall, and Ambassador Hatzfeldt supported Britain's request that Germany should represent British interests in Pretoria in the event of war.[46] For Bülow, however, this was going too far. Without some *quid pro quo* from London, for example in the Samoa question, he was not minded to support British policy in so demonstrative a manner, thus exposing himself to public criticism.[47] The excuse that Derenthall thereupon used with Ambassador Lascelles was that the German representative in Pretoria was a mere consul and not equal to such a task.[48]

Against a background of increasing readiness for war and intensified military preparations, London's anxiety about Germany's attitude visibly grew.[49] The British enquiry was a *ballon d'essai* designed to test the reliability of the neutrality that had ostensibly been promised. On the eve of the outbreak of hostilities, three aspects of this episode were seen by the British government as significant. First, the German neutrality could not remain devoid of tensions. Secondly, the German government would always so shape its political action as to take public opinion into account. Hence, thirdly, in the long term German neutrality would only be forthcoming in return for a recompense. Since a distribution of Portuguese territory had not materialized, German demands were already focusing on other colonial regions. To link the Transvaal question with the long-lasting Samoan conflict would, however, be to risk provoking yet another complete change in German policy. Hatzfeldt had already deployed this threat in September.[50]

It was primarily Chamberlain who, from a pragmatic assessment of the situation, realized how valuable to the interests of the British Empire, at that precise moment when the Transvaal crisis outweighed all other problems, an understanding with Germany over Samoa would be.[51] He and Hatzfeldt's subordinate, Hermann von Eckardstein, together drew up a provisional agreement on differences in the Pacific, completing their work by mid-October. Even though Bülow expressly rejected the suggestion that Germany was seeking to exploit Britain's difficulties in South Africa in order to obtain the desired concessions in Samoa, he yet did not deny that "the present moment [is] especially favourable".[52] And Holstein, too, pointed out that, without a war in South Africa, Germany could not hope to gain anything in Samoa.[53]

On 10 October, Bülow made it unequivocally clear to the British ambassador, Lascelles, that it was essential to come to terms quickly, since an agreement between Germany and Britain was indispensable to the "true interests" of the two countries. Deftly, Bülow brought in the topic of the Transvaal. German public opinion, he said, tended to be anti-British, although officially the German government was observing strict neutrality. Lastly, the State Secretary asked that his remarks should be viewed, not as threats, but as an indication of the difficulties with which he was faced, and that were preventing him from conducting "a policy of cordial understanding" with Britain. Of course, he added as a final thought, as long as the Samoa question was not settled it would be hopeless to contemplate such an accord.[54]

The outbreak, only a few days later, of war between Britain and the Transvaal would test the worth of the German promises. The Reich did indeed remain neutral throughout the war's duration. At the same time, however, the outbreak of hostilities increased Germany's leverage in the negotiations over Samoa. In the ensuing weeks, Bülow sought to force Britain to come to terms. The German negotiating position benefited from the fact that at this time the British Cabinet was growing increasingly concerned about the possible formation of a hostile coalition of continental powers, with the result that, in comparison with the tensions in South Africa, the Samoa problem rapidly receded into the background. From the German point of view, it was not only necessary to obtain clarification in advance of a long-planned visit to Britain by Wilhelm II; the German–British relationship also required to be clarified with an eye to the Tsar's visit to Berlin, due to take place on 8 November.[55]

Given the early, surprising defeats sustained by Britain in South Africa, Bülow's hopes seemed to bid fair to be fulfilled. Lord Salisbury in large part accepted a German treaty draft. He was aware that both a majority in the Cabinet and the growing pressure of anti-British feeling in Europe, together with fears of foreign intervention, at that stage left him very little room for manoeuvre. But even after the disaster of Ladysmith (30 October 1899) had finally compelled the settlement of the Samoa problem, and, following an urgent plea from Chamberlain, the British Cabinet had approved the draft treaty, not all contested questions were resolved. However, only speedy agreement on the Samoa problem could resolve the dilemma created by Wilhelm's travel plans, an anti-British public opinion and Russian proposals for an agreement on the Orient.[56] In a conversation with the British military attaché, Grierson, on 6 November, Wilhelm II complained with characteristic bluntness:

> I desire to remain friendly to England, but I have my duties as German Emperor to think of, and I cannot go on sitting on the safety-valve for ever. Does England not want my friendship, about the only one left her on the Continent? Some day when she is in trouble she will find that German patience has been tried too long.[57]

In the next two days a treaty was agreed on – only hours before the Tsar arrived in Berlin.[58] Formal signature took place in London on 14 November.

During the opening phase of the Boer War, Bülow acted under what proved to be the mistaken conviction that there was room for Germany to manoeuvre (enjoying a "free hand") between Britain and Russia, an asset that could be turned into negotiating successes without antagonizing either of the two powers. He let himself be guided primarily by the momentary access of prestige gained by his policy; territorial or economic considerations, in contrast, were not decisive for him. It became apparent in the course of the negotiations that it was no longer the Transvaal, the Boers or Samoa that mattered, but rather that it was the probable response to events of the Kaiser and German public opinion that were more and more moving into the foreground.[59]

It is to be presumed that the British did not altogether fathom the motives behind German policy formation during the relevant weeks. Yet the virtual use of force through which the German government had gained success in its negotiations on the Samoan issue certainly did not help to instil confidence. Nor did the 20–28 November visit to Windsor Castle by the German imperial couple, however much it was strictly a family occasion, change anything. Bülow, who was of the party, was lavish with assurances that the tone taken by the press did not reflect the views of the Kaiser and his government.[60] But when Chamberlain remarked "that he desired a general understanding between Germany, Britain and America", Wilhelm II replied, evasively and thus entirely in the same spirit as Bülow:

> A broad agreement of this kind would have its drawbacks for both sides. Whilst concluding formal alliances was not in accordance with British traditions, Germany's excellent relations with Russia meant that, at least for the present, she must observe certain political limits.[61]

How little Bülow was interested in an alignment with Britain may be seen from the comment with which Bülow closed his record of his conversations at Windsor Castle:

> I consider that it will in future be the task of the German government, having acquired a strong navy and whilst preserving good relations alike with the Russian and the British side, to await the further development of elemental events with patience and composure.[62]

This phrasing was entirely to the Kaiser's taste.

The state secretary's speech of 11 December 1899 to the Reichstag was for the consumption of the German public. In his address in justification of the Second Navy Law, which has gone down in history as the "hammer and anvil" speech, there remained no trace of a German–British accord, let alone of friendship or an alliance: "And where Britain is concerned, we are fully prepared to live with her in peace and harmony, on a basis of complete reciprocity and mutual consideration".[63] Chamberlain, who among the British leadership had been the most urgent in pressing for a *rapprochement* with Germany, was disappointed. In so far as any mention was made of Britain in Bülow's speech, the Colonial Secretary thought it "to be limited to *le plus strict[ement] necessaire*". He perceived that his German negotiating partner had duped him: "I feel", he wrote to Ambassador Lascelles, "rather as though I had been made to pull the chestnuts out of the fire for him".[64]

Bülow gave instructions that the affair should be dismissed as a misunderstanding, continued to hold out prospects of trustful and friendly relations, and promised continued neutrality in South Africa.[65] But the seeds of mistrust had now been sown. In his study of Germany, Britain and the Transvaal, Harald Rosenbach writes that it was at this point that the compatibility of Germany's theoretically pro-British South Africa policy and the in-practice anti-British demands for compensation were put to the test. This is undoubtedly correct, but may be an insufficiently exhaustive assessment. Let us therefore deliver a more severe verdict.

On 21 December, Ambassador Hatzfeldt reported that the question had been raised as to the circumstances under which Germany could accept the British desire for temporary control of Delagoa Bay. The retrocession of Zanzibar, which had been considered, appeared out of the question, but the cession of Walvis Bay did not. In addition, Berlin had its eye on the Bay of Tigers in the Southern part of Angola.[66] It may with confidence be assumed that its demands for compensation formed the true nub of Germany's policy; the neutrality that at bottom cost the Reich government nothing was merely a means to an end. Already in early December, in a report to Chancellor Hohenlohe, Hatzfeldt put the point very neatly:

> For us it can . . . only be useful if, without for our part entering into any obligations, Mr Chamberlain clings to the hope that ultimately we shall after all allow ourselves to be persuaded to meet his wishes concerning an alliance, or at least a close understanding. As long as he cherishes this hope, he will show a willingness to accommodate us in such colonial questions as may arise, and – as was the case over the Samoa question – will have to exert his influence in our favour, in Cabinet and especially upon Lord Salisbury.

In the margin of this report, Wilhelm II commented, "He is right, and this is what matters".[67] The German side had no intention of adopting a genuinely pro-British attitude, either for its own sake or with a mind to more far-reaching political prospects. Peter Winzen, who has studied Bülow's foreign policy in depth, describes this as the "lost chance of a century".[68] Bülow himself, years later, wrote merely, "Our neutral attitude during the Boer War was dictated by important national interests of the German Reich".[69] What was undoubtedly meant here was the build-up of the German Navy.

Indeed, at the close of 1899 Berlin was simply waiting for Britain, on account of its military reversals, to afford an occasion on the one hand for the pursuit of German expansion in Africa, and on the other for putting through the building up of the fleet despite domestic political resistance. The required pretext was provided when Britain seized three mail steamers: the "Bundesrath" affair, named after one of the vessels. Unfortunately, A. J. P. Taylor did not cite evidence for his claim that Bülow, Tirpitz and the Kaiser "drank champagne to the British naval officer who had given them such help in promoting the second Navy Law".[70] Nevertheless, the story is a plausible one in view of the policy pursued thus far, and of what Bülow wrote privately:

His Majesty has ordered that (without any impolitic venom or hate campaign against Britain, but objectively) the seizure of the "Bundesrath" is to be made use of, with emphasis and consistently, in the interests of the naval bill. In this connection reference may also be made to my recent speech on the Navy ("Nobody today can tell what results the war in South Africa will have etc.").[71]

What had happened?[72] On 28 December 1899, the German Consulate in Durban reported that the *Bundesrath* had been stopped outside Delagoa Bay, and escorted into Durban harbour by the British naval vessel *Magicienne*. The authorities had offered no justification for this action. Since, according to the shipping company, the *Deutsche Ostafrikalinie* in Hamburg, there had been no contraband of war on board, Bülow instructed his ambassador in London to clarify the factual background immediately and to require the British government to release the steamer without delay. No evidence of a breach of neutrality by the *Bundesrath* was produced; instead, on 3 January 1900, the news arrived that a second mail steamer, the *General*, had been seized outside Aden and compelled to unload its cargo. The atmosphere between Berlin and London became increasingly tense. Bülow particularly censured the clearly deliberate slowness and dilatoriness with which the British were dealing with the matter.[73] When, in addition, a third steamer, the *Herzog*, was impounded outside Durban, without the preceding cases having been cleared up, Bülow declared that the British must be more interested in damaging German trade than in fighting the Boers.[74] Writing to Hatzfeldt, Holstein even went so far as threaten the formation within days of an anti-British group of continental powers.[75] For days the diplomats argued about the rules of international law until, on 16 January, Salisbury put an end to the quarrel by announcing the impending release of the *Bundesrath*.[76] On the following day, the British prime minister set forth in detail his views on what had happened. In regard to the right to stop and search, he affirmed "that in case of steamers carrying mails, that right should be exercised with all possible consideration and only resorted to when the circumstances are clearly such as to justify the gravest suspicion".[77] That might have been the end of the matter, but, in light of the acrimony that had characterized his conversation with Hatzfeldt, Salisbury added:

I received with some surprise a communication from the Representative of a Power with whom Her Majesty's Government believe themselves to be on the most friendly terms, worded in so abrupt a manner and couched in language which imputed to Her Majesty's Naval Commanders, that they had shown a disrespect of International Law, and placed unnecessary impediments in the way of neutral commerce. There is no foundation for these imputations.[78]

It was not the three vessels that cast a cloud on German–British relations: it was the language held and the manner adopted, as was confirmed by the temporary representative of Ambassador Hatzfeldt, who had fallen ill. Paul von Wolff-Metternich had learned that "on no other occasion has Lord Salisbury voiced such displeasure as he evinced upon receipt of our Notes in this particular matter". In London – that is to say, no longer merely on the part of British public opinion, but also once again in the government – it was generally felt that in its difficult position Britain was being taken advantage of by Germany, and that this approach was to be seen, not as being the fault of German public opinion, but as the product of the anti-British policy being conducted by the government. Wolff-Metternich cited a Foreign Office confidant as saying that "this was undoubtedly the most regrettable aspect of the whole situation". Kaiser Wilhelm II did not agree with this analysis, commenting, "Metternich's friend seems to have no notion of the services which I have been quietly rendering to Her Majesty, her government, and the whole country".[79]

And yet: it was quite clearly the case that, for purely self-interested reasons, German neutrality now and then concealed the more deep-seated causes of German–British antagonism. Nor did the behind the scenes assistance referred to by Wilhelm II, for example forbidding German officers, even when retired, to take sides with the Transvaal, or the fact that the German government declined to receive either a Boer delegation or Paul Kruger himself,[80] make any difference to the British perception of German policy. None the less, it was undoubtedly of great assistance to Britain's war effort that Germany firmly rejected all proposed interventions by third powers. Between December 1899 and March 1900, that is in the most acute stage of the war, the Reich government on more than one occasion fended off proposals to intervene or to mediate.

The question of possible intervention by third powers in the events in southern Africa preoccupied all governments and the whole of public opinion from St Petersburg to Washington. Already in December 1899, financial circles in Paris were asking the German ambassador there whether he thought mediation was a possibility. His reply, "Not yet, and probably never by us", was a "correct" – thus, the Kaiser in a marginal note – expression of German policy.[81] To a suggestion by the Russian ambassador in Berlin that French, German and Russian vessels should be sent into Delagoa Bay in order to forestall a British occupation, Bülow at first returned no substantial reply.[82] When, in the middle of January, the same diplomat bluntly asked the Kaiser whether an anti-British coalition was on the cards, the latter replied equally bluntly "that he would not join such [a grouping], nor would he abandon the neutral attitude observed thus far".[83] In March, the Russian Foreign Minister, Muraviëv, renewed the suggestion that the Boer War should be brought to an end by the joint mediation of Russia, France and Germany. As the precondition for this, Bülow demanded a treaty in which the "Powers mutually guarantee one another's territorial integrity in Europe for a considerable number of years".[84] When the military situation in South Africa changed, and the initial Boer victories were followed by British successes, the defeated Boers, in mid-March 1900, asked the European powers to mediate. Bülow made it a condition for German cooperation "that the two opponents should both desire this".[85] He had, of course, reason to suppose that, now that the fortunes of war had been reversed, the British would reject any outside interference more firmly than ever. The Boer Republics were formally annexed that same summer, even though Boer resistance was to continue for another two years.

Bülow was, it is true, correct in what he had telegraphed to London, namely, that the German government had at no point sought to participate in intervention by France and Russia in the South African war, or to persuade these powers to intervene.[86] But, all the same, this did nothing to improve the bad overall impression that German foreign policy left on British minds. Holstein later summed it up: "But, by acting in a friendly manner and speaking in an unfriendly one, we fell between two stools (for 'we' read 'Bülow')".[87] Yet this belated recognition conceals the fact it was the common view, shared by all those on the German side who were involved in policy-making, that it was precisely in this way that most gain could be made in the national interest within the existing system of states.

In the nineteenth century, this international system consisted in a supranational framework of relationships, maintained by intensive reciprocal contact, among a small number of states who regarded themselves as forming part of that system and who on the whole could coexist with one another. Because, however, they were competitors for power within a hierarchically structured world of states, and because of their propensity for imperial expansion, the possibility of a general war between them was always present. In a chain of events perceived as a contest, the decision-makers in Berlin, to be sure, pursued the entirely legitimate aim of rapidly seizing the advantage in terms of national power. In those terms, it would be wrong to say Bülow's "global policy" (*Weltpolitik*) came no nearer to achieving its short-term goals. The building of the Grand Fleet, begun in 1898, was accelerated: on 12 June 1900, the Reichstag approved the enlargement of the navy desired by the Kaiser and the government. Bülow himself was soon appointed Chancellor. But these things came at a high cost. Any semblance of a rapprochement between Germany and Britain remained a semblance only, lacking a basis in substance, and consequently mutual differences became all the more starkly apparent. True, the alliance option was kept open for a while, but finally even Chamberlain wrote Germany off as a potential partner on the continent. What had, above all, been lacking on the German side, was a necessary and, most importantly, sincere willingness to enter an alliance. In retrospect we know that from that point on Britain would steer in another direction. Where the international system is concerned we may therefore conclude that, in step with the chronology and content of the Boer War, from 1897–98 down to the Entente Cordiale of 1904, that system underwent a quite decisive change, and that Germany failed to form an integral and cooperative part of this development. In other words, rather than being encircled in consequence of some master plan, Germany, over a period of years, brought about its own "excirclement".[88]

Notes

1. I should like to express my gratitude to Dr Eleonore C. M. Breuning for her translation, helpful comments and encouragement concerning this article.
2. Heinrich von Treitschke, *Deutsche Kämpfe. Neue Folge. Schriften zur Tagespolitik* (Leipzig, 1896), pp. 348–9; his article "Die ersten Versuche deutscher Kolonialpolitik" first appeared 27 November 1884. Cf. Peter Winzen, "Treitschke's Influence on the Rise of Imperialist and Anti-British Nationalism in Germany", in *Nationalist and Racialist Movements in Britain and Germany Before 1914*, P. Kennedy and A. Nicholls (eds), 154–70 (London, 1981).
3. Johann Jakob Sturz, *Der wiedergewonnene Weltteil, ein neues, gemeinsames Indien* (Berlin, 1875).
4. Ernst von Weber, *Die Erweiterung des deutschen Wirtschaftsgebietes und die Grundlegung zu überseeischen deutschen Staaten* (Leipzig, 1879), p. 38.
5. Friedrich Fabri, *Bedarf Deutschland der Colonien?/Does Germany Need Colonies?* translated, edited and with an introduction by E. C. M. Breuning and M. E. Chamberlain (Lewiston, Queenston, Lampeter, 1998), p. 129.
6. Julius Langbehn, *Rembrandt als Erzieher* (55th reprint, Leipzig, 1922), p. 191; the book first appeared anonymously in 1890.
7. Bernhard Schwarz, *Ein deutsches Indien und die Teilung der Erde – Colonialpolitische Randglossen zur Sachlage in Afrika und zur Congokonferenz* (Leipzig, 1884).
8. On the whole topic, see Matthew S. Seligmann, *Rivalry in Southern Africa, 1893–99: The Transformation of German Colonial Policy* (London, 1998); Harald Rosenbach, *Das Deutsche Reich, Großbritannien und der Transvaal (1896–1902: Anfänge deutsch-britischer Entfremdung* (Göttingen, 1993); Michael Fröhlich, *Von Konfrontation zur Koexistenz: Die deutsch-britischen Kolonialbeziehungen in Afrika zwischen 1884 und 1914* (Bochum, 1990). Further, see Iain R. Smith, *The Origins of the South African War, 1899–1902* (Harlow, 1996); Paul Kennedy, *The Rise of the Anglo-German Antagonism, 1860–1914* (London, 1980); A. N. Porter, *The Origins of the South African War: Joseph Chamberlain and the Diplomacy of Imperialism, 1895–1899* (Manchester, 1980); D. M. Schreuder, *The Scramble for Southern Africa, 1877–1895: The Politics of Partition Reappraised* (Cambridge, Mass., 1980); Leonard Thompson, "Great Britain and the Afrikaner Republics, 1870–1899", in *The Oxford History of South Africa*, vol. II (Oxford, 1971); D. W. Krüger, "The British Imperial Factor in South Africa from 1870 to 1910", in *Colonialism in Africa, 1870–1960*, vol. I, L. H. Gann and P. Duignan (eds), 325–51 (Cambridge, 1969); Jeffrey Butler, "The German Factor in Anglo-Transvaal Relations", in *Britain and Germany in Africa: Imperial Rivalry and Colonial Rule*, P. Gifford and R. Louis (eds), 179–214 (New Haven, 1967); C. D. Penner, "Germany and the Transvaal before 1896", *Journal of Modern History* 12, 31–58 (1940).
9. For what follows, see Jost Dülffer, Martin Kröger, Rolf-Harald Wippich, *Vermiedene Kriege: Deeskalation von Konflikten der Großmächte zwischen Krimkrieg und Erstem Weltkrieg 1856–1914* (Munich, 1997), pp. 441–56 ("Die Buren, der Kaiser und die deutsch-britischen Beziehungen in der Transvaalfrage 1895/96").
10. Martin Kröger, *"Le bâton égyptien" – Der ägyptische Knüppel: Die Rolle der "ägyptischen Frage" in der deutschen Außenpolitik von 1875/6 bis zur "Entente Cordiale". Europäische Hochschulschriften* III/470 (Frankfurt am Main, 1991), pp. 141–85.

11. Johannes Lepsius, Albrecht Mendelssohn-Bartholdy, Friedrich Thimme (eds), *Die Grosse Politik der europäischen Kabinette, 1871–1914* (40 vols, Berlin, 1922–27), vol. 11, no. 2577, memorandum by Marschall, 1 February 1895; G. P. Gooch and H. W. V. Temperley (eds), *British Documents on the Origins of the War, 1898–1914* (11 vols, London, 1926–38), vol. 1, p. 326, memorandum by the Assistant Clerk in the Foreign Office, J. A. C. Tilley, 5 January 1905.

12. Jean van der Poel, *The Jameson Raid* (Cape Town, 1951).

13. Lepsuis *et al.*, *Grosse Politik*, vol. 11, no. 2586, Marschall to Hatzfeldt, 28 December 1895.

14. Lepsuis *et al.*, *Grosse Politik*, vol. 11, no. 2610, Wilhelm II to Kruger, 3 January 1896.

15. Politisches Archiv des Auswärtigen Amts, Berlin (Political Archive of the German Foreign Ministry, Berlin; hereafter PA), R 14631, note by Wilhelm II on a report by Hohenlohe, 6 March 1897.

16. Rosenbach, *Das Deutsche Reich*, p. 76, Holstein to Hohenlohe, 9 April 1897.

17. Norman Rich and M. H. Fisher (eds), *The Holstein Papers*, vol. IV (Cambridge, 1963), no. 608, p. 22, Holstein to Hatzfeldt, 12 April 1897.

18. *Ibid.*

19. *Ibid.*

20. *Ibid.*, also no. 613.

21. Rich & Fisher, *The Holstein Papers*, vol. IV, no. 608, p. 24.

22. PA, London Embassy, vol. 1177, Hatzfeldt to Holstein, 20 May 1897.

23. Otto Becker, "Die Wende der deutsch-englischen Beziehungen", in *Festschrift für Gerhard Ritter zu seinem 60. Geburtstag*, Richard Nürnberger (ed.), 353–400 (Tübingen, 1950).

24. Lepsuis *et al.*, *Grosse Politik*, vol. 14/1, no. 3782, Hatzfeldt to Auswärtiges Amt, 29 March 1898.

25. Gregor Schöllgen, *Imperialismus und Gleichgewicht* (Munich, 1984), p. 89.

26. Imanuel Geiss, *Der lange Weg in die Katastrophe: Die Vorgeschichte des Ersten Weltkriegs, 1815–1914* (Munich, Zürich, 1990), p. 215.

27. Schöllgen: *op. cit.*, p. 90, Salisbury to Chamberlain, May 2, 1898.

28. Andreas Hillgruber: *Deutschlands Rolle in der Vorgeschichte der beiden Weltkriege* (3rd edition, Göttingen, 1986), pp. 21-2.

29. Lepsuis *et al.*, *Grosse Politik*, vol. 14/1, no. 3788, p. 212, Hatzfeldt to Hohenlohe, 7 April 1898.

30. Rosenbach, *Das Deutsche Reigh*, p. 109.

31. J. L. Garvin, *The Life of Joseph Chamberlain*, vol. III (London, 1934), p. 315, Chamberlain to Balfour (First Lord of the Treasury), 19 August and 23 August 1898.

32. Rosenbach, *Das Deutsche Reigh*, p. 109, Milner to his secretary G. V. Fiddes, 25 November 1898.

33. PA, R 2215, p. 27, memorandum by Bülow for Prince Heinrich (brother of Wilhelm II), 15 August 1899.

34. Lepsuis *et al.*, *Grosse Politik*, vol. 14/1, no. 3834, Richthofen to Hatzfeldt, 16 July 1898.

35. PA, R 14639, Bülow to Herff, 5 March 1898.

36. PA, personal files of Franz von Herff and Max Biermann (Herff's successor in Pretoria), transfer orders, 22 March 1898.

37. PA, R 14641, Richthofen to Metternich, 14 August 1898.

38. Rosenbach, *Das Deutsche Reigh*, pp. 39–40; Seligmann, *Rivalry in Southern Africa*, p. 146.

39. Rosenbach, *Das Deutsche Reigh*, p. 136.

40. *Ibid.*, p. 129, Holstein to Hammann (head of the press department of the Auswärtiges Amt), 9 September 1898.

41. PA, R 14641, Bülow to Auswärtiges Amt, 18 September 1898.

42. Uwe Kröll, *Die internationale Buren-Agitation, 1899–1902: Haltung der Öffentlichkeit und Agitation zugunsten der Buren in Deutschland, Frankreich und den Niederlanden während des Burenkrieges* (Münster, 1973).

43. Lepsuis *et al.*, *Grosse Politik*, vol. 15, no. 4382, Chamberlain to Eckardstein, 14 September 1899.

44. Lepsuis *et al.*, *Grosse Politik*, vol. 15, no. 4384, Bülow to Auswärtiges Amt, 20 September 1899.

45. Lepsuis *et al.*, *Grosse Politik*, vol. 14/2, no. 4098, Bülow to Auswärtiges Amt, 2 October 1899.

46. Lepsuis *et al.*, *Grosse Politik*, vol. 15, no. 4388, Lascelles to Derenthall, 3 October 1899; Lepsuis *et al.*, *Grosse Politik*, vol. 14/2, nos. 4099 and 411100, Derenthall to Hatzfeldt, 3 October 1899, Hatzfeldt to Derenthall, 4 October 1899.

47. Lepsuis *et al.*, *Grosse Politik*, vol. 14/2, no. 4103, Bülow to Hatzfeldt, 8 October 1899.

48. Lepsuis *et al.*, *Grosse Politik*, vol. 15, no. 4389, memorandum by Derenthall, 8 October 1899.
49. J. A. S. Grenville, *Lord Salisbury and Foreign Policy: The Close of the Nineteenth Century* (London, 1964), p. 267.
50. Paul Kennedy, *The Samoan Tangle: A Study in Anglo-German-American Relations, 1878–1900* (Dublin, 1974), p. 198.
51. Lepsuis *et al.*, *Grosse Politik*, vol. 14/2, no. 4089, Hatzfeldt to Auswärtiges Amt, 20 September, 1899.
52. Lepsuis *et al.*, *Grosse Politik*, vol. 14/2, no. 4091, Bülow to Auswärtiges Amt, 22 September 1899; no. 4094, Bülow to Auswärtiges Amt, 25 September 1899.
53. Holstein to Bülow, 3 October 1899. This document appears only in the German edition of the Holstein papers: Werner Frauendienst (ed.), *Die Geheimen Papiere von Friedrich von Holstein* (Göttingen, 1963), vol. IV, no. 709, n. 4, pp. 141–2.
54. Gooch & Temperley, *British Documents*, vol. 1, no. 150, Lascelles to Salisbury, 10 October 1899.
55. Peter Winzen, *Bülows Weltmachtkonzeption: Untersuchungen zur Frühphase seiner Außenpolitik, 1897–1901* (Boppard, 1977), pp. 202–5.
56. Lepsuis *et al.*, *Grosse Politik*, vol. 14/2, nos. 4115–17; Grenville, *Lord Salisbury*, pp. 269–324; Kennedy, *The Samoan Tangle*, pp. 230–33.
57. Gooch & Temperley, *British Documents*, vol. 1, no. 154, Grierson to Gough (Secretary at the British Embassy in Berlin), 6 November 1899.
58. Kennedy, *The Samoan Tangle*, pp. 236–8.
59. Dülffer *et al.*, *Vermiedene Kriege*, p. 315.
60. Winzen, *Bülows Weltmachtkonzeption*, p. 219.
61. Lepsuis *et al.*, *Grosse Politik*, vol. 15, no. 4398, p. 413, memorandum by Bülow, 24 November 1899.
62. *Ibid.*, p. 420.
63. *Stenographische Berichte über die Verhandlungen des Deutschen Reichstags*, 10th legislative period, 1st session, 119th sitting, p. 3293(C).
64. Rosenbach, *Das Deutsche Reigh*, p. 224, Chamberlain to Lascelles, 12 December 1899.
65. Rich & Fisher, *The Holstein Papers*, vol. IV, no. 722, Bülow to Hatzfeldt, 12 December 1899.
66. Lepsuis *et al.*, *Grosse Politik*, vol. 15, no. 4404, Hatzfeldt to Auswärtiges Amt, 21 December 1899; Winzen, *Bülows Weltmachtkonzeption*, pp. 286–92.
67. Lepsuis *et al.*, *Grosse Politik*, vol. 15, no. 4401, p. 426, Hatzfeldt to Hohenlohe, 2 December 1899.
68. Bernhard, Prince von Bülow, *Deutsche Politik*, Peter Winzen (ed.) (Bonn, 1992), p. 34.
69. Bernhard, *Deutsche Politik*, p. 140; Bülow's self-exculpatory book first appeared in 1913.
70. A. J. P. Taylor, *The Struggle for Mastery in Europe, 1848–1918* (Oxford, 1963), p. 390.
71. PA, R 2279, Bülow to Hammann and Esternaux (clerk in the press department of the Auswärtiges Amt), 31 December 1899.
72. Lepsuis *et al.*, *Grosse Politik*, vol. 15, ch. 102; Fröhlich, *Von Konfrontation zur Koexistenz*, pp. 216–19.
73. Lepsuis *et al.*, *Grosse Politik*, vol. 15, no. 4425, Bülow to Hatzfeldt, 6 January 1900.
74. Lepsuis *et al.*, *Grosse Politik*, vol. 15, no. 4426, Bülow to Hatzfeldt, 6 January 1900.
75. Lepsuis *et al.*, *Grosse Politik*, vol. 15, no. 4429, Holstein to Hatzfeldt, 7 January 1900.
76. Lepsuis *et al.*, *Grosse Politik*, vol. 15, no. 4446, Hatzfeldt to Auswärtiges Amt, 16 January 1900.
77. Lepsuis *et al.*, *Grosse Politik*, vol. 15, no. 4454, Salisbury to Lascelles, 17 January 1900; copied to Bülow 23 January 1900.
78. *Ibid.*
79. Lepsuis *et al.*, *Grosse Politik*, vol. 15, no. 4458, Wolff-Metternich to Hohenlohe, 24 March 1900.
80. Fröhlich, *Von Konfrontation zur Koexistenz*, pp. 218–19.
81. Lepsuis *et al.*, *Grosse Politik*, vol. 15, no. 4459, Münster (German Ambassador to Paris) to Bülow, 25 December 1899, enclosure.
82. Lepsuis *et al.*, *Grosse Politik*, vol. 15, no. 4463, memorandum by Bülow, 12 January 1900.
83. Lepsuis *et al.*, *Grosse Politik*, vol. 15, no. 4465, memorandum by Bülow, 13 January 1900.
84. Lepsuis *et al.*, *Grosse Politik*, vol. 15, no. 4472, Bülow to Radolin (German Ambassador to St Petersburg), 3 March 1900.

85. Lepsuis *et al.*, *Grosse Politik*, vol. 15, no. 4482, Bülow to Biermann, 10 March 1900.
86. Lepsuis *et al.*, *Grosse Politik*, vol. 15, nos. 4496 and 4497, Bülow to Wolff-Metternich, 31 March and 1 April 1900.
87. Friedrich von Holstein, *Lebensbekenntnisse in Briefen an eine Frau*, Helmuth Rogge (ed.) (Berlin, 1932), p. 214 (Holstein to his cousin Ida von Stülpnagel, probably 27 November 1902).
88. The concept of "excirclement" (*Auskreisung*) is borrowed from Geiss, *Der lange Weg in die Katastrophe*, p. 217.

CHAPTER THREE

Russian Foreign Policy and the Boer War

Derek Spring

On appointment as foreign minister in January 1897, Count N. V. Muraviev had been impressed with the strength of Russia's world position. He was pleased by French assurances that there could be no reconciliation between France and Germany until the return of Alsace-Lorraine and content to find both in Germany and France a distaste for Britain's "machinations". Nevertheless, he did not want cooperation of the continental powers to be seen as a programme for the isolation of Britain. There was a danger that Germany would use Franco–Russian hostility towards Britain to its own advantage.[1] However, the dramatic step forward by Russia in the Far East at the turn of 1897–98, with the occupation and then 25-year lease of Port Arthur and the Liaotung peninsula from China, decisively modified Russia's international position before and during the period of the Boer War. This overstretch of Russian expansion in the Far East urgently required the extension of the Manchurian railways, the building of naval and land defences for Port Arthur and the expansion of the inadequate Pacific fleet to face the Japanese. These placed huge demands over several years on the already overburdened state budget and required that Russia should stand aside from international complications.

Muraviev's proposal to the State Council (28 February 1898) for an agreement between the continental powers to limit military arms with the support of the ministers of war and finance already showed his awareness of the constraints on Russian policy for the time being.[2] This was the germ of the peace conference proposal in Muraviev's circular of 24 August 1898, which led to the Hague Conference itself in 1899. Meanwhile, an increasingly cautious policy was necessary. "Our state of unpreparedness naturally impels us now to extreme circumspection and caution" he advised in instructions to Peking on 23 August 1898.[3] In the light of the tensions between France and Britain over Fashoda, Muraviev warned the new war minister, Kuropatkin, in

43

November 1898, that "the present uncertain political situation shows the need to observe vigilance and extreme care, avoiding any conflict with England at any point where our joint interests come into contact, and in particular in the Far East".[4] While the growth of colonial disputes between Britain on the one hand and Germany and France on the other might give Russia some freedom of manoeuvre and "allow us to give essential support to France and draw Germany to the common cause", yet they should be "at the same time not getting into a hostile relationship with England".[5]

Britain remained the main rival internationally, but settlement of differences with it was not excluded. In the autumn of 1898 negotiations for spheres of railway building in China were taken up again and concluded in April 1899 with the Scott–Muraviev agreement recognizing Russian pre-eminence in northern China and British pre-eminence in the Yangtse valley. At the same time negotiations were taking place for a joint loan to Persia with Britain alone or together with France. Russia's wider financial interests, as perceived by the minister of finance, Sergei Witte, also favoured a reduction of tensions with Britain in the late 1890s. By 1897 the French were becoming concerned at the overloading of the Paris Stock Exchange with Russian stocks and more demanding in their financial relations. Witte sought to obtain greater freedom of manoeuvre by exploring the possibility of loans on the London and New York Stock Exchanges. But the key to opening the London market was a general political agreement and this was not forthcoming in spite of Salisbury's overtures. In late April 1899, Witte engineered the leaking to *The Times* of his speech to the State Council arguing the case for the encouragement of British capital investment in Russia. In June a small Russian railway loan was floated on the London market. It was not a great success, but Witte persisted in his efforts in this direction throughout 1899.

Meanwhile, signs of an Anglo–German rapprochement were seen as a serious danger to Russia and this is a key to understanding Russian policy in the Boer War. Ambassador Osten-Sacken reported from Berlin in June 1898: "the symptoms are still too vague to be the cause of accusations: nevertheless they demand from our part the most watchful attitude to keep Germany on our side and prevent her . . . from transferring to the camp of our enemies".[6] Muraviev instructed him to impress on the Germans, that "a sincere and unwavering agreement between Russia and Germany will be the best guarantee of the general peace".[7] This was not forthcoming, but when, in March 1899, the Germans secured a concession for a port on the Bosphoros as a terminal for the Baghdad railway, the need became urgent to confirm Russia's relationship with Germany by at least an agreement on their mutual interests in the Ottoman Empire. At the end of June 1899, Muraviev told Radolin that an arrangement on spheres of influence ought to be possible, together with a German recognition of Russia's claim on the Bosphoros in the event of the collapse of the Ottoman Empire. Otherwise Russia could look to Britain as

Russia had need for neither territorial expansion nor an outlet to the Persian Gulf, and was quite satisfied with the Afghan frontier. But Radolin failed to be moved by these threats and repeated Bülow's familiar views that there could be no agreement with either member of the Dual Alliance except in return for a guarantee of the territorial status quo in Europe. The summer of 1899 preceding the outbreak of the Boer War therefore saw not only a cooling of Russo–German relations, but also the clarification of the limited possibilities of cooperation with Germany.[8]

To understand the Russians' foreign policy during the period of the Boer War, we need to understand not only their perception of their interests and of the international situation, but also the internal tensions within the élite and apprehensions about the instability of the policy-making process, which also had an important bearing. At the end of the 1890s, Witte was the most outstanding and powerful figure in the Russian government. His responsibility for the negotiation of loans, for railway building and trade and for determining the size of the naval and military budgets gave him a powerful role in Russia's policy towards the outside world. On 17 March 1899 he successfully argued the case for his much criticized industrialization strategy before a committee chaired by the tsar.[9] His position was further strengthened in October 1899 with the dismissal of his rival, the interior minister, Goremykin.[10] But in spite of his strong position Witte was not a prime minister and was concerned at the volatility of the policy-making process. There were, he said, "no definitely established aims and definite means to attain them. We live from day to day and express our views as we think fit at the time".[11] Coordination of policy was in theory in the hands of the autocrat but this was no guarantee of the stable and coherent policy that Russia's economic development required. Nicholas II was young and inexperienced. He lost two foreign ministers in the first two years of his reign and the third, Muraviev, was not the man to turn the tsar into a statesman. Witte, in particular, had little confidence in Muraviev and looked to his deputy V. N. Lamsdorf as a more stable influence. The contradictions in the tsar's outlook meant that while he sought to solve problems by peaceful means, yet he "liked the idea of military glory" and the bold gesture according to Witte (in April 1900)[12] and was even "bellicose and arrogant (*voinstvennyi i samonadeyannyi*)" according to the former war minister, Vannovskii (in December 1896).[13]

Witte was conscious of two recent occasions in which the adventurism of the tsar had shown itself. In 1896 he had been prepared to give Nelidov, the ambassador in Constantinople, the right to call up the Black Sea fleet, when he saw fit, in order to occupy the Bosphorus.[14] Witte's intervention had played an important role in countermanding this. Similarly in November 1897, while a council meeting had decided against the occupation of Port Arthur, the tsar and Muraviev a few days later reversed the decision. Witte had been opposed but was unable to prevent the course of events and eventually reconciled himself to it. But the problem was inherent in the system where some ministers gave absolute priority to the decisions of the tsar as autocrat, while others, like Witte, were concerned to rely on good advice and persuasion, even if they were unwelcome. This source of instability of policy was exemplified in Muraviev's peremptory note to Witte in early 1898 about the occupation of Port Arthur, that his duty was simply to carry out the orders of his imperial master.[15] And again in 1900, Witte had to argue the case with his friend Sipyagin, minister of the interior, for a more critical and independent attitude towards the tsar.[16] These circumstances and experiences created tensions within Russian policy-making circles in the first phase of the Boer War, when the preoccupation of Russia's main rival seemed to create the opportunity for – or the danger of – some adventurous policy move.

Muraviev, however, was not inclined to an adventurous policy when the Boer War broke out in October 1899 in spite of the aggressive tone of Russian public opinion.[17] He was aware of the weaknesses of Russia's position and the limited possibility of cooperation between the continental powers. Muraviev's caution was evident in his talks with the Spanish queen and prime minister, Silvela, on 4 October.[18] Silvela had, since April 1899, been exploring the possibility of a secret, defensive continental coalition to strengthen the position of Spain against Britain.[19] Muraviev already knew, in any case, from conversations with the Germans in June 1899, that there could not be Franco–German cooperation on this issue either.[20] In his discussions with Silvela in October, Muraviev was "definitely cautious" about Britain, "as if he wanted to avoid saying anything in an unfriendly or hostile tone". Nothing concrete was said or promised on either side, and the Russian minister reminded him that a rapprochement between France and Germany, was "a very difficult problem", which could only be solved slowly.[21] In his talks with the Spanish Queen, Muraviev also emphasised the difficulties of achieving a Franco-German agreement.[22] His concern at this point was more to prevent Germany (or France) using the opportunity of the Boer war to strengthen their relations with Britain, than to set up an active anti-British coalition.[23]

On 6 October 1899, Muraviev left Biarritz for Paris to meet Delcassé and Loubet. A few days later he received a letter from Witte, which tacitly gave him a further reminder of the danger of using Britain's embarrassment for any policy of adventure. The St Petersburg Stock Exchange was suffering a serious crisis, with a general fall in prices from 23–27 September, worsening in October.[24] Delcassé had insisted that a financial arrangement between Witte and the Credit Lyonnais to raise money in France could not be allowed until the matter had been discussed with Muraviev. Witte wrote that it was becoming impossible to work with the French: "If France wants to close its market to us, let it say so – instead of making continual objections". In that case, Russia would have to apply for credit to the US and Britain. But "it would hardly be possible to find firm credit in America – and this will leave only England".[25] Undoubtedly Witte was frustrated with the French. But the onset of the Boer War made it *less* likely that Russia could find resources on the

London market, at least for the time being. His reference to Britain was evidently a warning to Muraviev that it was not in Russia's interests to excessively antagonize that power.

We do not have available either the reports of Muraviev or Delcassé on their discussions in Paris.[26] But the evidence of Muraviev's view of the situation of Russia and its relationships with the other powers in 1898–99, as well as such evidence as there is on his Paris visit, convinces that Muraviev did not make any adventurous proposals. The French agent Jules Hansen met Muraviev on 17 October and noted, "Conversation at Hotel Liverpool with Muraviev on the affairs of Transvaal. He does not have a very great interest in it, had not talked much on this subject with Delcassé . . . They will probably leave the English to do what they want".[27] Ten days later, Muraviev met Loubet and, according to the latter's secretary-general, "sounded the President to see if the French government was willing to join with Russia and Germany in joint action without, if not against England . . . Perhaps the three powers could intervene, before the end of hostilities, to arrange or to moderate the settlement".[28] Delcassé himself subsequently reported that he had agreed with Muraviev "to try to put an end to the war at an opportune moment". Muraviev was to "sound out" the Germans and "assure himself of their views" on his return journey to St Petersburg, via Berlin, where the tsar was also due to meet the Kaiser on 8 November.[29] All this amounts to rather less than a proposal by Muraviev for a continental coalition against Britain. The meaning of Combarieu's note on the talks with Loubet is not entirely clear, but the wording is significant: "joint action without, if not against England" emphasizes Muraviev's caution about antagonizing Britain. And Muraviev's task to "sound out" the Germans also falls far short of any intention to make a definite proposal or of any conviction about the German response.

In Berlin, on 8 November, both Muraviev and the tsar were scheduled to meet their German counterparts. The tsar had been in Darmstadt for the past month on vacation and from the beginning of the war had developed a keen interest in it, avidly reading the reports in the British press. Nicholas II shared the anti-English sentiments prevalent in the Russian military, modified by his personal relationships with the British royal family. At the beginning of November he declared to his sister the keen interest he had in every development of the war and the satisfaction he had at British setbacks.[30]

But as early as 20 October, the Russians were aware of the pro-British attitude of the Germans towards the Boer War.[31] In order to counteract this, the tsar saw his task in Berlin as "to set the Emperor on the British, reminding him of his famous telegram to Kruger".[32] This was appropriate action in Russian interests, given their apprehension of the danger of an Anglo–German rapprochement. But it can have been little surprise when the Anglo–German agreement on Samoa was announced on the morning of the arrival of the Russians in Potsdam, even before its signature. Muraviev was already aware of the limited possibilities of cooperation between France and Germany. His task, agreed with Delcassé, was only to "sound out" the Germans on their views rather than to make any proposals.[33] So the tsar declared his sympathy with the Boers, but insisted that African affairs did not interest Russia and it would remain simply an observer. Muraviev noted that public opinion in Russia, France and Germany was encouraging their governments to intervene against Britain , but such action was not appropriate.[34] That the meeting in Berlin was merely for a few hours was not a result of Russian disappointment at the results, as it had been agreed beforehand. In fact, Nicholas had been reluctant to go to Berlin at all, perhaps for security reasons.[35]

Muraviev was well aware of the difficulties of the Franco–German relationship for any significant action *against* Britain and nor was a directly anti-British policy in Russia's interests. At a time when Britain was in need of an ally, it was important to ensure that neither Russia's ally, France, nor its "friend", Germany, should move closer to Britain, thus weakening their ties with Russia. The discussion of any issues that would draw the continental powers together and emphasize their differences with Britain was important. But it was founded on the knowledge that no actual joint action against Britain was possible.

The private views of the tsar-autocrat showed that although there was no enthusiasm for collective action, there was some justification for apprehension in responsible Russian circles about independent Russian action as advised in parts of the press. The tsar had written to his sister on 2 November expressing his interest in the war and his sympathy for the Boers. He went on to tell her, revealingly:

> it is pleasant for me to know that only in my hands are the means finally to change the course of the war in South Africa. The means is very simple: to give the order by telegraph to all the forces of Turkestan to mobilise and move towards the frontier. That is all. No strongest fleet in the world can prevent us settling with England precisely in that most sensitive spot for her . . .

Certainly Nicholas did continue in a more cautious, if contradictory, tone that "the time has not yet come for that; we are not ready enough for serious action, particularly because Turkestan is not connected by a direct line with the interior of Russia".[36] This was a reference to the proposed Orenburg–Tashkent railway, a pet project of war minister Kuropatkin and of the French military as a weapon against Britain.[37] Witte was apprehensive about such talk in military circles and by Kuropatkin himself about a campaign towards India.[38] In spite of his criticism of the railway as essentially a stategic project likely to antagonize Britain, Witte had felt obliged, as a result of Muraviev's discussions with Delcassé in October, to agree to allocate 10 million roubles in the budget for 1900 to begin building the railway in return for allowing further Russian bonds on the French market.[39] This probably convinced Witte that for the time being a rapprochement with Britain was not possible. The tsar's deep hostility to British policy is evident from his family correspondence, although he was able to be polite and even congenial towards his English relations.[40] This antipathy was well known in court and official circles and gave free reign to the expression of anti-English sentiments that endangered the stability of policy in spite of his peaceful assurances.[41]

Witte's apprehensions for the present were exaggerated. Both Nicholas and Kuropatkin recognized that the time was not appropriate for action against Britain. But the tsar did like the idea of the bold gesture and the sense of Russia's potential power.[42] There could be no significant concentration in Central Asia to frighten Britain, but some play-acting was possible. In December 1899 troops were sent along the recently completed branch line of the trans-Caspian railway to Kushk on the Afghan frontier. It was a gesture that could be advertised to the anti-British public as showing Russia's potential to threaten Britain. But Kuropatkin told both the French and German ambassadors that in fact this only brought their forces to four battalions. And the Afghans and even the British were given reassurances.[43] In fact the line to Kushk was only just ready for normal traffic in 1900. And the report for 1899 on the state of the Central Asian Railway, which fed the Kushk branch, emphasized its poor condition with, for instance, few passing places to maximize the passage of trains.[44]

Witte was apprehensive that Kuropatkin still had in his mind the fantastic idea of a campaign to India. His lack of confidence in the war minister was to an extent subsequently justified by the latter's ill-considered behaviour over Russian intervention in the Boxer rising in the summer of 1900, when the military were given their head.[45] But Kuropatkin was less adventurist than he sometimes appeared to be and was aware of the value of agreement with Britain. In 1900 he noted:

> I am deeply convinced that the conquest of India in the 20th century would be a disaster and unbearable burden for Russia and at the same time I recognise as natural and desirable the establishment of as friendly relations as possible with England so that in the event of a revolt in India we will be on the side of the English.[46]

The almost universal anglophobia of the Russian press, and particularly of official and court circles, aroused the apprehensions of Witte, who again sought to emphasize the significance of Britain for Russia. On 14 December 1899 he declared his readiness "as a result of the desire expressed to me from England that the Russian [State] Bank should come to their aid" to lend £5–8 million in gold for a few months to help stabilize the London money market, whose difficulties were adversely affecting the St Petersburg exchange.[47] Through Muraviev, Witte asked Delcassé how the French would view such an action, which would, he thought, "conform to our mutual interests". Delcassé replied that in spite of French public opinion, they would not oppose Witte's idea.[48] However, already, on 18 December, Witte decided not to pursue the matter, ostensibly in view of the sensitivities of public opinion both in France and Russia.[49] But if Russian public opinion had been an issue, Witte would never have made the proposal at all. Witte and Muraviev were evidently not willing to displease French opinion. But there must be doubt about whether such a clear request for a short-term loan was in fact made by the Bank of England, particularly to Russia, which was itself short of capital. Evidence from the the Bank of England archives shows that it was quite secure about its position throughout the war and its policy of keeping its reserves relatively low.[50] In this light Witte's initiative was rather a means of reminding Muraviev once again that the London financial market had significance for Russia and any adventurous measures exploiting British embarrassment would not be politic.

Witte was apprehensive about any precipitate military action or seizure that could lead to a conflict, but was not averse to measures protecting Russia's commercial and financial interests by peaceful penetration. The Boer War coincided with the end of the 10 year agreement of 1890 with the Shah, which had effectively prevented railway construction in Persia. The situation was now more threatening for Russia, with the plans for the Baghdad railway reaching to the Persian frontier and the activities of foreign capitalists. Even Russian entrepreneurs put their proposals to Witte for a railway to a port on the Persian Gulf. Russia did not have adequate capital for such projects nor the state the resources. For Witte the continuation of the moratorium on railways in Persia was essential to prevent ill-considered adventures such as the one that had led to the occupation of Port Arthur. As a result, in mid-December, with Witte's approval, Muraviev gave instructions for the negotiation of a Russian loan to Persia in return for the renewal of the railway agreement. The loan was concluded at the end of January 1900 for 22½ million roubles on the security of most of the customs revenues, on condition that the Persians repaid all their other foreign debts.[51]

This loan did produce a significant strengthening of the Russian position in Persia, even though it was based on insecure foundations. It was not, however, simply a result of British preoccupation with the Boer War. The British minister in Teheran, and the (British) Imperial Bank of Persia had urged their government to give support to a loan in 1898–99, but the Treasury refused. British financiers were little interested without some guarantee or with actual control (rather than merely the security) of the customs revenues and Salisbury was inclined to think that north Persia at least was already lost to Russia. The Russian government, however, in spite of its straitened circumstances, was prepared to find ways to make a loan for the important political as well as economic benefits that accrued on its southern frontier. A joint loan with Britain was still a possibility as late as 29 September 1899, when Lamsdorf told the British ambassador that he would consult Witte further on the matter.[52] But on 14 December Muraviev issued instructions for the negotiation of a Russian loan in Teheran. At some point between those two dates, the idea of a joint loan was rejected.[53]

The coincidence of circumstances makes this appear as if Russia was simply taking advantage of the Boer War, but the situation was more complex. Already in August the Persians had made it clear to the British minister that they would not accept a joint loan, as they saw it as tantamount to the division of their country between the two powers and they were disappointed that the British had been unwilling to persuade their capitalists to make a loan.[54] Also, as a result of Muraviev's meeting with Delcassé in October 1899, Witte had felt compelled to accept the construction of the Orenburg–Tashkent railway on state resources in return for the placing of mortgage bonds of the Nobles Land Bank on the Paris market. For Witte the forwarding of this project, which was directed against Britain, removed the possibility for the time being of a working arrangement with Britain in Persia.[55]

Witte, as finance minister, had to play the key role in making the loan possible.[56] The Russian banks did not have the resources and the state budget was already under considerable pressure. Witte's novel solution was to find more than half of the loan from the private resources of the imperial family, including 11 million roubles from the tsar himself. This meant that an extra burden was not added to the state budget and also that the interest of the tsar and some members of his family was harnessed to the idea of expansion of Russia's influence by economic and financial means rather than military power.[57]

Action was also taken on the Afghan issue during the Boer War. On 6 February 1900 the British were informed that Russia intended to open "direct relations with Afghanistan for matters concerning frontier affairs". These would not have a political character and Russia would continue to regard Afghanistan as outside its sphere of influence. But now that a firm frontier had been established and trade was beginning to develop, the complete absence of relations was an anomaly.[58] Here, also, it is significant that the measure conformed to the priorities of Witte of the development of trade and commerce. Already, in 1895, Witte had convened a committee to discuss the conditions and development of Russo–Afghan trade. And Muraviev had informed Kuropatkin in November 1898 that "only by means of a possible easing of trade relations of Afghanistan with Russia . . . can we count on coming gradually closer to such a fanatical and anti-foreign country as Afghanistan".[59] Following the announcement to the British government, already on 9–21 February, V. I. Ignatiev, the Russian political agent in Bukhara, wrote to the Afghan trading agent expressing friendly feelings for the Emir and hoping that direct relations could be established for the mutual development of trade. He also took the occasion to explain that the recent troop movements to Kushk had only been to test the capacity of the new railway and had created a stir simply because of the difficulties the British had got themselves into in South Africa.[60]

However, the modesty of the measure must be noted. The Russians only declared their *intention* to establish such direct relations as were necessary for the development of trade. The note to the British government announcing this was couched in very friendly terms and the measure was not proposed in an aggressive manner. Lamsdorf's internal memorandum of 3 February shows that specifically diplomatic relations were not a matter for the present even though the British were in difficulties, but only for the future "when the situation was favourable".[61] Ignatiev's letter was not even addressed to the Emir and the Emir's trade agent in Bukhara had himself helped to precipitate the approach.[62]

In Ottoman Turkey, too, Russian policy did not stand still. The ongoing negotiations for a ten-year abstention on railway building in a zone along the southern Black Sea coast were brought to a successful conclusion on 31 March 1900, although Turkey could not be brought to commit itself against the fortification of the Bosphoros.[63] It is difficult to argue also that this measure was precipitated by the Boer War. The agreement was directed not so much against British activity in Turkey as against the German Baghdad Railway. Negotiations with Germany in the summer of 1899 had already shown that an agreement to protect their respective interests was not possible. Therefore, already in August 1899, Zinoviev in Constantinople had been instructed to demand the Turks should not offer railway or port concessions along the Black Sea coast to other powers. The issue became more urgent with the granting of the preliminary concession for the Baghdad Railway to the Germans in December 1899. And at the end of February 1900, Zinoviev was given instructions to press for an agreement, finally achieved with some difficulty by an exchange of notes on 31 March giving the Russians an exclusive right to build if the Turks could not build on their own resources in a large area of north eastern Anatolia bordering the Black Sea and the Russian frontier, in effect a veto on railways similar to that with Persia.[64] Again, it is significant that this had the strong support of Witte, who regarded the Baghdad Railway as a serious danger to Russia, while Russia was in no position to compete on the same terms with the Germans.

All the above initiatives were underway and some completed by 3 February 1900, when the Russian foreign ministry produced a document on "the tasks of the military policy of Russia in the Far East" to consider "whether Russia should use the favourable development of circumstances [the Boer War] . . . at least to achieve with the minimum expenditure of energy one of the pressing political tasks?"[65] Some other powers had hurried to secure benefits from the difficulties experienced by Britain, and this had raised hopes in public opinion that Russia would seek similar "compensations" by the seizure of territory or a port. However the memorandum, written by V. N.

Lamsdorf, Muraviev's deputy, firmly stated that Russia had no need of this. Any port would need to be defended, would be easy prey in war and would be very expensive.[66] As for the Bosphoros, however, everybody accepted the need to prepare for its occupation, but for the present it was only necessary to secure the recognition by Turkey of a sphere along the southern Black Sea coast where no foreign powers would build railways and an obligation not to fortify the Bosphoros. This would be enough to counterbalance the danger of Germany's Baghdad Railway concession.[67] Russia did not have the capital to build railways in Persia either and therefore the best policy was the recent renewal of the Shah's 1890 assurance not to allow other foreigners to build railways in Persia if Russia did not. The best means of struggle with Britain in Persia, the memorandum declared, was by the development of trade, roads, telegraph and the Caspian ports, and to this purpose they had just concluded a loan that would be a powerful instrument for Russia's political and economic influence.[68]

As for Afghanistan, the occupation of Herat, as suggested in the press as a strategic point for a future advance to India, was "extremely complicated and risky" and "extremely undesirable politically". However, the complete absence of relations with Afghanistan created problems now that Russia had a border with it. So the ambassador in London had already been instructed to inform the British government that it was no longer possible to refrain from direct relations with the ruler of Afghanistan.[69] In the Far East no new action was possible. The strengthening of the Russian position at Port Arthur required peace and complete abstention from any decisive actions that could create political complications, such as the occupation of the island of Kargodo (between Korea and Japan).[70] In conclusion, it was necessary to "*definitely clarify* the extremely serious question of the best means of preparing *the plan for the occupation of the Bosphoros Straits by Russia*" (original emphasis). But otherwise "the present political situation *does not raise* the need for any kind of urgent or extraordinary measures either to acquire by agreement any kind of harbour for our fleet or by means of military occupation any territory or strategic position at all". Nine other measures were proposed, none of which was expected to create any international complications or "infringe the peaceful course of Russian policy directed by your majesty's will".[71]

This memorandum has frequently been quoted, but its purpose and context have not been adequately explored. Such a broad statement of Russian policy aims and objectives across the Asiatic continent from the Bosphoros to the Pacific was unusual. Its purpose was evidently to carefully argue the case *against* any military seizures or precipitate action in Asia. Most of the measures proposed as appropriate had already been taken, such as the Persian loan, the renewal of the railways ban in Persia and the declaration of the right to open relations with Afghanistan. Others were already underway such as the negotiation of an agreement with Turkey on railways and the strengthening of Russia's position in the Far East. The rest of the proposals concerned merely the vague "speeding up" of projects, such as the Orenburg–Tashkent railway. The decision to *prepare* for the seizure of the Bosphoros was nothing new, but budget allocations had always been lacking and divisions in both the military and civilian élite about its relevance and priority continued to leave Russia unprepared for this eventuality to the end.[72]

The introduction refers to the need to consider the proposals for action made in the press or current in public opinion. But the autocrat and his ministers had no obligation to take account of public opinion and were generally resistant to it. Muraviev had recently dismissed any such influence and the memorandum itself rather belittles the Russian press as merely "echoing Europe".[73] Nevertheless, while rejecting the proposals made in the press for seizures of a port or territory as totally inappropriate, it is found necessary to spell out very carefully the arguments against them underlining the key points for the reader. But the readers of this top secret document, issued in a few numbered copies, were only to be the tsar himself and his ministers of foreign affairs, war, the navy and finance.

For whose benefit then were these arguments for strictly dipolomatic action? The danger, recognized by those ministers who were apprehensive about the instability of policy, was not the adventurous proposals of part of the press, but that those opinions and aspirations were shared in official and court circles near to the tsar. The Straits episode in 1896, and the seizure of Port Arthur in 1897–98, had shown the volatile potential and the uncertainty of the direction of policy that depended on who secured the ear of the young tsar among his competing ministers, family members and favourites.

Witte was apprehensive about adventurous influences on Russia's foreign policy. He confided his worries to his friend Polovtsov in seemingly more stable circumstances a few months later:

> Muraviev is no more than a courtier, thinking of pleasant things to say to the tsar and agrees with everything. Kuropatkin has quietened a bit but only thinks of the seizure of the Bosphoros or the invasion of India. The tsar likes the idea of such military glory and supports Kuropatkin.[74]

By January 1900 the anti-British attitudes of the Russian press and opinion were at their height. On 14–27 January 1900, Nicholas wrote in his diary about his sister's husband: "Sandro has gone completely mad about the war of the British against the Boers, though that is the case with all of us".[75] The tsar and Kuropatkin encouraged such measures as the rapid construction of the strategic Orenburg–Tashkent railway for the concentration of troops in Turkestan. Tyrtov, minister for the navy, hoped for some specific action, for instance the seizure of the island of Kargodo in the Straits of Korea.[76] In the second half of January 1900, the Kaiser also was encouraging Russia to take action against Britain. So in the early months of the Boer War, the heated atmosphere of court circles, public opinion and the Russian press created apprehension among the more sober policy-makers that the tsar's ear might be caught by the ideas of adventurous spirits and it was at this time that the decision to draw up the memorandum was made.

Muraviev had become aware of the need for a cautious policy and there is evident relief that the important task of drawing up the memorandum of 3 February had been so well executed in his effusive thanks to Lamsdorf, conveyed through the words of the minister of justice.[77] And Lamsdorf also had the confidence of Witte, who proposed him as foreign minister after Muraviev's sudden death in June 1900.[78] Witte was pleased with Lamsdorf's "completely calm assessment of the current situation" with its emphasis on diplomatic measures and economic competition. He underlined this, warning that the "preparations" and "speeding up" referred to in the proposals could not involve any new budgetary allocations.[79] The tax burden could not be increased, they were already overstretched and could not get into competition with "rich England". Witte, however, did still grudgingly recognize the need to "make preparations" for the seizure of the Bosphoros (which so excited Tyrtov and Kuropatkin). But this was because of the compelling argument in a hostile world that their seizure by a foreign power would be a disaster for Russia, which would impose an unbearable new burden on the budget for the defence of the Caucasian and Black sea coasts.[80]

The final summing up on this policy consultation precipitated by the Boer War concluded that the views expressed in the original memorandum coincided most nearly with the views of the minister of finance and underlined Witte's insistence that there could be no new budgetary allocations. But in apprehension that Kuropatkin's hope might still seem attractive, that they could secure the Bosphoros by entirely diplomatic means by pressure on Turkey, just as they had secured Port Arthur, it was spelled out that "the acquisition of the whole Kwantung province by peaceful diplomatic negotiations was such an exceptional event in history that we could hardly expect it to be repeated".[81] In this way the circumstances of the Boer War gave the opportunity for and even necessitated a clarification of Russia's major policy objectives and of the means to achieve them.

While Lamsdorf's memorandum was being prepared and discussed in the first two months of 1900, relations between the three major continental powers were in a state of flux. The issue of access to the Portuguese East African port of Delagoa Bay, so important to the British for access to the Transvaal, was under discussion in the new year between the Germans and the British. For the Russians, on 11 January, Osten-Sacken raised with Bülow the question of a joint Russo–German–French naval demonstration if the British should seize Delagoa Bay.[82] The Germans were not to be drawn to this proposal, which was hardly seriously meant, although it did clarify the German position. But in his Orthodox New Year interview with Osten-Sacken on 13 January, the kaiser hinted at a far broader proposal and gave the ambassador the impression that he would be prepared to take the initiative in concerted action against British aims in Egypt and South Africa (although he later vehemently denied it).[83] And a week later he showed great enthusiasm about Russian troop transports to Kushk on the Afghan frontier, volunteering the view that "only Russia could paralyse British power and deal her a mortal blow" and "if the tsar ever wanted to attack India, he would ensure that Europe would not budge".[84] A couple of days later the kaiser again spoke to Osten-Sacken, but this time expressing concern about a rumour that the British were to hand over their responsibilities in Egypt to Italian troops for the time being to enable them to transfer troops to South Africa. Bülow quickly denied there was anything in it. But for Muraviev, apprehensive about the closeness of Germany and Britain, it seemed to offer some slight opportunity. He added privately to his reply to Osten-Sacken:

> The raising of the Egyptian question by the Berlin cabinet would be beneficial to Russia in this respect: that it would create a new and serious cause of displeasure in London and thus remove the extremely serious danger for us of an entente between Germany and England.[85]

Muraviev undoubtedly got the impression that Germany might be prepared to take some initiative independently of Russia.[86] Perhaps the Germans were changing their mind in the face of the reverses of Britain in South Africa and the lack of British appreciation of their friendship.[87] But nevertheless he reacted very cautiously, suspicious of German aims. Osten-Sacken was to say that, as Russia had no interest to defend in South Africa, they would "examine any proposals from the point of view of justice and equity".[88] He then consulted his European ambassadors for their views. Nelidov from Rome advised that they should beware of the Bismarckian tendency "to direct our attention to more distant questions and away from those which are closest to us".[89] Muraviev's conclusion was that:

> the tendency of the Berlin cabinet to recommend hazardous enterprises from which Germany would be the first to benefit, is not new. But we have no reason to be drawn to it, while maintaining the best relations with the neighbouring empire, which is united with us by so many traditional and glorious ties.[90]

In mid-February the French ambassador, Montbello, reported that Muraviev considered there could be no real help from Germany.[91] But as the fortunes of the war turned in favour of the British at the end of February, Muraviev was brought to make a proposal for mediation. Delcassé entirely agreed, pointing out he had expressed the same view to the Russian ambassador several times over the past five months.[92] But the essential element of the

Russian proposal to Delcassé was that the Kaiser must take the lead: surely, Urusov told Delcassé, "the Emperor William cannot still have scruples about speaking to England of peace".[93] So on 3 March, Muraviev, through Osten-Sacken, raised the question of joint Russian–French–German friendly mediation to bring the conflict to a conclusion. Now that the British had achieved successes to satisfy their military honour, the time was appropriate for the three continental powers to exercise a "pression amicale" to prevent the complete crushing of the Boer republics, particularly in view of the heightened public opinion in favour of the Boers in all countries. It was to be a "humanitarian task conforming to the principles of the Hague Conference". But Muraviev's purpose was evident in his carefully worded language: "If the German and French governments sympathised with the idea of friendly pressure on Britain, the Imperial Cabinet, while co-operating in the entente between Germany and France, would not refuse, for its part, to exercise its moral support".[94] Undoubtedly there were high feelings in court and society circles in Russia about the David and Goliath struggle between "perfidious Albion" and the little Boer republics and the inability of Russia to make any impact on it.[95] But this was not enough to commit Muraviev or the tsar to take the lead even as the initiators of the Hague Peace Conference and as a party without significant interests in South Africa. Muraviev remained sceptical about the possibility of German cooperation with France in a continental bloc to make an approach to Britain. But given the anti-British statements of the kaiser, the proposal could clarify the German position and if it went ahead with a German initiative would prevent for the time being a closer Anglo–German relationship. Thus the essential element of the proposal was that Germany should take the lead, so for the Russians it was already a failure when the kaiser immediately suggested that the initiative should come from the tsar.[96] The further insistence by the Germans that there could not be cooperation with France, even on such a matter, without a confirmation of the Treaty of Frankfort, made it clear that the French and Russians would be left on their own to incur the displeasure of Britain, which was not the Russian objective at all.[97]

As early as 6 March, the tsar had told the Dutch ambassador that there seemed little likelihood of an intervention to save the Boers in which he thought the kaiser should take the lead; and Muraviev had already been told by the British ambassador that Britain would not accept any kind of mediation.[98] When the Kruger government itself asked for the mediation of the powers on 10 March, Muraviev told the Germans that Russia was still ready for a simultaneous *démarche* to offer their good offices to London.[99] But the Russian proposal had in fact already run into the sand with the German response. Muraviev's "initiative" was in fact no more than a proposal that the initiative should be taken by the Germans. And in so far as it was hoped it might contribute to a peaceful settlement, it was based on a failure to appreciate the Germans' concern not to harm their fragile relationship with

Britain. But the achievement of peace in South Africa was not the Russians' priority. Neither the tsar's personal sympathy for the Boers, nor his supposed commitment to the principles of the Hague Peace Conference were enough for Russia to be prepared to take the lead itself in approaching Britain. From this point, while Russian public opinion continued to follow British actions in South Africa with severe criticism, the issue fell away from the government agenda, only occasionally to emerge over the next two years, overshadowed by other developments.

The tsar did receive the Boer ambassador Dr Leyds discretely in August 1900. In May 1901 the tsar wrote to the new King Edward VII and in friendly and gently chiding terms suggested that honour had been satisfied and that the British ought to be able to bring the war to conclusion without further suffering. A Boer representative attended the marriage of the tsar's younger sister, in spite of Lamsdorf's efforts to forestall it, and the British ambassador's threats. These do show the continuing personal concern of the tsar about the war and his sympathy for the Boers.[100]

But by April 1900, while the war still continued in South Africa, Russia's international situation and policy seemed more secure. Witte commented to his friend Polovtsov that Russia did not have the best relations with other powers but there were no particular international questions and the tsar was peaceful.[101] However, this was the calm before the storm. In June the Boxer movement in China reached critical proportions. It drew attention away from Britain's predicament in the Boer War and forced Russia to exert itself to defend its interests in Manchuria. To Witte's chagrin, it introduced a volatile military element into the policy of "peaceful penetration", gave an excuse for his rival Kuropatkin to introduce a 150,000 strong army into Manchuria to protect the railways under construction and an opportunity for other, even non-ministerial influences to be heeded by the tsar. It was this military occupation and the subsequent difficulty of withdrawing that brought Russia to the disastrous Russo–Japanese war.

In the context of the developing international situation, therefore, the significance for Russia of the British involvement in the Boer War was that it presented the danger of either its ally France or its friend Germany using the opportunity to move closer towards Britain and thus reducing their dependence on good relations with Russia. In spite of the Franco–Russian alliance, Russia did not wish to be involved in a war and wished to maintain friendship with Germany as a firm point of its foreign policy. Yet the Franco–Russian alliance itself limited Russia's relationship with Germany and encouraged the latter to strengthen its ties with Britain, given the difficulty of resolving its differences with France. Britain's need of friends and support, particularly during the first six months of the Boer War, made this a particular danger for Russia. This to a substantial extent explains Russian concern about the German position in these months, not so much as a response to anglophobic opinion in Russia, nor with the view of realistically creating a continental coalition, but with the rather more negative aim of preventing the rapprochement of the strongest military power with the strongest naval power, while also resisting German encouragement to take some hostile action against Britain.

Notes

1. "Zagranichnoye puteshestvie M. N. Muravieva v 1897g.", *Krasnyi Arkhiv* 47–8, (1931), pp. 75–86, Muraviev's report to the tsar, 23 January/4 February 1897; *Documents Diplomatiques Français, 1871–1914* (hereafter DDF), series I, vol. 13, nos 87, 92, Hanotaux to Montebello, 31 January 1897 and Montebello (St Petersburg) to Hanotaux, 8 February 1897; Johannes Lepsius, Albrecht Mendelssohn-Bartholdy, Friedrich Thimme (eds), *Die Grosse Politik der europäischen Kabinette, 1871–1914* (40 vols, Berlin, 1922–27), vol. 13, nos 3425–8, note by Hohenlohe, 31 January 1897; note by Marschall, 31 January 1897; Hohenlohe to Radolin, 1 February 1897; Kaiser to Hohenlohe, 1 February 1897.
2. L. Telesheva (ed.), "Novye materialy o Gaagskoi mirnoi konferentsii 1899g.", *Krasnyi Arkhiv* 54–5 (1932), pp. 55–6, Kuropatkin diary, entry for 26 February/10 March 1898. DDF, I, vol. 14, nos 103 and 335, Moulin to Billot, 27 March 1898 and Moulin to Zurlinden, 8 September 1898.
3. L. Telesheva (ed.), "K istorii pervoi Gaagskoi konferentsii 1899g.", *Krasnyi Arkhiv* 50–51 (1932), pp. 67–8.
4. L. Telesheva in *Krasnyi Arkhiv* 51–2 (1932), pp. 69–70.
5. Draft report to Nicholas II, December 1898 in Telesheva, *Krasnyi Arkhiv*, 50–51 (1932), pp. 93–6. There was also concern about the threat to Russia's far eastern interests from the Anglo–American rapprochement: F. Kel'in (ed.), "Severo-amerikanskiye Soedinennyye Shtaty i tsarskaya Rossiya v 90x gg. XXv.", *Krasnyi Arkhiv* 52 (1932) pp. 133–40, Muraviev instructions to Cassini (Washington), 29 January–10 February 1898.
6. "Anglo-Germanskoye sblizhenie v 1898g.", *Krasnyi Arkhiv* 56 (1933), p. 69, Osten-Sacken to Muraviev, 29 May–10 June 1898. This is a collection of Muraviev's correspondence on the issue from June to December 1898.
7. *Krasnyi Arkhiv* 56 (1933), pp. 77–9, Muraviev to Osten-Sacken, 30 November–12 December 1898; *Krasnyi Arkhiv* 50–51 (1932), pp. 92–3, Muraviev report to Nicholas II, 30 November–12 December 1898; F. A. Rotshtein, *Mezhdunarodnyye otnosheniya v kontse XIX veka* (Moscow, 1960), pp. 498–500.
8. Lepsius *et al.*, *Grosse Politik*, vol. 14(ii), no. 3982, Radolin (St Petersburg) to Hohenlohe, 5 April 1899; *ibid.*, no. 4015, Bülow to Radolin, 24 March 1899; *ibid.*, nos 4017–18, 4020, notes by Bülow, 18 April, 26 April and 5 May 1899; *ibid.*, no. 4022, Radolin to Hohenlohe, 29 June 1899; DDF, I, vol. 15, no. 246, Montebello to Delcassé, 30 July 1899; W. L. Langer, *The Diplomacy of Imperialism* (New York, 1951), pp. 640–32; Rotshtein, *Mezhdunarodnyye otnosheniya*, pp. 561–7.
9. Rene Girault, *Emprunts et investissements francais en Russie, 1887–1914* (Paris, 1973), pp. 329ff.; *Materialy po istorii SSSR* (Moscow, 1959) vol. 6, pp. 159–222.
10. Dominic Lieven, *Nicholas II, Emperor of All the Russias* (London, 1993), p. 70.
11. "Iz dnevnika A A Polovtsova (1895–1900)", *Krasnyi Arkhiv* 46 (1931), pp. 126–7, entry for 14–26 April 1900.
12. *Ibid.*
13. V. N. Lamsdorf, *Dnevnik 1894–1896* (Moscow, 1991), p. 404, entry for 5–18 November 1896.
14. Lamsdorf, *Dnevnik 1894–1896*, pp. 403–4, entry for 5–17 November 1896. When warned that this would risk putting Russia in the same position as in 1854, the tsar replied, "They would never dare", and "We will deal with them".
15. D. M. McDonald, *United Government and Foreign Policy in Russia, 1900–1914* (Cambridge, Mass., 1992), pp. 17 and 226, n.51. According to Witte, Muraviev in June 1900 privately recognized the error of his policy in agreeing to the occupation of Port Arthur: S. Y. Vitte, *Vospominaniya* (Moscow, 1960), vol. 2, p. 176.

16. "Pis'ma Vitte k D. S. Sipyaginu (1900–01gg.)", *Krasnyi Arkhiv* **18** (1926), pp. 31–2.
17. My focus here is on Russian foreign policy. Public opinion had no formal way of influencing it in Russia at this time. The Russian press during the war was almost entirely pro-Boer, but its proposals for policy were various. The editor of the influential conservative-nationalist newspaper *Novoye Vremya* wrote in his diary as late as April 1900 of the high hopes of the Moscow public: "even a zemskii sobor [representative assembly], not to speak of a declaration of war on England for the Boers. But nothing came of it": A. S. Suvorin, *Dnevnik*, Moscow, 1923, p.238, entry for 9/21 April 1900. For public opinion see E. Kandyba-Foxcroft, *Russia and the Anglo-Boer War* (Roodepoort, 1981), pp. 29–51, 392–6; A. Davidson and I. Filatova, *The Russians and the Abglo-Boer War 1899–1902* (Cape Town, 1998), pp. 177–94; A. P. Vitukhnovskii, "Anglo-burskaya voina v otsenke russkoi periodicheskoi pechati", *Uchennye zapiski Petrozavodskogo gos. universiteta* **2**(i) (1962).
18. Lepsuis *et al.*, *Grosse Politik*, vol. 15, no. 4212, Radowitz (Madrid) to Hohenlohe, 5 October 1899.
19. Lepsuis *et al.*, *Grosse Politik*, vol. 15, no. 4205, Radowitz to Hohenlohe, 15 April 1899; see Christopher Andrew, *Théophile Delcassé and the Making of the Entente Cordiale* (London, 1968), pp. 146–9 on Spanish apprehensions. Also "Ispano-britanskii konflikt 1898g.", *Krasnyi Arkhiv* **60** (1933), pp. 3–59, for Russian despatches from the Madrid embassy from 16 May 1898 to 24 March 1899.
20. Lepsuis *et al.*, *Grosse Politik*, vol. 14(ii), no. 4022, pp. 552–3, Radolin to Hohenlohe, 29 June 1899.
21. Report of Radowitz of his discussion with Silvela: Lepsuis *et al.*, *Grosse Politik*, vol. 15, no. 4212, Radowitz to Hohenlohe, 5 October 1899.
22. Lepsuis *et al.*, *Grosse Politik*, vol. 15, no. 5214, Radowitz to Hohenlohe, 4 February 1900. Thus no attempt was made to "draw Spain into a continental coalition", as suggested by E. T. Corp, "Sir Charles Hardinge and the Question of Intervention in the Anglo-Boer War", *Journal of Modern History* **51** (1979), D. 1072. Much has been made of the report of the Austrian chargé in Madrid, Koziebrodzki, claiming that Muraviev had told Silvela that the time had arrived for the powers of Europe "to take common action against the ever-increasing aggressions and expansion of England" and that "there was every prospect of the conclusion of an understanding between Russia, France and Germany for the purpose": G. P. Gooch and H. W. V. Temperley (eds), *British Documents on the Origins of the War 1898–1914* (11 vols, London, 1926–38), vol. 1, no. 287, Monson (Paris) to Salisbury, 27 October 1899. Andrew, *Théophile Delcassé*, p. 164 accepts the validity of the report, as do Corp, "Sir Charles Hardinge"; J. A. S. Grenville, *Lord Salisbury and Foreign Policy: The Close of the Nineteenth Century* (London, 1964), pp. 270–74; and Kandyba-Foxcroft, *Russia and the Anglo-Boer War*, pp. 312–13. But the evidence of Muraviev's caution about not antagonizing the British by 1898–99, and in particular in not taking the lead in such action, gives more conviction to Radowitz's reports of Muraviev's meetings with Silvela and the Queen, as argued also by Rotshtein, *Mezhdunarodnyye otnosheniya*, pp. 581–4, who had some access to the archive of Russian foreign policy.
23. Reference has also frequently been made in the literature to the article of "Diplomaticus" in the *Fortnightly Review* for December 1899 purporting to reveal Muraviev's attempt to form a coalition for action against Britain. The author was Lucien Wolff, who admitted in 1908 in his paper the *Daily Graphic* that he had received the information from official sources with an indication that it would be in British interests if he could give Muraviev a rap over the knuckles: Rotshtein, *Mezhdunarodnyye otnosheniya*, p. 583 and note 7 referring to G. H. Perris, *Germany and the German Emperor* (London, 1912), p. 411 and footnote.
24. Girault, *Emprunts et investissements*, pp. 335–9.
25. B. V. Ananich, *Rossiya i mezhdunarodnyi kapital 1897–1914* (Moscow, 1970), pp. 38–41, quoting Witte to Muraviev not later than 29 September–11 October 1899.
26. Recent work in the Russian archives has also not yet revealed a report by Muraviev on this meeting. See for instance A. Davidson and I. Filatova, *The Russians and the Anglo-Boer War* (Capetown, 1998).
27. Pascal Venier, "Delcassé et les relations franco-britanniques pendant les debuts de la guerre des Boers" in Remy Pech *et al.* (eds), *Delcassé et l'Europe a la veille de la Grande Guerre* (Toulouse, 2000), note 30.

28. Andrew, *Théophile Delcassé*, p. 163, quoting the memoirs of Combarieu.
29. DDF, I, vol. 16, no. 90, Delcassé to Noailles (Berlin), 4 March 1900. Christopher Andrew emphasizes that Delcassé was keen to make use of the opportunity for a joint action against Britain. However, in a recent contribution to the debate, Venier, "Delcassé et les relations franco-britanniques", has more convincingly shown that Delcassé was in fact extremely cautious about arousing British hostility.
30. "Nikolai Romanov ob anglo-burskoi voine", *Krasnyi Arkhiv* 63 (1934), pp. 125–6, 21 October–2 November 1899; see Kandyba-Foxcroft, *Russia and the Anglo-Boer War*, pp. 291–3 for an English translation.
31. Lepsuis *et al.*, *Grosse Politik*, vol. 13, no. 3544, Tschirsky (charge, St Petersburg) to Ausamt, 20 October 1899.
32. "Nikolai Romanov ob anglo-burskoi voine", *Krasnyi Arkhiv* 63 (1934), pp. 125–6; Davidson and Filatova, *The Russians*, p. 210.
33. Rotshtein, *Mezhdunarodnyye otnosheniya*, pp. 574–6. Delcassé seemed to have been more disappointed and surprised by the result of this meeting, according to a despatch of Urusov, the Russian ambassador in Paris, 19–31 January 1900: A. F. Meyendorff (ed.), *La correspondence diplomatique de M. de Staal (1884–1900)* (Paris, 1929), vol. 2, pp. 452–3.
34. Lepsuis *et al.*, *Grosse Politik*, vol. 13, nos 3547, 3548, Notes by Bülow, 8 November 1899.
35. Lepsuis *et al.*, *Grosse Politik*, vol. 13, nos 3540, 3541, 3544. Nicholas only went to Berlin on the Kaiser's insistence that he could not be in Germany for a fifth year running without visiting its monarch in his capital. Tschirsky reported as early as 20 October that the view in St Petersburg was that the visit to Potsdam was only to be for a few hours as the Russians were annoyed (already then) at the German attitude to the Boer War and thus not because of the result of the meeting. This, however, does not explain the tsar's consistent reluctance to go to Berlin.
36. "Nikolai Romanov ob anglo-burskoi voine", *Krasnyi Arkhiv* 63 (1934), pp. 125–6. Nicholas II to Grand-Duchess Xenia Aleksandrovna, 21 October–2 November 1899. In contrast to the tsar's views, the despatches from the Russian embassy in London give a more balanced picture of the origins and beginning of the war: Meyendorff, *La correspondence diplomatique*, vol. 2, pp. 419–43.
37. Girault, *Emprunts et investissments*, pp. 335ff.; DDF, I, vol. 15, nos. 52, 63, 112, 128, 167, p. 268, Moulin to Delcassé, 30 Jan 1899 and Montebello to Delcassé, 4 February, 1 April and 5 May 1899; Ananich, *Rossiya i mezhdunarodnyi*, pp. 39–40, 62–3.
38. Kuropatkin emphasized that Russia was satisfied with its existing frontiers. Nevertheless he still referred to the possibility of a campaign towards India and what would be necessary for it, although "it would be a serious campaign and such an adventure of conquest does not suit us", DDF, I, vol. 16, no. 62, Montebello to Delcassé, 30 January 1900; *Krasnyi Arkhiv* 46 (1931), pp. 126–7, Polovtsov diary, April 1900,
39. DDF, I, vol. 16, no. 54, Montebello to Delcassé, 19 January 1900; Ananich, *Rossiya i mezhdunarodnyi*, pp. 39–40, p. 62 n.166.
40. For instance, he hosted a dinner with the British ambassador and his wife on 24 May 1900 for Queen Victoria's birthday, when he "was very gracious to them and made no mention of events in South Africa": Kandyba-Foxcroft, *Russia and the Anglo-Boer War*, p. 315.
41. On 29 March–11 April 1900 the tsar withdrew £167,240 in his name in the Bank of England relating to loans of 1822 and 1895, perhaps as a reflection of his views: Meyendorff, *La correspondence diplomatique*, vol. 2, p. 447. At the same time he contributed £1.1 million from his own resources to the loan to Persia.
42. It was widely accepted in Russian military circles that Britain's control of India was very fragile and that it would not require much to arouse native opposition to it. But real knowledge of the situation in India was lacking. In September 1900 in his instructions to the newly appointed first Russian Consul-General in Bombay, Lamsdorf noted that "there even exists a view that it would even be enough of a catalyst [*povod*], for instance, for the mere appearance of an enemy on the frontiers of India to provoke a mass uprising of the natives against the English" and added that "you should carefully assess this situation and 'be on the alert'": A. Popov, "Angliiskaya politika v Indii i russko-indiiskiye otnosheniya v 1897–1905gg.", *Krasnyi Arkhiv* 19 (1926), p. 60.
43. DDF, I, vol. 16, no. 62, Montebello to Delcassé, 30 January 1900; Lepsuis *et al.*, *Grosse Politik*, vol. 17, no. 5334, Radolin to Hohenlohe, 30 January 1900; *The Letters of Queen Victoria*, 3rd

series, vol. 3, G. E. Buckle (London, 1930), pp. 439 footnote and p. 461. In December 1899 the tsar told the British ambassador to let the Queen know of his most friendly feelings, that he deplored the tone of the Russian press and that "nothing was further from his thoughts than to take advantage of [Britain's] difficulties". Also Kandyba-Foxcroft, *Russia and the Anglo-Boer War*, p. 75; Davidson and Filatova, *The Russians*, p. 219.

44. *Zapiska o sostoyanii zakaspiikoi zheleznoi dorogi i glavneishikh potrebnostyakh eyo uluchshenii*, St Petersburg, 1899.

45. *Krasnyi Arkhiv* **46** (1931), pp. 126–7, Polovtsov diary entry, 14–26 April 1900. The idea of a campaign towards India was also referred to in the Russian press, for example *Novoe Vremya*, 28 October–9 November 1899 as quoted by Davidson and Filatova, *The Russians*, p. 221.

46. E. L. Shteinberg, "Angliiskaya versiya o russkoi ugroze Indii v xix I xx vv", *Istoricheskiye Zapiski* **33** (1950), p. 62. Kuropatkin also in February 1900 expressed the view that there would need to be an agreement with Britain about Persia, but only when the Orenburg–Tashkent railway was completed. *Krasnyi Arkhiv* **18** (1926), pp. 21–2, Kuropatkin to Muraviev, 16–29 February 1900.

47. DDF, I, vol. 16, no. 28, Vauvineux (charge St Petersburg) to Delcassé, 14 December 1899.

48. DDF, I, vol. 16, p. 47, note 2, giving a partial quotation of Delcassé to Vauvineux, 15 December 1899.

49. NS GB 43, Vauvineux to Delcassé, 18 December 1900: I am grateful to Pascal Venier for this reference from the French archives. According to a report in *The Times*, 23 December 1899, col. 6a, Muraviev considered that it would be a breach of Russia's neutrality and was reluctant to agree.

50. Iain Smith, *The Origins of the South African War 1899–1900* (London, 1996), pp. 411–12. The report in *The Times* (23 December 1899, col. 6a) makes no reference to a Bank of England request and shows that financial circles found this "rumour" of a loan from capital-short Russia, rather puzzling.

51. Davidson and Filatova, *The Russians*, p. 222 conclude that this was a result of the Boer War and quote the liberal Russian journal *Russkoye Bogatstvo* of January 1900 for confirmation of this view. But see Lepsuis *et al.*, *Grosse Politik*, vol. 17, no. 5336, Tschirsky note, 27 February 1900, for an informed contrary contemporary assessment.

52. R. L. Greaves, "British Policy in Persia, 1892–1903", *Bulletin of the School of Oriental and African Studies* **28**(ii) (1965), p. 286.

53. F. Kazemzadeh, *Russia and Britain in Persia, 1864–1914* "New Haven, 1968", pp. 323–4.

54. Rotshtein, *Mezhdunarodnyye otnosheniya*, p. 640 n.66.

55. B. V. Ananich, *Rossiiskoye samoderzhaviye i vyvoz kapitalov, 1895–1914* (Leningrad, 1975), pp. 27–8.

56. Witte was able to impose his priorities as is clear from his finding a way to make the Persian loan, while in the spring and summer of 1900 he stubbornly and successfully insisted that he could not find the resources for a loan to Bulgaria. A. K. Martynenko, *Russko-bolgarskiye otnosheniya v 1894–1902gg.* (Kiev, 1967), pp. 247–57. In September 1900 he was even prepared to make a small foreign loan of 30,000 roubles to the chief lama of Mongolia, but the terms were rejected: Rotshtein, *Mezhdunarodnyye otnosheniya*, p. 645, n.86.

57. On this and the Persian loan in general, see Ananich, *Rossiiskoye samoderzhaviye*, pp. 18–28; Kazemzadeh, *Russia and Britain in Persia*, pp. 311–27; Greaves, "British Policy in Persia", pp. 284–307 (particularly pp. 285–8); Geoffrey Jones, *Banking and Empire in Iran: The History of the British Bank of the Middle East* (Cambridge, 1986), vol. 1, pp. 83–7.

58. Gooch and Temperley, *British Documents*, vol. 1, no. 376, p. 307, Memorandum of the Russian Embassy, London, 25 January–6 February 1900. The Russians had given assurances about Afghanistan being outside their sphere of interest, but they had never formally recognized the Anglo-Afghan Treaty of Gandamak of 1879, on which the British claim to control the foreign relations of Afghanistan was based.

59. P. Kotlyar, *Istoricheskii ocherk afgano-russkikh otnoshenii v 1870–1919* (Moscow, 1963), p. 189. In 1900 the railway to the Afghan frontier was taken over by the Ministry of Communications, whose interest was to maximize its commercial traffic.

60. For the original letter in full see M. A. Babakhodzhaev, *Russko-afganskiye torgovo-ekonomicheskiye svyazi* (Tashkent, 1965), appendix, pp. 115–16. For partial qotation see Gooch

and Temperley, *British Documents*, vol. 1, p. 309, "Precis by A. Parker on Russo-Afghan relations", October 1903.

61. Davidson and Filatova, *The Russians*, p. 222 wrongly states that diplomatic relations were established.

62. In early 1899 the agent had approached E. P. Kovalev, who was in charge of the Kelif custom post, proposing that the Russian government should send the Emir a letter with a request to appoint representatives for discussions on trade matters. In spring 1899 the agent had reported back that the Emir had nothing against agreement with Russia but favoured private negotiations. However, Kovalev was given strict instructions not to enter into negotiations fearing complications with Britain and even that it might be a provocation. So when, in 1900, Afghan merchants came to Kelif, Kovalev backed out of his promise to take them to Moscow, St Petersburg and the Nizhnyi Novgorod fair and claimed to be ill. M. A. Babakhodzhaev, *Russko-afganskiye torgovo-ekonomicheskiye svyazi*, pp. 53–5; B. N. Iskanderov, *Iz istorii bukharskogo emirata* (Moscow, 1958), pp. 109–10.

63. These were not actual railway concessions, as stated by Davidson and Filatova, *The Russians*, pp. 221–2. Lepsuis *et al.*, *Grosse Politik*, vol. 17, nos 5217, 5218, 5221, Marschall (Constantinople) to Ausamt, 26 and 28 February 1900 and Marschall to Hohenlohe, 4 April 1900; Rotshtein, *Mezhdunarodnyye otnosheniya*, pp. 642–5.

64. G. L. Bondarevskii, *Bagdadskaya doroga i proniknovenie germanskogo imperializma na Blizhnyi Vostok. 1888-1903* (Tashkent, 1955), pp. 216–24; Rotshtein, *Mezhdunarodnyye otnosheniya*, pp. 641–2.

65. *Krasnyi Arkhiv* 18 (1926), pp. 4–18, quotation here from p. 6. Generally known as the Muraviev memorandum. The copy in the Lamsdorff archive is dated 22 January–3 February 1900: TsGIA f. 568, op. 1, d. 159.

66. *Krasnyi Arkhiv* 18(1926), p. 9.

67. *Ibid.*, pp. 10–11.

68. *Ibid.* pp. 11–14.

69. *Ibid.*, pp. 14–15.

70. *Ibid.*, pp. 15–16.

71. *Ibid.*, pp. 16–18.

72. The crises at the Straits in November 1912 and April 1913 still found Russia with inadequate facilities for a viable expedition.

73. *Krasnyi Arkhiv* 18 (1926), p. 5.

74. *Krasnyi Arkhiv* 46 (1931), pp. 126–7, Polovtsov diary, entry for 14–26 April 1900. The Germans also had rather a poor opinion of Muraviev: e.g. Lepsuis *et al.*, *Grosse Politik*, vol. 15, no. 4492, note by Bülow, 20 March 1900, and the kaiser's comments on despatches in this period.

75. Davidson and Filatova, *The Russians*, p. 215; Sandro was Grand-Duke Alexander Mikhailovich, who was married to the tsar's younger sister, Grand-Duchess Xenia Aleksandrovna.

76. Tyrtov and Kuropatkin, however, found it difficult to argue with the memorandum as it had been given preliminary approval by the tsar before submission to them. Already on 7 February the tsar noted, "I fully approve the main ideas of this excellently compiled memorandum", TsGIA, f. 568, op. 1, d. 159, l. 19.

77. The minister of justice (also a Muraviev) told the foreign minister that "he had never read a notice more admirably edited, of an exemplary purity of style and a reasoning as sober and eloquent as it is categorical". Muraviev told Lamsdorf:, "I have never known him to be so enchanted" TsGIA, f. 568, op. 1, d. 159.

78. Witte's account of his discussion with the tsar about Muraviev's successor in S. Y. Vitte, *Vospominaniya* (Moscow, 1960), vol. 2, p. 177. At the height of the crisis over the Boxer rising, Witte remarked, "the appointment of Count Lamsdorf is a very reassuring fact", *Krasnyi Arkhiv* 18 (1926), p. 37, Witte to Sipyagin, 31 July–13 August 1900.

79. Kandyba-Foxcroft, *Russia and the Anglo-Boer War*, p. 316, refers to a Russian document passed to the British about Russian military preparations in Turkestan to be completed by June 1900 "in the event of complications in Afghanistan". This may well have been one of the "preparations" referred to in the memorandum, eagerly set in motion by the military. But Witte's refusal of new credits should be noted.

80. *Krasnyi Arkhiv* 18 (1926), pp. 22–5, Witte to Muraviev, 10–23 February 1900. Witte's influence

on the February 1900 memorandum to clarify and coordinate Russian foreign policy is also suggested by his own memorandum presented to the tsar in the same month, proposing the uniting of all matters relating to the economy in the hands of the Ministry of Finance: Ananich, *Rossiya i mezhdunarodnyi kapital*, p. 26.

81. Ananich, *Rossiya i mezhdunarodnyi kapital*, pp. 25–9, note compiled in the Ministry of Foreign Affairs on the basis of the ministers' comments, submitted to the tsar, 27 February–11 March 1900.

82. Lepsuis *et al.*, *Grosse Politik*, vol. 15, no. 4463, note by Bülow, 12 January 1900; no. 4464, Bülow to Hatzfeldt (London), 12 January 1900; no. 4465, note by Bülow 13 January 1900. Meyendorff, *La correspondence diplomatique*, vol. 2, pp. 447–8, Muraviev to Staal (London) 13–26 January 1900.

83. *Ibid.*

84. Meyendorff, *La correspondence diplomatique*, vol. 2, pp. 448–9, Osten-Sacken to Muraviev 7–19 January 1900. Bülow's note on the kaiser's new year discussion with Osten-Sacken is, in contrast with the ambassador's report, very cautious. However, Bülow was not actually present and made his note only from what the kaiser told him: Lepsuis *et al.*, *Grosse Politik*, vol. 15, no. 4465, note by Bülow, 13 January 1900.

85. Muraviev to Osten-Sacken, 13–25 January 1900, in the Archive of Russian Foreign Policy, as referred to by Rotshtein, *Mezhdunarodnyye otnosheniya*, p. 606.

86. Meyendorff, *La correspondence diplomatique*, vol. 2, pp. 447–8, Muraviev to Staal, 13–26 January 1900. Also DDF, I, vol. 16, nos 64 and 78, Montebello to Delcassé, 1 February and 15 February 1900.

87. DDF, I, vol. 16, no.64, Montebello to Delcassé, 1 February 1900.

88. Meyendorff, *La correspondence diplomatique*, vol. 2, pp. 447–8, Muraviev to Staal, 13–26 January 1900.

89. Meyendorff, *La correspondence diplomatique*, vol. 2, pp. 451–2, Nelidov (Rome) to Muraviev, 18–30 January 1900.

90. Meyendorff, *La correspondence diplomatique*, vol. 2, pp. 450–51, Muraviev to Osten-Sacken, 27 January–8 February 1900.

91. DDF, I, vol. 16, nos 62 and 78, Montebello to Delcassé.

92. Venier, "Delcassé et les relations franco-britanniques", has also recently emphasized the moderation of Delcassé's policy in contrast to Andrew, *Théophile Delcassé*, ch. 8, pp. 158–79, who argues that Delcassé was prepared to go much further than the Russians in action against the British.

93. DDF, I, vol. 16, no. 90, Delcassé to Noailles, 4 March 1900.

94. Lepsuis *et al.*, *Grosse Politik*, vol. 15, no. 4472, Bülow to Radolin, 3 March 1900.

95. See, for instance, Lepsuis *et al.*, *Grosse Politik*, vol. 15, no. 4395, Tschirsky (charge St Petersburg) to Hohenlohe, 30 October 1899; and no. 4486, Radolin to Hohenlohe, 11 March 1900.

96. Lepsuis *et al.*, *Grosse Politik*, vol. 15, no. 4476, Radolin to Ausamt, 5 March 1900; and no. 4479, Pourtales (The Hague) to Hohenlohe.

97. Lepsuis *et al.*, *Grosse Politik*, vol. 15, no. 4463, note by Bülow, 12 January 1900. Andrew, *Théophile Delcassé*, ch. 8, emphasizes the significance of this for the trajectory towards the Anglo–French entente.

98. Lepsuis *et al.*, *Grosse Politik*, vol. 15, no. 4479, Pourtales to Hohenlohe, 6 March 1900.

99. Lepsuis *et al.*, *Grosse Politik*, vol. 15, no. 4491, Radolin to Ausamt, 14 March 1900.

100. Kandyba-Foxcroft, *Russia and the Anglo-Boer War*, pp. 88–99; Davidson and Filatova, *The Russians*, pp. 223–5, 231–5; A. Maylunas and S. Mironenko, *A Lifelong Passion: Nicholas and Alexandra – Their Own Story* (London, 1996), p. 205. The tsar's letter to Edward VII does show a certain sensitivity in his personal relationships (even if this was lacking in so many other respects) in his admission that he had not raised the matter of the Boer War with Queen Victoria in the previous year because of the delicacy of her health.

101. *Krasnyi Arkhiv* 46 (1931), pp. 126–7, Polovtsov diary, entry for 14–26 April 1900.

CHAPTER FOUR

French Foreign Policy and the Boer War[1]

Pascal Venier

I

After the outbreak of the Boer War, anglophobia reached its climax in *fin de siècle* France. The pro-Boer feelings of French public opinion are well established.[2] By sharp contrast, the orientation of French government policy during the early stages of the conflict remains unclear. This is particularly the case with France's attitude towards Britain and the role of Foreign Secretary Théophile Delcassé in the so-called question of intervention in the Boer War. The latter has been the subject of heated controversies, both at the time of the *Daily Telegraph* affair in 1908 and in the inter-war period.[3]

In the late 1960s, Christopher Andrew challenged the traditional interpretation of Delcassé's foreign policy, and dismissed the claim laid by the French foreign secretary's collaborators that he was convinced, as early as February 1899, of the need to alter radically the course of French foreign policy by seeking an understanding with Britain, and consistently took steps to implement it.[4] In a masterful reassessment of French foreign policy during the period 1898–1905, considered at the time as the definitive study of Delcassé's foreign policy, the Cambridge historian argued that Delcassé no longer believed, at the beginning of the Anglo-Boer war, in the possibility of an amicable settlement of pending issues with Britain. Favouring intervention in the conflict as an opportunity to reopen the Egyptian question, he sought an alliance with Germany.[5] According to Andrew, he was therefore instrumental in "two separate attempts to persuade Germany to join with the Dual Alliance (France and Russia) in demanding that England end her military occupation of Egypt", in November 1899 and again in March 1900.[6] Only after the failure of the second attempt is he supposed to have realized the impossibility of France reaching an understanding with Germany without prior acceptance of the Treaty of Frankfurt.

This seemed to settle the question and Andrew's interpretation has generally been accepted for the past 30 years. However, a careful analysis of available sources suggests a rather different reading of the events. The purpose of this chapter will therefore be to re-examine French foreign policy during the early stages of the Boer War.

II

It is generally believed that in the autumn of 1899, Count Muraviev, the Russian foreign minister, attempted to form a continental coalition with a view to intervening in the Boer War.[7] It has been argued that this initiative was actively supported by Delcassé, who saw in a triple intervention of France, Russia and Germany an opportunity to reopen the question of Egypt.[8] During Muraviev's visit to Paris in October 1899, it has been supposed that both men agreed that the Germans should be sounded during the forthcoming visit of the tsar to the kaiser.[9] On 8 November, at Potsdam, Muraviev is thought to have proposed to Kaiser Wilhelm II and Count von Bülow an intervention of the three continental powers in the conflict and supposedly attempted to overcome German fears of British naval superiority, but to no avail, as the Germans were not then disposed to consider intervention.[10] There is however little documentary evidence to back up this version of events.

The general impression given by French Foreign Secretary Théophile Delcassé, in the fall of 1899, is that he was undoubtedly aware that the position of France was not favourable to an adventurous policy. Not only was France, in the context of the Dreyfus affair, in acute political turmoil and the regime fighting for its survival,[11] but ensuring the success of the forthcoming Paris Universal Exhibition of 1900 was also a major preoccupation for the government.[12] Furthermore, the Fashoda crisis had all too cruelly revealed that the state of preparedness of the French Navy was inadequate to risk a confrontation with the Royal Navy.[13]

It had become clear, in the summer of 1899, that a Franco–German détente was taking place, illustrated, for example, by the highly symbolic visit made by Wilhelm II to the French ship L'Iphigénie, in the Norwegian port of Bergen,[14] which was not without causing some concern in Britain.[15] It is also well established that after the outbreak of the South African war Germany made a number of overtures to the French, expressing an interest for an understanding between the two countries.[16] Delcassé remained, nevertheless, extremely cautious, having no illusions as to the likely outcomes of the German advances and fearing a possible manoeuvre of the Kaiser to discredit France in the eyes of London. The failure of his own attempt to initiate a rapprochement with Germany in December 1898, at the time of the Fashoda crisis, had clearly revealed that the question of Alsace-Lorraine remained an insurmountable obstacle to any understanding between the two countries.[17] When approached by the French, Wilhelm II had not only asked for guarantees for Alsace-Lorraine but would have gone, in what would not have been out of character for a sovereign notorious for his extravagant and clumsy diplomacy, as far as suggesting a personal union of France and Germany under his authority![18] Two important issues probably also weighed significantly in the French evaluation of the situation. First, it was extremely difficult to combine a possible entente with Germany with the Franco–Russian alliance. Secondly, although Anglo–German relations went through a phase of tension in October 1899 because of the Samoan question, the French remained seriously concerned that Germany had already reached a diplomatic understanding with Britain.[19]

Despite Delcassé's reservations, steps were nevertheless taken to probe German intentions. A secret envoy, Jules Hansen, was dispatched to Berlin in October 1899 to further enquire into the German government's intentions,[20] but his mission was unsuccessful as Bülow refused to meet him.[21] Noailles was nevertheless instructed to find out more and to ask him to be more specific, but Bülow remained more elusive than ever.[22] The kaiser for his part, while expressing his concern at the rise of British power, left no ambiguity about his appraisal of the situation: "When I sent my telegram to Krüger, it was still time. But, in the last four years the English have developed their navy to such an extent that I am paralysed. It is impossible to risk ourselves against them: my trade, my ports, Hamburg, are too exposed".[23] Germany's support in any intervention of the continental powers in the South African question was therefore clearly out of the question.

When, immediately before the outbreak of the Boer War, Muraviev, who was visiting Biarritz, met the Spanish queen and prime minister in neighbouring San Sebastian, and later went on to Paris to hold discussions with the French leaders, rumours that he was orchestrating a continental coalition against Britain were running high, especially in the British press. Derek Sping's contribution to the present volume, however, shows very convincingly that the Russian foreign minister was not inclined to such an adventurous policy. This is confirmed by the testimony of Jules Hansen, who, after meeting him on 17 October, revealingly deplored his lack of interest for the question of South Africa.[24] On the French side, the outbreak of the war had brought back the recurrent fear of a British preventive strike against France or its colonies.[25] Reporting a conversation with the French ambassador, Paul Cambon, the French naval attaché revealingly commented that:

> *Above everything, England seems to be prepared to reject any intervention.* She knows that there is little love for her in Europe and is bitterly concerned about it. She feels she cannot do much against Germany or Russia; but considers, rightly or wrongly, that France is vulnerable in several points, especially when it comes to her navy, her

ports and her colonies. She would be all too happy to use her navy against *France alone*.[26]

It is very difficult to have a precise idea of the content of the discussions that took place with French officials during Muraviev's stay in Paris, because no detailed documentary evidence subsists in the French diplomatic archives.[27] This visit came a couple of months after Delcassé's trip to St. Petersburg during which the alliance between the two powers had been reshaped[28] and the main subject of discussion seems to have been a projected Russian loan of 560 million francs.[29] The question of Egypt was discussed at some stage, but Delcassé was not in favour of an initiative in this respect at the time.[30] It seems clear that the French authorities were determined to refuse to follow any adventurous course and to stay aloof from any idea of a hostile intervention against Britain.[31] The account of Muraviev's talks with French President Emile Loubet on 27 October, appears to be significant in terms of of the spirit in which the negotiations were conducted on the French side. It shows, revealingly, that the French president, when sounded out by Russia's foreign minister on the French willingness to engage in a joint action with Russia and Germany, without completely discouraging him, engaged in vague and dilatory talk.[32] For his part, all Delcassé agreed to was to make a vague and half-hearted commitment, and as he later revealed, "to try, should the right moment arise, to put a end to the war between England and the Transvaal".[33]

Much has been made of the meetings between the two emperors and their ministers, but no proposal for a common diplomatic intervention was actually made.[34] The Germans were firmly determined to decline any proposal.[35] Accordingly, on the eve of the visit, a semi-official note was inserted in the semi-official press, notably the *Kölnische Zeitung*, denying that any intervention scheme had been put to the German government, in a hint that such a proposal would not be welcome.[36] On the very morning of the Russians' arrival in Berlin, the Anglo–German agreement on Samoa, a great success for Bülow's Free Hand policy, was announced even before it was actually signed.[37] The only document ever produced as evidence in support of the claim that an actual proposal for intervention was ever made by Muraviev to the Germans on this occasion is a letter from Delcassé to Noailles of 4 March 1900.[38] This document, however, reveals unequivocally that "Count Mouravieff who was to meet Emperor William and M. de Bülow had undertaken to sound out the imperial Government and to enquire of their dispositions. They seemed to him such that no conversation could be engaged on this matter."[39] This is confirmed without any possible ambiguity by the testimony of the other party in these meetings, Count von Bülow himself, who reported that Muraviev commented on the impossibility to attempt anything about the conflict and that the French thought likewise.[40]

III

If anglophobia was reaching its high point in France during the early months of the Boer War, there seems however to be a sharp contrast between the attitudes of the French public opinion and official policy. If, at a personal level, the empathy of the majority of ministers went to the Boers, the French government's official policy during the conflict was to remain strictly neutral.

The French government was far from serene at the end of 1899. Wilhelm II's visit to Britain in late November was undoubtedly of a nature to raise further concerns about the state of Anglo–German relations. This was the more so as the colonial secretary, Joseph Chamberlain, ventured within days of the kaiser's departure to publicly call for an "alliance of the Anglo-Saxon and Teutonic races" in a speech given in Leicester. As Delcassé wondered in a letter to Camille Barrère, the French ambassador to Italy, "London and Berlin are linked and confess to be linked. In what way and how far? This is the great unknown hanging over general policy".[41] The rise of hostility towards France in British public opinion seriously preoccupied Paul Cambon, who didn't dissimulate his fears.[42] It is a fact that the rise of British jingoism in Britain combined with the concomitant climax of anglophobia in France created an explosive mix.[43]

Delcassé resisted the pressure of public opinion and took great care to dissociate himself clearly from the attacks of the press against Britain.[44] His speech on foreign policy at the Chamber of Deputies in November 1899 was meant to be extremely reassuring for the British, and was an attempt to defuse a potentially explosive situation. He went a long way, and probably as far as he possibly could, to promote a spirit of *détente* with Britain, and during a meeting with the British ambassador made plain that he felt that the "policy of France should be that of friendship with England" and that there were "undoubtedly outstanding questions to be settled between the two countries; but looking all round the world, he could not see one which could not be arranged amicably, if both parties are actuated by an honest wish for peace."[45]

While taking to heart the need to protect French economic interests in South Africa,[46] Delcassé appears to have been rather well disposed towards Britain when it came to financial and business relations between the two countries. When, in mid-December 1899, Witte, the Russian finance minister, who was considering lending 5–8 million pounds worth of gold to the Bank of England in order to contribute to stabilize the London money market, asked Delcassé for his point of view in the question,[47] the French foreign secretary was rather supportive.[48] The Russians, however, decided a few days later not to further the matter.[49] It also seems significant that at a time of great tension between the two countries, Paul Cambon felt that "business people, the *City*, do not want a conflict. We must seek their support" and suggested promoting economic collaboration between French and British economic interests in the Yunnan.[50] During the Boer War, French banks made important investments in London where the interest rate was higher.[51] Paul Cambon could, in 1903, go as far as stating that "the costs of the South African war were, so to speak, paid with French gold".[52] It is clear that financial ties contributed significantly to bringing France and Britain closer together, as the City remained dependant on French capital.[53]

The conflict encouraged some of the leaders of the *Parti colonial*, the influential French colonial lobby, to press the government to take steps to exploit the situation of British relative weakness. In an article published in *Le Figaro* on 7 November 1899, Eugène Etienne, the unchallenged leader of the French colonial party, expressed the view that while it was not incumbent on France to intervene in the conflict, it had interests of its own to defend and that the moment would seem to be favourable for pushing them. To this end, he would have liked to see France embark on "a diplomatic conversation" with Britain with a view to assuring the predominance of French influence in north-west Africa and to bringing about a settlement of the various questions pending in Asia.[54] However, such were not the intentions of the French Cabinet; on the contrary, the stated official policy was to mark a pause in imperial expansion. This was made plain by Albert Decrais, the minister for colonies, in a speech to the Chamber of Deputies on 11 December 1899, in which it was stated that the era of conquests was now closed. [55] According to one of its leading figures, Joseph Chailley-Bert, the director of the *Union coloniale française*, this speech was the direct cause of the creation by a group of colonial expansionists of the *Déjeuner du Maroc*, later renamed the *Déjeuner Etienne*, which actively campaigned in favour of French expansion in Morocco and urged the government to review its policy.[56]

Overall, the attitude of the French foreign secretary appears to have been consistent with the official stated policy, as he attempted to restrain the expansionist ambitions of both the French colonies of Indochina and Algeria. He not only held in check the designs of the governor-general of Indochina, Paul Doumer, on the neighbouring Chinese province of the Yunnan,[57] but he also promoted collaboration between French and British economic interests within the Anglo-French Yunnan Syndicate.[58] The task proved more difficult in the case of Algeria as both Governor-General Edouard Lafferrière and the *Armée d'Afrique* were in favour of expansion into Morocco. The South African war provided the "men on the spot", always prone to disregard instructions from Paris, with an opportunity to foment an incident in In Salah that enabled the French penetration of the oases of the Tuat in late December 1899, soon followed by the occupation of the Souara and Zousfana valleys.[59] While the French foreign minister was very critical of the fact that "the Saharan policy has been conducted without the knowledge of Parliament", he had to put on a brave face. Fully understanding that it was totally impractical for the French troops to withdraw, as their involvement on Moroccan soil had provoked a pan-tribal movement of reaction against the French, Delcassé had no option but to agree to maintain the occupation of the Tuat and other occupied Moroccan territories.

The attitude of the French government in the controversial question of the *droit de visite* by the Royal Navy of French merchant vessels in the Indian Ocean is also revealing of the rather conciliatory attitude of the French government, in the winter of 1899–1900.[60] It was in sharp contrast with that of the German government, which aimed at exploiting tensions on this issue to create public support for the naval bill. The fact that the minister for the navy, Jean-Marie de Lanessan, was pro-British, as one of the founders of the *Comité de l'Entente Cordiale*, perhaps contributes to explain the positions taken by the department of the navy.[61] In any case, had Delcassé been inclined to seek an understanding with Germany as has often been argued, it was the ideal time to make a common stance with it.

In mid-January 1900, in the context of the *Bundesrath* affair, which had created a climate of acute tension between Britain and Germany, von Bülow and Wilhelm II made overtures that the Russian Ambassador, Count Osten-Sacken, interpreted as indicating that Germany would be prepared to consider the eventuality of a continental coalition against Britain.[62] Delcassé, however, unambiguously refused to envisage an entente with Germany.[63] Approached by Urusov about the possibility of reopening the Egypt question, the French minister was extremely reserved, stressing, on 25 January, how damaging such a move could potentially be for the "prestige and the dignity of the Powers who would have attempted it."[64]

It is nevertheless clear that, as Christopher Andrew has shown, Delcassé did seriously envisage, in early February 1900, the possibility of reopening the question of Egypt.[65] He did so after Cogordan, the French consul-general in Cairo, suggested pressing London not to evacuate Egypt, but, more modestly, to enforce the dispositions of the international convention on the Suez Canal of 1888. This convention provided for its "neutralisation" and "internationalisation", but the British had refused to implement it since 1889.[66] The Parisian daily *Le Matin*, Delcassé's mouthpiece, was employed, as was often the case, to float a trial balloon, by publishing, on 6 February, a leader entitled "L'Egypte", which encouraged Germany to take part with the support of France and Russia in an initiative to secure the neutralization of the Suez Canal, from which it would itself benefit directly.[67]

The French foreign secretary seems not to have pursued the matter, as the Germans were clearly not receptive to his overture. Much to the contrary, it was reported from Berlin that a violent anti-French campaign, believed to be orchestrated by the *Wilhelmstrasse*, was developing in the German semi-official press.[68] Furthermore, Montebello, the French ambassador, reported from St Petersburg that both Muraviev and the Russian war minister, General Kuropatkin, "believe that we cannot count on any real and efficient support from Germany, in any circumstance, at least in the current state of affairs, and they both seem . . . to be in perfect agreement on this matter".[69]

IV

It is well established that the Russian ambassador in Berlin approached von Bülow on 2 March 1900 and submitted a note suggesting that Germany join in a tripartite initiative to end the war between Britain and the Boer Republics.[70] It has been argued that this *démarche* was conceived by its protagonists as a way of bringing about a hostile intervention and as a step towards the formation of a continental coalition against Britain.[71] Supposedly, Delcassé's desire to profit from Britain's difficulties and his hopes to broaden the scope of a possible intervention to include the question of Egypt and force the British to evacuate the Khedivate, remained strong.[72] There are difficulties in following this interpretation.

On the evening of 28 February 1900, Prince Urusov, the Russian ambassador, met Delcassé and told him of his government's intention to ask Germany to join with France and Russia in an offer of *bons offices* to Britain in order to end the South African conflict.[73] Such an idea seems to have originated with the tsar himself. Nicholas II, who had already played a decisive role in bringing about the Hague peace conference of 1899, saw, after a series of British victories, the possibility of a peaceful resolution of the conflict.[74] It was also presented by the Russians as a response to earlier suggestions for intervention made by the Kaiser and Bülow.

Delcassé was convinced of the need to end the bloodshed in South Africa but was also, like the Russians, eager to force the kaiser to clarify his position once and for all. He decided to follow the Russians but with great caution, as he wanted to ensure that the initiative was not misinterpreted. A *modus operandi* was defined by the two parties. The Russian ambassador alone was to approach the Germans and the proposal would take a non-political form. Interestingly, in this respect, the French foreign secretary drew a parallel between this initiative and that of France in the conflict between Spain and the US in 1898.[75] He personally suggested that the US should be associated with the *démarche* in order to avoid any ambiguity as to its nature.[76]

One of the main arguments put forward in support of the thesis of Delcassé's hostility towards Britain is the fact that at a Cabinet meeting on 28 February 1900 the possibility of a war with Britain, and the action to be taken should it arise, were discussed.[77] However, it seems difficult to see in the positions taken by Delcassé during the meeting an indication that he was in favour of a hostile policy towards Britain, as has been argued,[78] and even less that he was planning a preventive strike against Britain.[79] A first objection to the whole argument is the simple one of chronology, as it is possible to establish that Delcassé was only told by Urusov of the Russians' intentions on the evening of the day in which the Cabinet had met.[80] The discussion that took place during the Cabinet meeting, therefore, could not possibly be a consequence of the meeting with Urusov.

The discussion in question should, in fact, primarily be interpreted as a response to the phenomenon of the *war scares* or *"psychoses de guerre"*, which reached their high point on both sides of the channel from mid to late February 1900.[81] After the relief of Ladysmith, rumours had spread in the press of a possible war with England and alarmist articles were published in the French press.[82] At the same time in Britain, William T. Stead in the *Review of Reviews* was involved in organizing an invasion scare.[83] This feeling of war in sight went far beyond journalistic pranks as respectable politicians took the matter very seriously. Lord Rosebery felt sufficiently strongly about it to raise the issue in the House of Lords on 15 February, and less than a week later the Royal Navy mobilized its reserves.[84] From Paris, Sir Edmund Monson reported hearing:

> from such different quarters the same story of a belief in the hostile intention of England that I cannot too forcibly insist upon its existence. I was told yesterday by a Member of the Senate that many of his colleagues in that body have the strongest conviction that an Anglo-French war is inevitable, and that it will be brought on by England at the close of the war in South Africa.[85]

It is also important to stress that the measures advocated by Delcassé were essentially defensive in nature and most of them were in fact part of an ongoing programme of reform of the colonial defence, initiated after the Fashoda crisis. It is a fact that the idea of landings in England or Egypt, or threatening Burma from French Indochina, were mentioned in the debates, but they seem to have been more expressions of wishful thinking than serious discussions of strategic planning likely to be implemented. In any case, the Fashoda crisis of 1898 had already revealed French naval shortcomings and that France did not have the capability to fight a war against Britain, with a chance to win. The decision-makers were under no illusions that the conflict in South Africa had opened a window of opportunity for France. In any case, the only practical decision taken was, at the suggestion of Delcassé, to call for a meeting of the *Conseil Supérieur de la Guerre*, extended to the president and the war and navy ministers, which met 19 days later primarily to discuss defensive measures in case of war.[86]

It is also difficult to accept the statement that Delcassé intended to take the opportunity of the *démarche* to reopen the Egypt question. There are indications that during his meeting with Urusov on 28 February, this possibility was ruled out by the Russian ambassador.[87]

On 3 March, Wilhelm II announced that he thought that London should be sounded out about Urusov's suggestion. But the Kaiser also asked for a prerequisite to any negotiation in the form of a guarantee of the territorial status quo in Europe for the three powers.[88] This was politically impractical for France as it would have meant renouncing its claim to Alsace and

Lorraine, and this immediately brought the initiative to an end so far as the French were concerned. The German emperor, who had let the British ambassador to Berlin know of the initiative on the day,[89] attempted to exploit the initiative by writing to his uncle, the Prince of Wales, to keep him fully informed of the recent developments.[90]

Far from having been initiated in a hostile frame of mind, the *démarche* seems to have genuinely been conceived in a very different spirit from what is often assumed. Delcassé stressed in his correspondence that it was primarily intended as a "friendly *démarche*" inspired by humanitarian motives,[91] undertaken in the spirit of Article 3 of The Hague Convention, which provided for third parties to engage in *bons offices*, mediation and arbitration.[92] The French ambassador in St Petersburg, the Marquis de Montebello, convincingly emphasized that it was neither an offer of "intervention", nor even of "mediation", but was strictly and solely "an offer of *bons offices*", meant as "a peaceful and friendly *démarche*".[93] It is also interesting to stress the similarities with two other Russian initiatives, such as the plea for the cessation of the war sent by the tsar to King Edward VII in June 1901,[94] or the Russian *démarches* for a proposition of arbitrage between London and the Boer Republics.[95]

It is also revealing that the German response did not prevent Muraviev from persevering, for on 14 March he developed the project to send a circular proposing to the powers an intervention in favour of the Boer Republics.[96] The Russian foreign minister only gave up after the president of the South African Republic sent a request to eight European powers and the US to seek their friendly intervention.[97]

Conclusion

Far from having been as hostile towards Britain as has been argued, the policy followed by Théophile Delcassé was far more moderate. It is interesting to note that after a rather tense period in Franco–British relations in February–March, marked by war scares, Delcassé's speech to the Senate on 3 April 1900 significantly contributed to dissipate misunderstandings between the two countries and opened a clear phase of *détente* between the two powers in the spring of 1900,[98] so much so that the French foreign minister was violently criticized not only by the French nationalist opposition, but also, more revealingly, by the German semi-official press. On 4 March 1900, *Die Post*, in an article inspired by the *Wilhelmstrasse*, went as far as to state that Russia "has the right to be surprised to see her ally 'begging' the trust of England . . . But one must say that M. Delcassé has always been in favour of the English alliance".[99] The possibility of a rapprochement between Britain and France was becoming a matter of some concern to the German government, so much so that in early June 1900, von Bülow instructed the German ambassador to St Petersburg, Tschirschki, to draw the attention of Muraviev to the risk of an *entente* between the two powers for which Morocco would be the price.[100] The Russian foreign minister appeared to share this concern.[101]

Could it be suggested that more credit be given to the traditional interpretation of Delcassé's foreign policy and to the assertion of his collaborators that Delcassé was already developing one of the main axes of his *Grande Politique* by seeking a rapprochement with Britain? A major objection to this argument is perhaps the new orientation given to the Franco–Russian alliance by the protocol of 2 July 1900, signed by the French and Russian heads of general staff. Britain was treated for the first time as a potential enemy, giving the alliance "an anti-English twist".[102] Such an extension of the provisions of the Franco–Russian alliance, which nevertheless remained intrinsically a defensive alliance, was a way for the French to both satisfy the Russians that the alliance remained the cornerstone of their foreign policy and take precautions against a British threat.[103] This new dimension given to the alliance, coming after the reshaping of August 1899, can perhaps best be understood as reflecting a major concern for both parties, namely the risk of a possible Anglo–German alliance. From a French perspective such an alliance between the main maritime power and the main continental power, would undoubtedly have been a worst-case scenario.

Notes

1. I should like to thank Professor John Keiger and Dr Derek Spring for their comments and encouragement.
2. Jean-Guy Pelletier, *L'opinion française et la guerre des Boers (1899–1902)*, thèse de doctorat de 3° cycle, Université de Paris X-Nanterre (1972); and Philip M. H. Bell, *France and Britain, 1900–1940: Entente and Estrangements* (London, 1996), pp. 10–11.
3. See André Mévil, *De la Paix de Frankfort à la conférence d'Algéciras* (Paris, 1909), pp. 46–7 and Edward T. Corp, "Sir Charles Hardinge and the Question of Intervention in the Boer War: An Episode in the Rise of Anti-German Feeling in the British Foreign Office", *Journal of Modern History* 51(2) (June 1979), On-Demand Supplement, D1071–84.
4. Albéric Néton, *Delcassé (1852–1923)* (Paris, 1952), pp. 204–206.
5. Christopher M. Andrew, *Théophile Delcassé and the Making of the Entente Cordiale* (London, 1968), pp. 158–79.
6. Christopher M. Andrew, "The Entente Cordiale From Its Origins to 1914", in *Troubled Neighbours, Franco–British Relations in the Twentieth Century,* Neville H. Waites (ed.) (London, 1971), p. 15.
7. William L. Langer, *The Diplomacy of Imperialism* (New-York, 1951), p. 652; John A. S. Grenville, *Lord Salisbury and Foreign Policy: The Close of the Nineteenth Century* (London, 1964), p. 270; and Andrew, *Théophile Delcassé,* p. 164.
8. *Ibid.*
9. *Ibid.*
10. Grenville, *Lord Salisbury,* p. 272; and Andrew, *Théophile Delcassé,* p. 164.
11. Jean-Baptiste Duroselle, *La France de la "Belle Epoque"* (Paris, 1992), pp. 200–201.
12. *La Politique extérieure de l'Allemagne, 1870–1914, Documents officiels publiés par le ministère*

allemand des Affaires étrangères (hereafter PEA), (Paris, 1932), vol. 17, no 4292, pp. 111–12, Below-Schlatau to Hohenlohe, Paris, 19 October 1899.

13. Renée Masson, *La Marine française lors de la crise de Fachoda 1898–1899*, Université de Paris, DES thesis, 1955.

14. Archives de la Marine, Vincennes, BB3 1106, Delcassé to Lanessan, Minister for the Navy, 7 July 1899.

15. See, for example, Diplomaticus [Lucien Wolf], "Bergen and the coalition nightmare", *Fortnightly Review*, 1 September 1899, pp. 536–46.

16. Ministère des Affaires Etrangères (MAE), NS Allemagne 26, Telegram from Noailles to Delcassé, 18 October 1899 and letter from Noailles to Delcassé, Berlin, 29 October 1899, *Documents Diplomatiques Français, 1871–1914* (hereafter DDF) series 1, vol. 15, no 287, pp. 502–3.

17. Note from Arthur von Huhn, Berlin correspondent of the *Koelnische Zeitung*, 5 December 1898, PAE, vol. 15, no 3821, pp. 124–30; and Jamie Cockfield, "Germany and the Fashoda Crisis, 1898–99", *Central European History* 16(3), 267–72 (1983).

18. According to the testimony of the Austro-Hungarian ambassador in Berlin, 14 January 1899, quoted in Pierre Guillen, *L'Allemagne et le Maroc de 1870 à 1905* (Paris, 1967), p. 572.

19. Abel Combarieu, *Sept ans à l'Elysée avec le Président Emile Loubet* (Paris, 1932), p. 41.

20. Andrew, *Théophile Delcassé*, p. 161.

21. Johannes Lepsius, Albrecht Mendelssohn-Bartholdy, Friedrich Thimme (eds), *Die Grosse Politik der europäischen Kabinette, 1871–1914* (40 vols, Berlin, 1922–27), vol. 15, p. 407, note 2, Wilhelm II to Bülow, 29 October 1899.

22. DDF, 1, vol. 15, no. 288, pp. 503–4, Delcassé to Noailles, Paris, 30 October 1899; and DDF, 1, vol. 15, no. 291, p. 508, Noailles to Delcassé, Berlin, 6 November 1899.

23. DDF, 1, vol. 15, no. 287, pp. 502–3, letter from Noailles to Delcassé, Berlin, 29 October 1899.

24. MAE, Hansen papers, 3, cahier de notes.

25. John F. V. Keiger, "La perception de la puissance française par le Foreign Office", in *La Puissance française à la Belle Epoque*, Pierre Milza and Raymond Poidevin (eds) (Brussels, 1992), pp. 183.

26. Marine, BB4 1750/4, account of a conversation with Paul Cambon given by the French naval attaché, Captain Albert Fiéron, in a letter to the minister for the navy, Lanessan, London, 29 October 1899. The emphasis is Fiéron's.

27. Andrew, *Théophile Delcassé*, p. 163; and the note from the editors in DDF, 1, vol. 16, no 4, p. 9.

28. Pierre Renouvin, *La Politique Extérieure de Th. Delcassé 1898–1905* (Paris, 1953), pp. 12–14.

29. Jean-Claude Allain, *Joseph Caillaux* (Paris, 1978), vol. I, p. 311.

30. DDF, 1, vol. 16, no. 59, pp. 85–6, Delcassé to Montebello, 25 January 1900.

31. This was revealed a few weeks later by an article written by Delcassé's confidant, Louis Jesierski, under his usual pseudonym: Jean Fontaine, "L'accord anglo-allemand", *La Dépêche de Toulouse*, 14 November 1899.

32. Combarieu, *Sept ans à l'Elysée*, p. 41.

33. DDF, 1, vol. 16, no. 90, p. 140, letter from Delcassé to Noailles, 4 March 1900.

34. It is perhaps not irrelevant to note that in 1908, in the context of the *Daily Telegraph* affair, when the question of intervention in the Anglo–Boer war was the subject of a heated controversy, Wilhelm II never claimed to have received any such proposal. Much to the contrary, an anonymous article inspired by the *Wilhelmstrasse* was published in the *Deutsche Revue* explicitly confirming that no proposal was made on this occasion. Cf. Mévil, *De la Paix de Frankfort*, pp. 48–9. In the 1920s, German revisionist historian Erich Brandenburg reached the same conclusions and stated that "on the Czar's visit to Potsdam on November 8th, 1899, nothing happened beyond an exchange of mutual assurances of goodwill", Erich Brandenburg, *From Bismarck to the World War* (Oxford, 1927), p. 135.

35. P. M. Kennedy, *The Samoan Tangle: A Study in Anglo–German–American Relations, 1878–1900* (Dublin, 1974), p. 232.

36. Diplomaticus [Lucien Wolf], "Count Muraviev's Indiscretion", *Fortnightly Review*, December 1899, pp. 1036–45.

37. Kennedy, *The Samoan Tangle*, pp. 225–39.

38. Cf. Grenville, *Lord Salisbury*, p. 271; and Andrew, *Théophile Delcassé*, p. 164.

39. DDF, 1, vol. 16, no. 90, p. 140, letter from Delcassé to Noailles, 4 March 1900.

40. PEA, vol. 17, no. 4310, p. 135, note from Bülow, Berlin, 8 November 1899.

41. DDF, 1, vol. 16, p. 73, Delcassé to Barrère, Paris, 17 January 1900.
42. DDF, 1, vol. 15, no. 297, pp. 514–15, Paul Cambon to Delcassé, London, 11 November 1899; and Delcassé papers 3, Paul Cambon to Delcassé, 23 November 1899.
43. P. J. V. Rolo, *Entente Cordiale* (London, 1969), pp. 102–3.
44. John F. V. Keiger (ed.), *France 1891–1904, British Documents on Foreign Affairs*, part I, series F, vol. 11, (Frederick, 1989), p. 239, Monson to Salisbury, 1 December 1899.
45. *Ibid.*
46. Michel Maubrey, "Les Français et le *veau d'or* : la question sud-africaine (1896–1902)", in *La France et l'Afrique du sud: Histoire, mythes et enjeux*, Daniel Bach (ed.), 37–66 (Paris, 1990).
47. MAE, NS Grande-Bretagne 43, Vauvineux to Delcassé, St Petersburg, 14 December 1899.
48. MAE, NS Grande-Bretagne 43, Delcassé to Montebello, 15 December 1899.
49. MAE, NS Grande-Bretagne 43, Vauvineux to Delcassé, 18 December 1899.
50. Delcassé papers 3, Paul Cambon to Delcassé, 23 November 1899.
51. Samir Saul, *La France et l'Egypte de 1882 à 1914: Intérêts économiques et implications politiques* (Paris, 1997), p. 666.
52. *Ibid.*, Paul Cambon to Stephen Pichon, 27 January 1909.
53. *Ibid.*
54. Eugène Etienne, "L'Angleterre devant l'Europe", *Le Figaro*, 7 November 1899.
55. Joseph Chailley-Bert, "Les Origines du protectorat français au Maroc", *Revue Parlementaire et Politique*, 10 May, 295 (1923).
56. *Ibid.* See also Christopher M. Andrew and A. Sydney Kanya-Forstner, "The French Colonial Party: Its Composition, Aims and Influence, 1885–1914", *Historical Journal* 14, 110 (1971).
57. MAE, Delcassé papers 26, Delcassé to Waldeck-Rousseau, 18 July 1900.
58. MAE, Delcassé papers 3, Paul Cambon to Delcassé, 23 November 1899; and Michel Brugière, "Le Chemin de fer du Yunnan, Paul Doumer et la politique d'intervention française en Chine, 1899–1902", *Revue d'Histoire Diplomatique*, 70(3), 252–5 (1963).
59. Franck E. Trout, *Morocco's Saharan Frontiers* (Geneva, 1969), p. 31; and Jacques Thobie, *Histoire de la France coloniale, II. L'apogée* (Paris, 1991), p. 165.
60. Marine, BB3 1115, Paul Cambon to Delcassé, 4 July 1900.
61. Marc Michel, *La Mission Marchand 1895–1899* (Paris, 1972), p. 193.
62. Baron A.-F. de Meyendorff, *Correspondance diplomatique de M. de Staal, 1884–1900* (Paris, 1929), vol. 2, pp. 447–51, Muraviev to Staal, 26 January 1900.
63. Combarieu, *Sept ans à l'Elysée*, pp. 50–52.
64. DDF, 1, vol. 16, no. 59, pp. 85-6, Delcassé to Montebello, 25 January 1900.
65. Andrew, *Théophile Delcassé*, pp. 166–9.
66. DDF, 1, vol. 16, pp. 89–91, Cogordan to Delcassé, Cairo, 29 January 1900.
67. "L'Egypte", *Le Matin*, 6 February 1900.
68. MAE, Paris, NS Allemagne 15, Noailles to Delcassé, 6 February 1900; and *The Times*, 7 February 1900.
69. DDF, 1, vol. 16, no. 78, p. 122–3. Montebello to Delcassé, St Petersburg, 15 February 1900.
70. DDF, 1, vol. 16, no. 91, p. 142, Noailles to Delcassé, Berlin 5 March 1900; Combarieu, *Sept ans à l'Elysée*, p. 52; and Lepsuis *et al.*, *Grosse Politik*, vol. 15, no. 4472, p. 516, telegram from Bülow to Prince Radolin, Berlin, 3 March 1900.
71. Andrew, *Théophile Delcassé*, p. 172.
72. *Ibid.*
73. MAE, NS Allemagne 15, telegram from Delcassé to Montebello, 2 March 1900.
74. Meyendorff, *Correspondance diplomatique*, p. 446; PEA, vol. 18, no. 4423, p. 35, Bülow to Radolin, Berlin, 3 March 1900; PEA, vol. 18, no. 4440, pp. 48–9, Radolin to Hohenlohe, 11 March; and MAE, Delcassé papers 10, Montebello to Delcassé, St Petersburg, 15 March 1900.
75. DDF, 1, vol. 16, no. 90, p. 140–41, telegram from Delcassé to Noailles, Paris, 4 March 1900.
76. MAE, Delcassé papers 10, telegram from Montebello to Delcassé, 3 March 1900; and PEA, vol. 18, no. 4425, pp. 35–6, Bülow to Radolin, 3 March 1900.
77. MAE, NS Grande-Bretagne 12, note by Delcassé, 28 February 1900.
78. Andrew, *Théophile Delcassé*, pp. 170–71.
79. For Grenville, Delcassé went as far as considering, at the end of February 1900, no less than a "preventive war" against it! Grenville, *Lord Salisbury*, pp. 269–90.

80. MAE, NS Allemagne 15, telegram from Delcassé to Montebello, 2 March 1900.
81. Arthur J. Marder, *The Anatomy of British Sea Power: A History of British Naval Policy in the Pre-Dreadnought Era, 1880–1905* (New York, 1940), pp. 372–80; and Baron Pierre de Courbertin, "The Possibility of War between England and France", *Fortnightly Review*, 1 May, 719–29 (1900).
82. Keiger, *France 1891–1904*, p. 257, Sir Edmund Monson to Salisbury, 9 March 1900.
83. Langer, *The Diplomacy of Imperialism*, p. 663.
84. Marine, BB4 1750/4, Captain Fiéron to Lanessan, London, 21 February 1900.
85. Keiger, *France 1891–1904*, p. 257, Sir Edmund Monson to Salisbury, 9 March 1900.
86. Service Historique de l'Armée de Terre, Vincennes, 1 N 8, minute of the meeting of the CGS of 19 March 1900.
87. DDF, I, vol. 16, doc. 90, p. 137, Delcassé's minute of Paul Cambon dispatch of 2 March 1900. Interestingly, this point was made by Christopher Andrew in his doctoral thesis, *The Foreign Policy of Théophile Delcassé to 1905*, PhD thesis (Cambridge University, 1965), p. 84.
88. DDF 1, vol. 16, no. 102, pp. 161–2, Delcassé to Paul Cambon, 14 March 1900; and DDF 1, vol. 16, no. 107, pp. 172–3, Delcassé to Noailles, Paris 26 March 1900.
89. Cf. Grenville, *Lord Salisbury*, p. 288.
90. Sir Sydney Lee, *King Edward VII: A Biography* (London, 1925), vol. 1, p. 769.
91. DDF, 1, vol. 16, no. 102, p. 161, telegram from Delcassé to Cambon, Paris, 14 March 1900.
92. *Ibid*.
93. MAE, Delcassé papers 10, letter from Montebello to Delcassé, St Petersburg, 15 March 1900.
94. Lee, *King Edward VII*, pp. 765–6.
95. MAE, NS Transvaal-Orange 25, Montebello to Delcassé, 6 December 1901.
96. PEA, vol. 18, no. 4445, p. 53, Radolin to *Auswärtiges Amt*, 14 March 1900.
97. MAE, NS Transvaal-Orange 24, Montebello to Delcassé, St Petersburg, 13 March 1900.
98. MAE, Delcassé papers, 14, Paul Cambon to Delcassé, London, 10 April 1900.
99. MAE, NS Allemagne 15, "Analyse d'un article de la 'Post' du 4 mars 1900."
100. Bülow to Tschirschky, Berlin, 5 June 1900, quoted in Guillen, *L'Allemagne et le Maroc*, p. 570.
101. Tschirschky to Bülow, St. Petersburg, 9 June 1900, quoted in Guillen, *L'Allemagne et le Maroc*, p. 570.
102. Pierre Renouvin, "L'orientation de l'alliance franco-russe en 1900–1901", *Revue d'Histoire Diplomatique* 80, 193–204 (1966).
103. Renouvin, *La Politique Extérieure*, p. 33.

CHAPTER FIVE

Austria-Hungary and the Boer War[1]

F. R. Bridge

"Dans cette guerre je suis complètement Anglais." Thus the Emperor Franz Joseph, in the presence of the French and Russian ambassadors, to their British colleague, Sir Horace Rumbold, at a court ball on 9 January 1900.[2] The emperor went on to express his regret at the "difficulties" that the British had recently encountered, and his hope that the campaign would soon take a more favourable turn. In this attitude to the war, Franz Joseph remained absolutely consistent to the end. As matters improved in the summer he spoke to the British military attaché "in the most hearty and enthusiastic manner of our recent successes in South Africa";[3] and he was in turn particularly gratified to discover, from the "more than friendly tone of the leading English papers", on the occasion of his seventieth birthday in August, "how well his sincere friendship for England was understood by English public opinion".[4] True, by December he was impressed by the "extraordinary mobility of de Wet and his continuous supply of ammunition", but he remarked "at the same time on the exceptional marching powers and endurance of our men",[5] "alluded with evident satisfaction" to Kruger's flight, and "said he considered [the] solution favourable to Great Britain which he had always so earnestly desired was fast approaching".[6] As the war dragged on, the emperor "gave free expression to his regret at the unfortunate obstinacy of the Boers",[7] but he was "immensely pleased" at, and took the lead among the European sovereigns in offering the British his congratulations on, their eventual victory.[8] As Rumbold's successor, Sir Francis Plunkett, observed, "His Majesty has throughout been our staunchest friend".[9]

This spirit of harmony was characteristic of the reactions of the Austro-Hungarian decision-making elite towards the Boer War in several respects: in terms of the general consensus that marked Anglo–Austrian relations at the turn of the century; in terms of the data supplied to Vienna by Austrian officials in Cape Town and London; and in terms of the elite's own unspoken political and social assumptions about the dangers confronting a friendly fellow-imperial power.

In terms of the broad issues of world politics at the turn of the century, with the continent divided between the Triple Alliance and Franco–Russian Alliance, and with both Great Britain and Germany facing potential threats from Russia and France overseas, neither Vienna nor London was inclined to write off altogether the much-vaunted "traditional friendship" between Great Britain and Austria-Hungary. As Balfour reminded Lansdowne in December 1901, it was: "a matter of supreme moment to us that Italy should not be crushed, that Austria should not be dismembered, and that Germany should not be squeezed to death between the hammer of Russia and the anvil of France".[10]

Austro-Hungarian diplomats were delighted to find the Monarchy's role as "a necessary element in the balance of power in Europe and therefore of the peace and order of the world" endorsed in the British press;[11] just as they were flattered when the Foreign Office asked for advice about Balkan questions, in which "the British government attaches great importance to proceeding in agreement with us".[12] The Austro-Hungarian ambassador in Berlin was equally gratified to hear from his British colleague that:

> it has always been a tradition of British diplomats to keep in closer touch with their Austro-Hungarian colleagues, and this custom has only recently been affirmed by the British Foreign Office, which has urged on its heads of mission confidential co-operation and closer contact with their Austro-Hungarian colleagues.[13]

For the Austrians, such sentiments were no mere empty words. After all, for a decade after 1887 their diplomatic position had rested on the Mediterranean Agreements with Great Britain and Italy, designed to resist Russian and French encroachments in the Ottoman Empire and North Africa. It is true that by 1897 these agreements had lapsed, and that the Austrians had taken refuge in a bilateral agreement with Russia that pledged the two powers to respect the status quo in the Near East. However, Vienna was not entirely comfortable with this arrangement. The foreign minister, Agenor Count Goluchowski, suspected adventurous elements in St Petersburg of trying to steal a march on the Monarchy: for much of 1901, for example, they seemed to be encouraging the unreliable King of Serbia – "un fou avec lequel il est impossible de compter"[14] – to turn his country into a Russian satellite. At the same time, the brutal disregard shown by the Monarchy's German ally for the grievances of Poles and Czechs, not only in Polish Prussia but in Galicia and Bohemia, both threatened to exacerbate racial conflicts within the Monarchy and brought home to Vienna the disadvantages of too exclusive an association with Berlin. In these circumstances, the Austrians were anxious to make what they could of what remained of the traditional friendship with Great Britain.

On 2 February 1900, for example, Rumbold found Benjamin Count Kállay, common finance minister and, along with the foreign minister, one of the two leading civilian authorities in the Monarchy, "in perfect despair" over the news of British disasters in South Africa: after all, Russia was rumoured to be moving in Central Asia, and "under given circumstances a British fleet at Salonica or Besika Bay was a factor of the highest importance".[15] "Next to the Emperor Franz Joseph", the ambassador declared, "we have no more valuable friend in this Monarchy than M. de Kállay who in his own words describes himself as English to the backbone in his opinions and sympathies".[16] Kállay feared that after the end of the war Great Britain might relapse into its "old sense of security" instead of reorganizing its army to become "formidable as a land Power . . . stronger than either Germany or Russia". Distrusting Germany and fearing Russia, Kállay was very concerned about "England's national revival and probably hopes, though by no means confidently, that in us Austria-Hungary may yet find the mightiest of allies in the final settlement of what to this Monarchy is a question of life and death", the Eastern Question. Similarly, for Count Mensdorff in London it was "very much to be hoped, in the interests of the future great Power status of the British Empire", that after the war Lord Roberts would be able to convince the government and parliament of the need for a through modernization of the army.[17] Meanwhile, Goluchowski himself assured the British that an accommodating successor would be found for Baron Heidler at the Cairo legation, as Vienna wanted to show the greatest possible regard for British wishes in Egypt, "in view of the relationship that exists between Austria-Hungary and England".[18]

Even Baron Aehrenthal in the St Petersburg embassy – by no means an anglophile – recognized that a serious weakening of Great Britain as a result of the Boer War might make her embarrassingly inclined towards a rapprochement with Russia; whereas:

> everything which makes for a strengthening of England's dominating position at sea will also suit the Monarchy, because in this fashion the expansionist tendencies of our most powerful neighbours, Germany and Russia, are to some degree held in check . The value of our alliance for these two countries increases automatically as soon as there is any worsening of Anglo-German or Anglo-Russian relations.[19]

Goluchowski was less Machiavellian, sincerely welcoming the German emperor's gestures of homage at Queen Victoria's deathbed as "the crowning of the rapprochement" between Great Britain and Germany that Austria-Hungary so much desired;[20] and like his imperial master, he lost no time in congratulating the British on the final conclusion of peace:

> it was a relief for the whole of Europe that England should have her hands free again, for as long as she had been hampered by the heavy

calls on her military resources in South Africa, it was difficult for her to maintain, as visibly as was desirable, her position in the Mediterranean . . . Count Goluchowski said he attached the greatest importance to Great Britain's not allowing the idea to get general that she was beginning to attach less importance to her position in the Mediterranean; he sincerely hoped that the end of the War in South Africa, by an arrangement so satisfactory to HMG [His Majesty's Government], would enable Great Britain to resume the predominance in that sea which he most sincerely desired her to have. [21]

As for the issues at stake in the South African conflict, the authorities in the Dual Monarchy attached less importance to the chorus of indignation in the continental press than to the official reports of their observers in Cape Town and London; and these were consistently sympathetic to the British. Emil Edler von Hirsch, for example, consul-general in Cape Town, was an avowed admirer of Cecil Rhodes, "to whose energy and enterprising spirit South Africa owes so much";[22] while his second-in-command, Egon Baron von Ramberg, was on the most cordial terms with Milner's secretary, not surprisingly given his open avowal to the latter in June 1899 that:

the interests of the Austro-Hungarian Monarchy in South Africa are exclusively commercial, and would be best served if the present confused political circumstances [in the Boer republics] were to give way to orderly conditions under the present English regime, which represents progress and free trade.[23]

Indeed, von Ramberg was soon a great favourite with Milner himself, reporting at length to Vienna on the basis of long after-dinner conversations with the governor: Milner was "a strong supporter of the imperialist idea in South Africa who has set himself the task of fully restoring the prestige and supremacy of England in South Africa".[24] On the eve of the war, Milner was at some pains to explain to von Ramberg that he was no:

warlike hothead. Not at all. He was peace loving, but he had recognised that the disloyalty of the Cape population nourished by the Transvaal government represented an ever-growing threat to the existence of English possessions in South Africa. Sir Alfred Milner described the government of the Transvaal as a military oligarchy, an oligarchy that was all the more dangerous as it had huge sums of money at its disposal which it was using, on the one hand to arm its citizens to the teeth, and on the other to support the anti-English party in the Colony. People unjustly accuse England of having started this crisis out of greed; the causes are not financial but purely political. The mines are already more or less in the hands of English capitalists, but the menace that comes from the neighbouring state, so strongly armed, and from its armed citizens is an evil that must be removed if England does not wish to run the risk of some day losing its South African colonies.[25]

In 1900, von Ramberg was Milner's favoured incumbent for a consulate that might be established in Johannesburg. As Lansdowne told the Austrians, "it would be very agreeable to the English officials if he could be employed in the Transvaal. He is one of the very few members of the foreign consular body at Cape Town who is well disposed towards us".[26]

In London, the Austro-Hungarian ambassador, Franz Count Deym, in post since 1888, was *persona gratissima* both with the government and the royal family; while the chargé d'affaires, Albert Count Mensdorff-Pouilly-Dietrichstein was, with his Coburg connections, a blood relation of Queen Victoria and on particularly easy terms with the Prince of Wales. Not surprisingly, their reports were uniformly sympathetic to the British case. In the summer of 1899, for example, Deym was in no doubt that Kruger's offers at the Bloemfontein conference had been "inadequate";[27] while Mensdorff emphasized that:

> despite all the press talk, people understand very well that the Uitlander population for whose rights such a great display of power is demanded are mostly adventurers of varied nationality and provenance, without patriotism or loyalty to any fatherland and who are only interested in making a fortune as quickly as possible. As a government MP said to me, the Uitlanders are "the scum of the earth".

It was not a question of

> the Uitlanders, not a question of the Transvaal Republic alone, but of the whole of South Africa and the English possessions there. England's prestige is in danger and the subjects of Dutch descent must be prevented from getting the idea that the Dutch can successfully oppose the English in South Africa. The spectre of a "United States of South Africa" with a predominantly Dutch population and leadership must be banished, and people seem to regard the present moment as a decisive one for the future shape of South Africa.[28]

Mensdorff was actually at Balmoral with his royal relatives in the final crisis, and he made sure that the emperor in Vienna was fully acquainted with their views:

> Her Majesty stressed that no blame at all could attach to England; the Boers were pressing and forcing things towards war with their

unreasonable attitude. Altogether Her Majesty spoke in very deroga-
tory terms of the Boers. They were ignorant, bigoted and outra-
geously cruel towards the natives. The whole difficulty went back to
1881, "Majuba Hill" which had made the Boers arrogant:
"Gladstone's fault , I fear", Her Majesty added . . . Her Majesty
seemed to me certainly averse to any war, but less strongly opposed
to this war than I had expected. The Prince of Wales spoke in the
same sense . . . only more decisively, as befits his temperament, and
in violent terms against Herr Kruger and the Boers.[29]

The sympathies of these Austro-Hungarian diplomats were well illustrated
by two incidents arising from the presence in London of Austrian aristocrats
returning from South Africa. The arrival, in March 1900, of Count Adalbert
Sternberg, who at first claimed to have been simply a war correspondent with
the Boers who had been captured by the British, at first attracted little attention. When he proceeded to boast, however, in an interview with the Viennese *Neue Freie Presse*, that he had actually been serving as a military adviser
to the Boer forces, the British authorities, headed by an infuriated Prince of
Wales, took the matter up with the embassy. Eventually the exertions of the
increasingly exasperated Deym and Mensdorff, backed up by Goluchowski in
Vienna, succeeded in persuading Sternberg to withdraw to France.[30] In
February 1902, by contrast, Deym was delighted to report the arrival in
London of Feldmarschall-Leutnant Count Hübner, who spoke "in particularly favourable terms about the so ill-famed concentration camps". When he
mentioned the matter to the under-secretary at the Foreign Office, the upshot
was a luncheon at the Austrian embassy at which Balfour arranged for Hübner
to be interviewed by Ivan Müller of the *Daily Telegraph*, biographer of Sir
Bartle Frere and a friend of Hübner's father. According to Balfour, "such a
favourable account of the concentration camps from an Austrian general (and
son of the ambassador and world-traveller so popular in America) would
make a specially great impact in the United States of America and would be
of great help to the British government". After the interview had been
published, the king (informed by Balfour) asked Deym at dinner to arrange
for Hübner to see him; but the general had by that time left for Paris. "It
would have been very easy to make him the lion of the day here", Deym
contentedly observed, "as the English are above all grateful for any sign that
the slanders that circulate about them are not believed".[31]
Indignant disbelief was certainly the reaction they evoked in the higher
reaches of the Austro-Hungarian establishment. Not only the emperor, but
the war minister and the chief of staff, were wont to speak "in the highest
terms of admiration of the gallantry" of the British army.[32] Franz Joseph had
an enormous personal regard for Queen Victoria, ordering double the normal
length of court mourning when she died, and taking the opportunity of the
opening of the Austrian parliament in February 1901 to deliver a fulsome

eulogy of the late queen who as "a shining example of the sovereign virtues was bound to me by the sentiments of a true friendship".[33]

This solidarity had recently found practical expression: when the Duke of Orleans, who resided in England but who had written an open letter congratulating *Le Rire* over an obscene cartoon of Queen Victoria, was expelled from all his London clubs and forced into social exile across the channel, Franz Joseph immediately made it clear that "until the Queen had forgiven the Duke, he would himself continue not to receive him".[34] Nine months later, Edward VII, whose anger against the Duke was unabated, claimed to "know that the Emperor thinks just as I do about the Duke of Orleans".[35] Indeed, hostility to attacks on the British monarchy was fairly widespread in the Austrian establishment, perhaps because it savoured of an attack on monarchy in general: Count Szögyény, ambassador in Berlin, for example, was beside himself at the "totally irresponsible" remissness of the police authorities who had failed to confiscate an issue of *Kladderadatsch* containing "a quite incredible defamation [*Verunglimpfung*] of a friendly sovereign who is an uncle by blood of the reigning German emperor".[36] Franz Joseph was, in fact, the only sovereign to take effective action against these scurrilous productions, sending an official from the Ministry of the Interior to arrange with the British embassy for the necessary legal procedures for the confiscation of the offending materials; and Rumbold was later to boast in the *National Review* that "I believe I may claim to be the only one of HM representatives who was at that time able to contribute to the putting down of an abominable nuisance".[37]

Another establishment demonstration of monarchical solidarity and antipathy to the Boer cause was afforded by Franz Joseph's absolute refusal to grant audiences to either President Kruger, on his sympathy-seeking tour of European capitals in October 1900, or to the Boer generals who embarked on a similar mission after the end of the war. On the first occasion, Rumbold was informed that on receipt of a dispatch from Paris reporting Kruger's intentions, the emperor had minuted, without waiting for news of William II's reaction, "let steps be taken at once to prevent Kruger coming here".[38] In the Ballhausplatz, under-secretary Szécsen confidently assured Plunkett that Kruger "knew well enough he had nothing to expect from this government and was not likely to ask"; and Lansdowne felt he "need not say how satisfactory it is to me to be aware of HM's attitude in regard to this troublesome matter".[39] Meanwhile, Szécsen and Plunkett entirely concurred as to the "subversive, anti-monarchical nature of the pro-Boer movement".[40] Even in pro-Boer St Petersburg, Austrian diplomats were alive to a certain nervousness about the way in which "the human sympathy which everyone must feel for this valiant people is being daily exploited for attacks on the government for its inactivity".[41] Hence, perhaps, the government's ban on newspaper reporting of the arrival of a Boer delegation: "this kind of subversive tendency can hardly count on approval and toleration in aristocratic Russia".[42] On the second occasion, while the Germans bothered the Foreign Office for some weeks with a clumsy proposal that the British ambassador might present the Boer generals to the kaiser, the fact that "the Emperor of Austria has intimated that he will not receive the generals if they come to his country, and there are other sovereigns who would probably do the same and whose position would be rendered extremely difficult if the German Emperor were to take as different line"[43] encouraged the British to stand firm.

In marked contrast to these concerns of the decision-making elite were those of the general public. Individuals such as Prince Clary Aldringen or Herr Frederick Suess, owners of the baths at Teplitz-Schoenau and Franzensbad respectively, who approached the Foreign Office with offers of free cures for wounded British officers[44] were very much the exception. For the most part, even in Hungary, where memories of British support in 1849 still lingered, the British ambassador had to admit that, although "in the Upper and Government circles the feeling towards England is apparently most friendly and hearty . . . among the bourgeoisie and the Professor class the anti-English, or perhaps I might say, the pro-Boer feeling is very general".[45] In Austria, hostility to Great Britain was even more pronounced, and not only, as Rumbold sometimes implied, among German nationalists inspired by the ravings of the pan-Germans in the neighbouring Empire. It was certainly sanguine of him to claim in February 1900 that a pro-Boer meeting in the capital was "chiefly got up for pan-Germanic purposes" and "in no way represented the sentiments of the population of Vienna".[46] Before the month was out he was having to admit that the public interest in the Boer War was "very remarkable": in Prague both Czechs and Germans were so absorbed by it "as almost to forget for a time the internal dissentions which so closely concern them". Slovene and southern Slav opinion was also "extremely violent against England": a committee of the Croatian diet had "unanimously adopted" a motion of sympathy with the Boers before the authorities had stepped in to halt its progress. Altogether, "the most reactionary and most clerical elements as well as the great body of extreme Radicals and Social Democrats" had come together in an unholy alliance, united in their "instinctive hatred of conservative and Protestant England".[47]

Fortunately for Anglo–Austrian relations, of course, the foreign policy of the Dual Monarchy was determined solely by the emperor and his foreign minister, entirely independently of the parliamentary bodies. Although the minister might choose to explain himself retrospectively to annual meetings of the delegations selected from the Austrian and Hungarian parliaments, he never appeared before those latter bodies. Nor was the emperor inclined to defer to them: as he defiantly informed the British military attaché at the end of the war, "from the first he had never for one moment allowed himself to be misled by the popular opinions and sentiments prevailing on the continent".[48] Prince Charles Kinsky, second-in-command at the St Petersburg embassy, and a great favourite in English society ever since he had won the

Grand National on his own horse in 1883, was even more dismissive of public opinion:

> I am all the more pleased at the success of the English as it gives me a certain inner satisfaction, in that I . . . have always held Lord Roberts to be a really able soldier – by continental standards too . . . May things go on like this, and may they soon finish the whole business. When it is all over, people will be able to look back with admiration at the so robustly patriotic and steely [*nervengesunde*] attitude of the English people and of the parliamentary parties. Above all, the real strength of the English people has shown itself once again, and at the same time it makes one really sad to see by contrast the political immaturity of our parliamentary circles and our so-called intelligent-sia. So immature that they are not even capable of appreciating their own immaturity and the political maturity of another people and of drawing conclusions from it. There are some great asses in our coun-try!! (Es gibt doch große Ochsen bei uns.)[49]

In short, Rumbold was not wide of the mark when, on his retirement in September 1900, he bore:

> grateful testimony to the faithful adherence of the Imperial Govern-ment to their traditional policy of friendship to Great Britain. During the last dark winter, when an ignorant and corrupt press servilely following the lead of our worst enemies in Germany were doing their best to malign and turn opinion against us, . . . the sympathies of the Government were never led astray. We have no better friend in the world than the Emperor Franz Joseph and the distinguished men who serve HM. Count Goluchowski and, above all, M de Kállay, are sincere admirers and favourers of England, even though the old intimacy and the time-honoured alliance have lost some of their value for this country in the great change that has come over the Eastern Question.[50]

With the direction of Austro-Hungarian foreign policy safely in the hands of an anglophile elite, the handling of such practical questions as arose from the Boer War served to only to enhance the harmony prevailing between London and Vienna. Goluchowski and his colleagues at the head of the Austrian and Hungarian cabinets, Koerber and Szell, displayed a lofty disre-gard for the attacks of the opposition, which concentrated essentially on two issues: the government's refusal to reconsider any kind of mediatory interven-tion to stop the war, and its alleged breaches of neutrality by permitting the sale of Hungarian horses for use by the British against the Boers. It is true that, as the anglophobe press had been quick to take up the issue, Goluchowski in

January 1900 asked the British War Office to manage its purchases of horses discreetly, without letting it be seen that either government was involved, whereupon Rumbold hastily instructed all British consuls to lie low.[51] This done, Goluchowski was happy to instruct Szell to see to it that nothing was done to hamper shipments from Fiume; and he ignored the protests of the Boer agent Dr Leyds over the government's breach of neutrality.[52] As Koerber blandly explained to the Austrian parliament in March, the sales were "a purely business matter" for private individuals that did not impinge on the government's stance of neutrality.[53] Although his critics found this "totally unsatisfactory" and even launched a "most unseemly attack" on the "so-called chivalrous Emperor" for his role in the affair,[54] Franz Joseph was supremely unconcerned, expressing his pleasure to Rumbold "at our having been able to obtain from Hungary a supply of what he believed to be very useful animals".[55]

Goluchowski was equally serene, explaining to the delegations at Budapest in May that "as regards the possibility of an amicable intervention, he saw no present prospect" of it, as neither Great Britain nor the Boers would agree. As for alleged supplies of arms to the British by Skoda, the government's neutrality was not infringed by its "noninterference with the supply of arms by private persons", even to the British government; and "he did not propose to press his police investigations further".[56] In the end, the Hungarian Foreign Affairs Committee accepted the government's position of strict neutrality but – according to what the British consul-general heard from a confidential source – Goluchowski could not persuade it to adopt "a sentence congratulating England upon the success of her arms and expressing a general sympathy with her policy in those regions of Africa".[57] It was much the same story when the delegations met in Vienna the following year: states and governments might be bound by neutrality, Goluchowski blandly explained, "but individuals had the right to continue supplying the belligerents with war materials" at their own risk; and the government "had no right to enquire where the horses were destined for" as their sale was "a private transaction". As for a tender of mediation: Great Britain had made its position quite clear "and we have really no reason . . . to commit any unfriendly act against the British government . . . with whom we wish to live in peace and friendship".[58]

The British were certainly grateful for these demonstrations of the Austro-Hungarian government's "friendly attitude" and Salisbury was careful to express his thanks to Vienna.[59] They were particularly appreciative of the language in which, on 12 December 1901, the Hungarian prime minister answered a parliamentary interpellation about the sale of horses to Great Britain. Although even Szell admitted "a natural sympathy with every nation combating for its freedom", and although he only took the usual line – that as the government had no official knowledge of the sales, it had no grounds for interfering – he went on to condemn the language of his critics about "a friendly nation, and one whose sympathy Hungary had enjoyed in the days of her troubles . . . Hungary entertained a high respect for England, besides an admiration of her greatness".[60] It was perhaps a measure of Lansdowne's sensitivity about the extent of Great Britain's unpopularity on the continent, that even this fairly anodyne speech moved the rather dry foreign secretary to write, in his own hand, an effusive personal letter to Deym: Szell's words would "I am sure be greatly appreciated here. The more so because we are not used to such kindly and sympathetic words. The courage and straightforwardness of the speech are as remarkable as the goodwill which it exhibits. M. Szell will occupy a warm corner in our hearts".[61] Meanwhile, a *Times* leader of 13 December, paid public tribute to Hungarian "chivalry": Szell was "the only statesman who has so far had the courage to stand up to the mania of Anglophobia . . . The British people will never forget that he has given public expression to the feelings of the noble Hungarian people".

The war gave rise to only one direct confrontation between London and Vienna, and even that ended in a cordial agreement. In August 1900, the military authorities in South Africa expelled a number of continentals, including 55 Austrian employees of the Netherlands Railway Company; and when these arrived home, according to under-secretary Lützow, "in very destitute condition", the Austrian press began to denounce the British and to taunt Goluchowski with the gratitude he was now receiving.[62] When Rumbold confirmed that the minister was indeed "very sensitive about the attacks that may be made on him here for his English sympathies",[63] Salisbury promised to ask the War Office for a report and to consider cases for compensation. By November, nothing had happened, however, and a rather sceptical Lansdowne was confronted by an "eloquent" plea from Deym on behalf of the "undesirables": "it would be good policy on our part to treat those expelled with consideration . . . for the complaints put Count Goluchowski , who was most friendly to Great Britain, in a difficult position".[64] The Austrians objected to the proposed time limit for claims, and to the summoning of impecunious claimants – many of whom lived in remote parts of the Monarchy – to London to give oral evidence.[65] Their own proposal of a simple lump sum payment was not well received in London, however, even when it was backed up by a crude reminder from under-secretary Szécsen, that "considering the great friendliness displayed by the Austro-Hungarian Government in spite of the popular prejudices here in favour of the Boers, he considered it would be good policy to grant the sum without delay".[66] Lansdowne insisted that it was impossible "that large sums of public money should be paid to those persons without any attempt to test the trustworthiness of their statements".[67] In the end, however, after the Italians, Germans and Russians had also added their protests, Lansdowne decided to settle for lump sum payments after all; and although the sum offered to the Austrians (£15,000) was only one quarter of what they had been claiming, Goluchowski professed himself "extremely glad".[68] Indeed, in comparison with the Dutch and the Germans, whose enormous claims had been reduced to one twentieth, and one tenth respectively (while the overall claim of £1,232,625 had been reduced to £106,950) the Austrians had indeed done remarkably well.[69] At any rate, Goluchowski fulsomely assured the Hungarian delegations that it was thanks to the "especially considerate attitude" (*besonderen Entgegen-kommen*) of the British government that the outcome had been "in every way satisfactory".[70]

The same readiness to understand the point of view of the other party helped to moderate the exchanges between Vienna and London over the behaviour of the Austro-Hungarian press. Here, the British felt themselves to be the aggrieved party; but they were generally ready to accept the explanations or excuses advanced by the Austrians. The latter, it must be admitted, proved quite skilful in directing British wrath on to allegedly even more culpable parties, particularly Germany; certainly a somewhat questionable tactic, given their general desire for closer cooperation between Great Britain and the Triple Alliance, including Germany.

In the very first weeks of the war, for example, Rumbold had commented on the "spitefully malignant satisfaction" with which the Viennese press – inspired, he suggested, from Germany – had greeted recent British defeats in South Africa.[71] At the same time, Baron Alfred de Rothschild approached Count Mensdorff in London: Chamberlain had recently written to him to complain about the language of the Austro-Hungarian press, which he particularly regretted "because Austria-Hungary enjoyed warm sympathies in England and people had hitherto been accustomed to regard us as friends of England". The minister was therefore asking Mensdorff to move his government "at least to influence the Austro-Hungarian press to adopt a less unfriendly tone towards the present war and England". Mensdorff, for his part, professed his surprise at Chamberlain's complaint:

> as Lord Salisbury, who had recently mentioned to me the hostile language of the German newspapers, had admitted that he could not level this charge against the Austro-Hungarian press, apart from a few exceptions; and that, on the contrary, the sympathy for England that exists in Austria-Hungary repeatedly found expression, particularly in the newspapers close to the government.

Although he agreed to report to Vienna, he pointed out that "in our country too it was not in the government's power to influence all the newspapers, and not at all those that were controlled by the opposition". In fact, he suggested to Goluchowski, the problem lay partly with the British press: he had already been:

> struck by the way in which the English newspapers, as if deliberately, reproduce all the articles from our newspapers that are unfriendly to England, while failing to publish commentaries that are definitely

friendly, and that as a result I am repeatedly questioned in society here as to why Austria is now so suddenly hostile to England.[72]

Matters had not much improved two years later, by which time Mensdorff was beginning to agree with the Russian ambassador that, thanks to the prolonged display of pro-Boer feeling on the continent, in government circles and high society a certain "bitterness and hostility towards the foreigner has in the long run taken possession of English opinion".[73] In October 1901, at Balmoral, Mensdorff was treated to a great show of indignation by Edward VII himself, "still enraged at the pro-Boer attitude of the continent". After producing a number of coarse postcards of the kind he received every day, and one of which came from Trieste:

> His Majesty again complained bitterly about the press and claimed that despite all the friendliness between England and Austria-Hungary, our newspapers were the most unfriendly of all. I permitted myself to contradict this , and pointed out, as so often before, that this unfriendly atmosphere had its origin in an ill-conceived sentimentality [*eine schlecht verstandene Sentimentalität*]; the general public was in fact not well informed about the true origins of the war and only saw two little states that were defending their independence against one of the greatest Powers on earth. With the end of the war the Anglophobe feeling will disappear, insofar as it exists in our country at all.

On this occasion, too, however, the Monarchy escaped with its reputation fairly unscathed, all the more so as Mensdorff:

> further pointed out that the Imperial and Royal government has always observed a most friendly attitude, often under very difficult circumstances, and has prevented as far as possible every anti-English demonstration or publication. The King admitted this and spoke in terms of the highest recognition and gratitude of [Franz Joseph] who had always proved himself a true and good friend of the King and of England.[74]

British and Austrian attitudes were well illustrated in the furore that broke out in Germany in the wake of Chamberlain's Edinburgh speech of 25 October 1901, comparing the South African campaign to those recently undertaken by the continental powers (including that by Austria-Hungary in Bosnia in 1878), and which dragged on into the new year with a haughty reply by Bülow in the Reichstag and a further defiant speech from Chamberlain. From the start, Deym feared that the row might "annihilate for a long time all prospect of closer co-operation between England and Germany"; but he was if anything even more concerned to dissociate Austria-Hungary from what he termed the "quite unreasonable" German reaction.[75] He managed in fact to get Chamberlain to admit "that our press, even those papers that do not hide their sympathies for the Boers, had by no means followed the example of the German press".[76] Indeed, although the minister (who said he had taken care to study all the military orders in question before making his speech) could not remember to which Austrian measures in Bosnia he had been referring, he assured Deym that he would "not object if you asked me, to declaring that I did not intend to insult Austria-Hungary or to accuse it of cruel treatment of the enemy". (The ambassador did not take him up on this, sensing that such a declaration would only be likely to fan the flames in Germany.)[77] In Vienna, meanwhile, Plunkett emphasized that although angry public meetings had denounced Chamberlain's "infamous accusation" that the Austrians in Bosnia had perpetrated atrocities like those to which the "heroic Boer people" were being daily subjected by what the *Vaterland* termed "the mercenary levies of England", "the Emperor and the government quite disapprove of these unseemly manifestations".[78]

It was not simply that the Austrians found in Germany a useful whipping boy, however. They were in fact genuinely angered by the "quite incorrigible" arrogance of the German officials (who had recently embarrassed Vienna enormously by their harsh measures against their Polish subjects).[79] If Count Berchtold at the London embassy questioned Germany's wisdom in alienating a friend such as Chamberlain, "the strongest and most influential statesman . . . for the sake of their foolish public opinion", Goluchowski was even more scathing: "friend Bülow richly deserved" the verbal drubbing he had received at Chamberlain's hands.[80] As for the emperor, he made a point of accosting Plunkett at a court ball, with an "eager and pleased look", to tell him of the:

> pleasure with which he had seen the spirited answer given by England to the extraordinary attack made by the German Chancellor, and agreed with me that the energy displayed in refuting the unmerited and offensive remarks made in Germany would have a salutary effect on our detractors abroad . . . The Emperor said he could not understand how Count Bülow should have used such extraordinary language, for it was in the clear interest of Germany to remain on good terms with His Majesty's government; it certainly was of the greatest importance to Austria-Hungary that there should be no friction between England and Germany.[81]

Clearly, the incident had done nothing to impair Anglo–Austrian relations in their narrower, bilateral aspect; and with the conclusion of peace at Vereeniging, followed by the coronation of Edward VII, even the Austro-Hungarian press began to adopt a more friendly tone.[82] "Justice and culture", the formerly violently hostile *Vaterland* declared: "have in King Edward a powerful supporter ... Our warmest sympathies accompany the high-minded King". True, some of the encomia were rather double edged: as the *Neues Wiener Tageblatt* pointed out, King Edward had been "an active factor in the conclusion of peace ... It will always be to his renown that under his reign the devastation of Africa came to an end".[83] Archduke Franz Ferdinand, as ever completely at loggerheads with his imperial uncle and with the establishment, was anything but taken with the prospect of having to attend the lengthy coronation celebrations planned in London. "I must tell you", he informed a harassed Mensdorff in May:

> that I am quite *shattered* about the programme. Apart from the fact that, strictly between you and me, I find it a scandal that, during a war in which thousands of sons of the Empire [*Landeskindern*] are bleeding to death for the sake of a stock-exchange speculation and the army is getting one defeat after another, they should be putting on celebration after celebration for weeks, it shows a really English lack of consideration, to keep the foreign princes in London for eleven days with dinners and similar entertainments, and shorten or ruin their summer holidays.[84]

As far as the people who really counted were concerned, however, Anglo–Austrian relations were, if anything, even more cordial at the end of the Boer War than at the beginning. Although, after the war was over, Rumbold's publicistic activity earned him "a wigging" from Lansdowne (who seems even to have considered stopping his pension)[85] this was really because his *National Review* article, appearing on the very eve of William II's visit to London, had drawn embarrassing comparisons between the chivalrous Franz Joseph and "other rulers who now pose as our friends", and went on to describe the Germans as "our most dangerous and unrelenting foes".[86] With Rumbold's remarks about Franz Joseph nobody had any quarrel, either in Vienna[87] or in London, where the permanent under-secretary at the Foreign Office assured Mensdorff that:

> no term of praise is too high, and the whole of England knows what deep gratitude this country owes to His Majesty. Nowhere in the world does His ... Majesty receive more respect and admiration than here in England. HRH the Prince of Wales and several other personalities spoke to me in the same terms.[88]

In short, Anglo–Austrian relations during the Boer War were redolent of an era in which the chancelleries of Europe were controlled by a small cosmopolitan elite with shared values, making policy with a lofty disregard for the passions of the masses and the demands of press and public opinion. It was, however, an era that was drawing to a close. In the next decade, confronted by growing pressures from mass movements, the increasingly ominous militarization of diplomacy, and the drift towards a Europe polarized in two camps – in which Austria-Hungary appeared increasingly as a helpless instrument of, even a willing accomplice in, German hegemonial ambitions – the small cosmopolitan elites that had managed Anglo–Austrian relations during the Boer War began to lose control. The next war in which Great Britain was involved was to be a very different affair.

Notes

1. My thanks are due to the officials of the Haus-, Hof-, und Staatsarchiv, Vienna, and of the Public ecord Office (PRO), and the British Library, London, for permission to use the archives within their care.
2. PRO Foreign Office (hereafter PRO FO) 7/1297, Rumbold to Salisbury, no. 11, 10 January 1900; G. P. Gooch and H. W. V. Temperley (eds), *British Documents on the Origins of the War* (11 vols, London, 1926–38), vol. 1, no. 305; H. Rumbold, "An English tribute to the Emperor Franz Joseph", *National Review*, November, 364–72 (1902).
3. PRO FO 7/1298, Wardrop to Rumbold, no. 28, 8 June 1900, enclosed in Rumbold to Salisbury, no. 124, 9 June 1900.
4. PRO FO 7/1299, Rumbold to Salisbury, no. 182, 28 August 1900.
5. PRO FO 7/1299, Wardrop to Plunkett, no. 64 confidential, 23 December 1900.
6. PRO FO 7/1300, Plunkett to Salisbury, telegram 32, 19 September 1900
7. PRO FO 7/1309, Plunkett to Lansdowne, no. 1, confidential, 3 January 1900.
8. PRO FO 800/117, Lansdowne MSS, Plunkett to Lansdowne, private, 5 June 1902.
9. *Ibid.*
10. Balfour, BL Add. MSS 49727, Balfour to Lansdowne, 12 December 1901.
11. Haus-, Hof-, und Staatsarchiv, Vienna, Politisches Archiv (hereafter PA) VIII/Karton 125, Deym to Goluchowski, no. 39A, 24 May 1901 and encl. *Morning Post*, 24 May 1901.
12. PA VIII/125, Deym to Goluchoski, no. 87D, 7 December 1900.
13. PA III/157, Szögyény to Goluchowski, no. 18C, 17 May 1902.
14. PRO FO 7/1309, Plunkett to Lansdowne, no. 39 confidential, 14 February 1901.
15. PRO FO 7/1297, Rumbold to Salisbury, no. 28 confidential, 2 February 1900; Gooch and Temperley, *British Documents*, vol. 1, no. 249.
16. PRO FO 7/1297, Rumbold to Salisbury, no. 71 confidential, 31 March 1900
17. PA VIII/ 125, Mensdorff to Goluchowski, no. 74A, 12 October 1901.
18. *Ibid.*, Goluchowski to Deym, no. 70, 13 March 1900.
19. PA X /118, Aehrenthal to Goluchowski, private, 16 January, 26 February 1902.
20. PRO FO 7/1309, Milbanke to Lansdowne, no. 33, confidential, 8 February 1901.
21. PRO FO 120/785, Plunkett to Lansdowne, telegram 4, Africa, 4 June 1902; PRO FO 7/1324, Plunkett to Lansdowne, no. 156 confidential, 13 June 1902.
22. PA XXXVIII/259, Hirsch to Goluchowski, no. 2, Pol., 8 May 1899.
23. *Ibid.*, Ramberg to Hirsch, 23 July 1899, encl. in Hirsch to Goluchowski, no. 14, Pol., 25 July 1899.
24. *Ibid.*
25. *Ibid.*, Ramberg to Hirsch, 23 October 1899, encl. in Hirsch to Goluchowski, no. 31, Pol., 24 October 1899.
26. Quoted in Erwin A. Schmidl, "Zur Geschichte der k.(u) k. Konsularvertretungen im südlichen Afrika bis zum ersten Weltkrieg", in *Mitteilungen des Oesterreichischen Staatsarchivs* 38, 223–73; "Biographische Angabe", p. 272. In due course Ramberg succeeded Hirsch in Cape Town,

before moving on to Pretoria and Johannesburg to become, with a total of 15 years' service, the longest serving I & R official in South Africa; *Ibid.,* pp. 272–3.

27. PA VIII/122, Deym to Goluchowski, no. 24A, 12 June 1899.
28. *Ibid.*, Mensdorff to Goiluchowski, no. 32A, 17 July 1899, no. 38A, 17 August 1899.
29. PA VIII/ 123, Mensdorff to Goluchowski, no. 48A, 3 October 1899.
30. PA VIII/ 125, Deym to Goluchowski, private, 20 March 1900.
31. PA VIII/128, Deym to Lützow, private, 10 February 1902.
32. PRO FO 7/1298, Wardrop to Rumbold, no. 28, 8 June 1900, enclosed in Rumbold to Salisbury, no. 124, 9 June 1900.
33. PRO FO 7/ 1309, Milbanke to Lansdowne, no. 321, 5 February 1901.
34. PRO FO 7/ 1309, Plunkett to Lansdowne, no. 22, very confidential, 17 January 1901.
35. PA VIII/ 126, Mensdorff to Goluchowski, private, 24 October 1901.
36. PA VIII / 156, Szögyény to Goluchowski, private, 4 February 1901.
37. Rumbold, "An English tribute".
38. PRO FO 800/117, Lansdowne MSS, Plunkett to Lansdowne, private, 20 December 1900.
39. *Ibid.*, minute, and PRO FO 7/1299, Plunkett to Lansdowne, no. 249, confidential, 6 December 1900.
40. *Ibid.*
41. PA X/116, Kinsky to Goluchowski, no. 57B, 28 October 1901.
42. PA X/116, Aehrenthal to Goluchowski, no. 56F, 24 August 1900.
43. Balfour MSS, 49727, Balfour to Lansdowne, 8 October 1902, secret.
44. PRO FO 120/ 763, Rumbold to Salisbury, no. 24, Africa, and no. 26, Africa, 6 May and 23 May 1900.
45. PRO FO 7/1323, Plunkett to Lansdowne, no. 133, 20 May 1902.
46. PRO FO 120/763, Rumbold to Salisbury, no. 9, Africa, 4 February 1900.
47. *Ibid.*, Rumbold to Salisbury, no. 16, Africa, 27 February 1900.
48. PRO FO 7/1323, Fairholme to Plunkett, 16 May 1902, encl. in Plunkett to Lansdowne, no. 131, 20 May 1902.
49. Haus-, Hof-, und Staatsarchiv, Vienna, Aehrenthal MSS, Kinsky to Aehrenthal, private, 3 March 1900.
50. PRO FO 7/1299, Rumbold to Salisbury, no. 191, confidential, 8 September 1900.
51. PRO FO 120/763, Rumbold to Salisbury, telegram 5, Africa, 22 January 1900; PRO FO 120/766, Thornton to Rumbold, telegram, 10 February 1900.
52. PRO FO 120/763, Rumbold to Salisbury, no. 15, Africa, 22 February 1900.
53. PRO FO 7/1297, Rumbold to Salisbury, no. 66, confidential, 27 March 1900.
54. *Ibid.*, and PRO FO 120/763, Rumbold to Salisbury, no. 16, Africa, 27 February 1900.
55. PRO FO 7/1297, Rumbold to Salisbury, no. 66, confidential, 27 March 1900.
56. PRO FO 7/1302, Thornton to Rumbold, no. 30, 29 May 1900.
57. *Ibid.*, Thornton to Rumbold, no. 28, 28 May 1900.
58. PRO FO 7/1310, Plunkett to Lansdowne, no. 145, 8 June 1901.
59. PRO FO 120/762, Salisbury to Rumbold, no. 5, Africa, 6 March 1900.
60. PRO FO 7/1315, Thornton to Plunkett, no. 38, 12 December 1901.
61. PRO FO 800/117Lansdowne MSS, Lansdowne to Deym, 17 December , Deym to Lansdowne 18 December 1901; PA VIII/126, Deym to Goluchowski, no. 97A, 20 December 1901.
62. PRO FO 120/763, Milbanke to Salisbury, no. 30, Africa, 30 August 1900.
63. *Ibid.*, Rumbold to Salisbury, telegram 12, Africa, 30 August 1900.
64. PRO FO 800/117, Lansdowne MSS, Lansdowne to Plunkett, private, 14 November 1900.
65. PRO FO 120/773, Lansdowne to Plunkett, no. 5, Africa, and no. 6, Africa, 23 April and 1 May 1901.
66. PRO FO 120/774, Plunkett to Lansdowne, no. 2, Africa, 11 April 1901.
67. FO 120/773, Lansdowne to Plunkett, no. 6, Africa, 1 May 1901.
68. PRO FO 120/774, Plunkett to Lansdowne, no. 26, Africa, 19 November 1901.
69. PRO FO 120/773, Lansdowne to Plunkett, no. 20, Africa, 28 September 1901.
70. PRO FO 120/785, Plunkett to Lansdowne, no. 8, Africa, 27 May 1902.
71. PRO FO 7/1286, Rumbold to Salisbury, no. 256, 10 October 1899; Gooch and Temperley, *British Documents*, vol. 1, no. 295.

72. PA VIII/123 Mensdorff to Goluchowski, private, 14 November 1899.
73. PA VIII/126, Mensdorff to Goluchowski, no. 80A, 10 October 1901.
74. *Ibid.*, Mensdorff to Goluchowski, private, 10 October 1901.
75. PA VIII/126, Deym to Goluchowski, no. 92C, 22 November 1901; PRO FO 120/773, Lansdowne to Plunkett, no. 21, Africa, 26 November 1901.
76. PA VIII/126, Deym to Goluchowski, no. 93A, very confidential, 26 November 1901.
77. *Ibid.*
78. PRO FO 120/774, Plunkett to Lansdowne, no. 25, Africa, 13 December 1901; PRO FO 7/1322, Plunkett to Lansdowne, no. 17, 16 January 1902.
79. PA III/158, Szöyény to Goluchowski, private, 12 February 1902.
80. Aehrenthal MSS, Berchtold to Aehrenthal, 25 February 1902; PA I/480, Goluchowski to Szögyény, private, 17 January 1902.
81. Gooch and Temperley, *British Documents*, vol. 1, no. 333, Plunkett to Lansdowne, no. 24, Africa, 19 January 1902.
82. PRO FO 7/ 1324, Plunkett to Lansdowne, no. 192, 31 July 1902.
83. *Ibid.*, Milbanke to Lansdowne, no. 204, 10 August 1902.
84. Mensdorff MSS, Franz Ferdinand to Mensdorff, 4 May 1902.
85. PL Add. MSS. Balfour MSS 49727, Lansdowne MSS, Verney to Sandars, 8 November 1902; see also PRO FO 7/1333, Lansdowne to Sanderson, 5 November 1902 and minute, Lansdowne to Law Ofiicers, 12 December 1902.
86. Rumbold, "An English tribute".
87. PA VIII/128, Deym to Goluchowski, private, 19 December 1902.
88. PA VIII/128, Mensdorff to Goluchowski, no. 58, 7 November 1902.

CHAPTER SIX

Italy and the Boer War

Gilles Ferragu

Of the European powers, Italy was probably the most troubled by the conflict in South Africa. Could Italy, traditionally on friendly terms with Great Britain, and without territory in southern Africa, view the war other than through British eyes? Memories of the Risorgimento, however, pushed the Italians towards supporting the Boers. As a result, Italian policy seemed hesitant, divided between national interests and popular sentiments.

There is little Italian writing on this subject: few historians have been interested in it, except to explore the participation of Italian volunteers on the Boer side.[1] The war was followed at a distance because Italy was engaged in a complex foreign policy that had to reconcile friendship with Great Britain, maintenance of the Triple Alliance, and rapprochement with France. Nevertheless, lack of interest was not complete: Britain was important in the diplomatic life of Italy, and what affected it could not leave indifferent the Italian ministry of foreign affairs, the Consulta. Beyond the reaction of Italy to this conflict there is the question of the consequences of this reaction for the policy and interests of Italy itself.

Part I of what follows will address Anglo–Italian relations up to 1899, and it will be seen that these relations, traditionally good, had become strained since 1890. Part II will analyse the immediate reactions of Italy and of the Vatican to the conflict, through their views of the belligerents and of the causes of the war, both on the level of policy and on that of public opinion. Part III will examine the diplomatic consequences of the crisis.

I. Anglo–Italian relations on the eve of the war

On the eve of the conflict in South Africa, Anglo–Italian relations were, officially at least, excellent. Good relations with London was a dogma of Italian foreign policy. This tradition was based on history and notably on the role of Great Britain in the Risorgimento. It took equally into account British naval power in the Mediterranean, and the political affinities between constitutional monarchies. Italian anglophilia was a mixture of tradition, respect, admiration and gratitude. It is impossible, however, to separate Anglo–Italian relations from the European context. Italy had been allied, since 1882, to the continental rival of Great Britain, Germany, who while acknowledging the intimacy between London and Rome, hoped to use it to breach British isolationism and bring Britain into the Triplice of Germany, Austria-Hungary, and Italy. Rome was torn between the model of friendship with Britain and the model of membership of the Triplice. Thus, when the treaty of December 1897 ending the Greco–Turkish war delivered Crete, the cause of the quarrel, to the European powers, the Italian government ranged itself with the liberal powers (Britain and France) in opposition to Germany and Austria-Hungary. In this it was supported by public opinion. In the chancelleries of Europe, this was seen as proof of British influence on Italian policy, and attributed to the return to the Consulta, after an absence of over 20 years, of Visconti Venosta.[2] It was believed that if London had not intervened in the affairs of Crete, Italy would have sided with the other members of the Triplice. To no one did Italy seem to be an entirely solid support, and the French minister for foreign affairs, Delcassé, was told that London seriously envisaged that the fall of the House of Savoy would coincide with that of the government of Rudini.[3]

The Mediterranean Agreements of 1887, between Italy, Great Britain and Austria-Hungary, had been able to reconcile the two models of Italian policy, as well as encouraging Italy in the Mediterranean ambitions that it was developing. Those agreements, however, were not renewed in 1897, partly because of the reaction in Europe to the Jameson Raid of 1895. When the Boer War finally broke out, it was once again as regards the Mediterranean that Italian policy reacted. In effect, Anglo–Italian relations suffered from the weight of British imperialism and the policy of Joseph Chamberlain. In Africa, Anglo–Italian relations were affected by Anglo–French rivalry. The Fashoda crisis of July to November 1898, a diplomatic victory for Britain,[4] disturbed Italy, who saw in it a future menace to its own ambitions. The Anglo–French agreement of 21 March 1899, following the evacuation of French forces from the Nile, only confirmed this concern. The prospect of an eventual rapprochement between Paris and London based on a division of Tripoli was even more alarming for Italian diplomatists, because Italy had for some time wished to acquire this province of the Ottoman Empire, just as until 1881, and the establishment of a French protectorate, it had coveted Tunisia. The Anglo–French agreement of 21 March 1899 delimited the zones of influence of Britain and France between the Congo and the Nile. Canevaro, the Italian foreign minister, had been kept in the dark by the British and the French, and the Italian government had been unable to prepare the population for the news.[5] Continuing British silence was as troubling as the fact that under the agreement the region given to France, to the north and west of Lake Chad, contained the hinterland of Tripoli, namely Borkou and Tibesti.[6] Moreover, Lord Salisbury refused to proclaim that Britain had no designs on Ottoman territory, and Germany and Austria-Hungary abandoned Italy on this issue.

Almost simultaneously, Great Britain conspicuously failed to support an Italian demand for a naval base in China. Canevaro, breaking with Visconti Venosta's and Rudini's policy of inactivity, had, in February 1899, instructed the Italian representative at Peking, de Martino, to demand a naval base in the bay of San Mun and the recognition of Italian interests in the region. The Chinese rejection of this demand caused Canevaro, on 8 March, to issue an ultimatum, which was cancelled on the same day when Salisbury made it known that Britain would support only pacific action. A mistake in the receipt of instructions caused the ultimatum to be delivered, only to be rejected by the Chinese. To a country sensitive to its power image this was a distinct blow. It brought into disrepute the Consulta and the government, and did not leave even the king untouched. The affair was comparable with the Italian defeat at Adowa, in Ethiopia, in 1896.

The San Mun affair and the Anglo–French agreement were, for the Italians, disappointing results of their sentimental attachment to the British. The reaction of the press was moderated by the government, through the agency of *Populo Romano*. Italy had no wish to publicize the injuries to its pride, but in private the ministry was furious with the British for bringing about a political crisis that it was unable to survive. Anglo–Italian relations had been distinctly compromised. The new coldness was accentuated when the British Mediterranean squadron avoided Cagliari, where it had been expected to participate in celebrations attending a visit to Sicily by King Humbert, and cruised instead along an uninhabited coastline. The tone of the royal toast reflected the Italian reserve.

Yet another matter weakened the traditional links between Italy and Great Britain, and this risked creating a new field of irredentism. Only recently unified, Italy was sensitive about the condition of Italian-speaking populations under foreign rule. There had been several collisions with Austria-Hungary over Trieste and the Trentino. By a decree of 22 March 1899, London broke the linguistic *modus vivendi* between Italian and English that had prevailed in Malta since the British arrival there in 1814, and tried to impose English: in 15 years' time Italian was to disappear from official use, and English was to become compulsory. The leaders of the Italian community in Malta protested and appealed for help to the society Dante Alighieri, the Italian equivalent of the British Council, which in turn appealed to the Italian government.[7] The matter threatened to become a diplomatic issue, but the government in Rome distanced itself from the press denunciations of the change. In London the Italian chargé d'affaires, Costa, reported that the British press was fully aware that a blunder had been committed, but justified it in the name of the higher interests of the British Empire.[8] A visit to Malta by the colonial secretary, Chamberlain, in November 1900, gave the Maltese the opportunity to raise the matter again, all the more so as Italy, after a period of stupor, had officially announced its astonishment. An injury obliged Chamberlain to return by train, via Rome. There he met Visconti Venosta but, through lack of a common language, the two ministers discussed nothing concrete.[9] In a speech of 11 December Chamberlain did respond to questions and criticisms, maintaining that only a small fraction of Maltese spoke Italian.[10] This piece of economy with the truth caused *la Tribuna*, on 13 December, to speak of "provocation to irredentism". Nor was this all: a tax increase finally pushed the Maltese into resistance. In May 1901 the Italian consul at Malta, Grande, reported public demonstrations of up to 30,000 people, and four petitions demanded a referendum on the language issue.[11] Britain only slowly registered the size of this problem, and in October 1901 offered only an extension of five years, beyond the original 15, before the elimination of Italian as a language of administration was complete.[12] In 1903 Grande was to speak of "a long and inexorable war" conducted by Chamberlain against the Italian language.[13]

II. Italy, the Vatican and the Boer War

The first question to be examined is that of the image, in Italian opinion, of the belligerents. Britain manifestly embodied a model of civilization at its height. Thus, in the *Nuova Antologia* of 16 February 1902, the senator F. Nobili Vitelleschi compared the British to the ancient Romans. However, fearing a tendency in British policy towards imperialism and isolationism, he considered Britain to be menaced by pride and by a feeling of invincibility. Moreover, his judgement was that in the world as it was, such an empire could not last for long. The same image is to be found with the sociologist C. Lombroso, who accused Britain of being imperialist and falsely liberal, and contrasted the "impure" England of Chamberlain and Rhodes with the "great Britain of Gladstone and Spencer".[14] Haunted by their memory of the Roman empire, the Italians had a tendency to see in the Boer War one of those frontier struggles that had exhausted the "virtue" of their ancestors. Another image of Britain, put forward in Vitelleschi's article, was common in Italy: that of the liberal power, loved for its support at the time of the Risorgimento. Here again, however, Britain's recent silence on other popular and national causes, such as the Greeks and the Armenians, and its support for the US in 1898 against Spain, a latin and European country, had caused offence in many quarters. Such matters, together with disputes over the Red Sea, lengthened the list of disappointments already catalogued: San Mun; the Anglo–French agreement of 21 March 1899; Malta. From this point of view, the heyday of Anglo–Italian friendship was clearly over, and it was only prudent on the part of Italy to cultivate other connections.

The Boers, in contrast, were perceived as a people adapted to Africa and to its savagery. The historian T. Filesi has stated that the Boers were regarded as pioneers, with a strong faith, brave and with a sense of duty.[15] Lombroso, for his part, saw in the Boers a triumph of Darwinism: the white "pseudobarbarians" were the best fitted to survive in the milieu of Africa and would evolve as soon as conditions of life improved. The analogy with the Roman empire and its barbarians was clear. Lombroso went on the compare the Boers with the American colonists of 1776 and the Italians of 1860. They were accused all the same of religious fanaticism: Filesi saw the dark side of this people, while the liberal deputy Pantaleoni, in *la Tribuna* of 21 January 1900, considered that a defeat of Britain would be a defeat for liberalism at the hands of a religiously intolerant society. Lombroso, more favourable to the Boer cause, also remarked on the strict religion, but justified it as a pure form of Calvinism.

The question of representations poses that of reactions. Faced with a suspicious public opinion in Britain, the Italian government wished to control the reactions of its own population and to avoid hostile demonstrations. The ministries of the interior and foreign affairs drew up a sort of *cordon sanitaire* in order to discourage initiatives favourable to the Boers. King Victor Emmanuel III set the example, reading *The Times* rather than the national press.[16] But in Italy, as in the rest of Europe, pro-Boer manifestations increased through 1901. In March 1901, for example, Boer committees were set up in Turin and Venice.[17] In the tradition established by Garibaldi and his red shirts there was also to be a problem with volunteers. Surveying the numerous foreign volunteers arriving in Pretoria in September–October 1899, the Italian consul there, Morpurgo, was happy to note that there were no Italians, something he pointed out to the British authorities. Later on, the Italian government tried to play down rumours of the departure of young Italians for the war.[18]

Distinct from the neutral stance of the government, Italian public opinion was pro-Boer. Catholic opinion rallied to the thesis put forward by the *Osservatore Romano*, the quasi-official organ of Saint-Siege, which held the cause of the war – the interference by Britain in the internal affairs of another state – to be immoral, and hence the war itself morally indefensible.[19] In this war between two non-Catholic peoples, the Vatican could address the question on a purely theoretical level without making any official pronouncement other than to call for peace. The Italian ambassador in London, de Renzis, reported the unhappiness there with the fact that the Curia was overtly favourable to the Boers. The Duke of Norfolk, one of the most prominent English Catholics, sent a letter denouncing this stance to Cardinal Rampolla, secretary of state at the Vatican, who replied that the *Osservatore Romano* was not an official publication. The *Nuova Antologia* was closer to the general mood: divided between admiration for Britain and enthusiasm for what Kaiser Wilhelm II called "a courageous little people", it evoked both the greatness of the British colonial enterprise and the struggle of the Boers to free their nation.

Advised by the government, the Italian press remained neutral, contenting itself with providing information rather than comment.[20] Only such publications as *L'Unita* departed from this stance. The press, however, was not representative of Italian opinion. Foreign diplomats stressed in their reports that anglomania was out of fashion, heralding a fall in anglophilia, especially among republicans and radicals. This sentiment seemed to be shared even by some, for example Fortis and Nasi, who were close to Francesco Crispi, one of the most anglophile of Italian politicians, which testified to its strength.[21] In the background there arose a general fear – "apocalyptic", according to T. Filesi – of uprising on the part of the indigenous population of Africa, profiting from the war between the whites. Senator Vitelleschi, in September 1899, worried about the reaction of Africans to a fratricidal war which would set back civilization in Africa.[22]

More than what was at stake in the Boer War, which, of course, included gold fields, it was the military methods followed by the belligerents that caught Italian attention. For war correspondents and military journalists, the war was interesting from several points of view. In the first place it was a matter of observing an army reputably the best in the world, on which the Italians counted so far as a European conflict was concerned. The theatres of operations, the strategy and the tactics of Lord Roberts invited comparison with those of General Baratieri in Ethiopia in 1896.[23] In October 1899, the Italian ambassador in London stressed the enthusiasm of the British people for the war, as well as the excellence of the preparation of the expedition as it made its way to what ought to be a walkover. The first British victories of Glencoe and Elandsgate suggested a short war and only the attitude of the the Franco–Russian alliance disturbed Rome.[24] On 31 October, however, a first British defeat astonished the Italians. In December, the situation of the British seemed incontestably bad: Costa noted on 12 December the reversal of British fortunes after the Cape passed into Boer hands; a week later he considered that the campaign was a disaster.[25] Early in 1900 Rome was concluding that the British army, confronted by tactics that it was unable to match, was not invincible and that victory would be both difficult and costly in human lives.[26] This engaged Italian sympathy: Italy was reminded of its own checks in Ethiopia, and in particular its defeat at Adowa in 1896. As a result, a rumour emanating either from Berlin or from Egypt had a certain success in the Italian press. The rumour was that Italy had agreed to help Britain by sending its own troops to replace British forces in Egypt, which would then be sent to the war. Foreign diplomats were sceptical, estimating that Italian public opinion would oppose such a move, while for Britain to treat Italy as an equal was inconceivable. Denials swiftly arrived, in *la Perseveranza*, which had links with the government, and after a statement by Salisbury on 23 February nothing remained of this rumour except a suspicion of an effort on the part of the British to draw Italy into a discussion of Mediterranean matters.[27]

III. Mediterranean consequences

The year 1899 was a decisive one for Anglo–Italian partnership. The setbacks over San Mun and the Anglo–French agreement of March had demonstrated to Rome the ambiguities of a policy based too much on the friendship of a Britain whom the Italians continued to respect and whose power they continued to fear. By contrast, the peaceful outcome of the Fashoda crisis and the declaration by France of its disinterest in Tripoli conferred on the latter a pacific image.

Its setbacks in the war against the Boers clearly damaged the image of Britain, for it was no longer simply diplomacy that was in question, but the power that underpinned that diplomacy and the isolationism of the British. The initial British reverses, together with the general European resentment of it – something understood by Italy's ally, Germany – made it difficult for Italy to decide where to place itself on the diplomatic chess board. When criticism of the expedition made itself clear in London, the enthusiasm of Italian diplomatists declined. De Renzis wrote, in February 1900, "The grandeur of [British] imperialism in fact lacks the support of a large, war-hardened and well-trained army. The country will perhaps see to it now that it has found out how weak its armour is".[28] A month later, the troops of Lord Roberts having retrieved British fortunes, he reported a new intransigence on the part of the British: "chauvinism has crossed the Channel".[29] Roberts' taking of Pretoria, on 5 June 1900, effectively put an end to the war: the military losses of the expedition were redressed. But the weaknesses that had not been suspected either by London or by Rome caused Italian diplomatists to view British policy in a new way.

Visconti Venosta had written, in January 1900:

> If the failure of British arms in South Africa becomes definitive, the diminution of her prestige and power could provide great temptations to Powers which would stand to benefit from that. If, on the other hand, British arms were to finish up having the better of the Boers the enormous sacrifices of the war will oblige the British government to want a definitive solution, with the annexation pure and simple of the South African Republics; and this important territorial change in southern Africa could raise for an interested

Power some question of compensation in other regions of Africa . . . These possibilities cannot be excluded from our forward planning, for they might be such as to alter the present conditions in the Mediterranean and hence touch Italy's interests directly.[30]

De Renzis predicted, in May 1900, that "a reformed England will emerge, which will pursue a very different policy from that which it did in the past".[31]

The image of France naturally profited from the revelations of British weakness, and there were some in Rome who considered leaning towards France for its support. Even so, Britain remained the last resort of Italy in the case of a conflict with France. As the question posed for Italy by the British difficulties in South Africa was that of the balance of power in the Mediterranean, France, and the intentions ascribed to it, returned to the centre of the debate on Italian foreign policy. As during the Spanish–American crisis of 1898, Italy was placed between two camps. The Boer War revived Italian fears of a France suspected of seeking domination of the Mediterranean. As Barrère, the French ambassador in Rome, reported to his foreign minister, Delcassé, early in November 1899:

In a word, the balance of power in the Mediterranean means for the majority of Italians the preponderance of Britain. The preponderance of France appears intolerable to them, even though France wishes to take nothing from Italy, not even what she wishes to acquire from the Ottoman Empire. It is the predominance of the British Empire that reassures the Italians.[32]

Some Italians saw the Boer War as the prelude to a Franco–British war, in which the Mediterranean would be at stake. Barrère believed that even if Italian politicians were still anglophile, public opinion was not. He commented on the benevolent neutrality of Visconti Venosta, in contrast to the more anti-British position assumed by Rudini. At the very end of 1899, he claimed that Rudini believed that Britain would not wait for the increase in the French fleet and the creation of a German navy before attacking France; having examined the situation that such an eventuality would create for Italy, Rudini believed that Italy ought to join a continental coalition against Britain and, if necessary, help to put one together.[33] The attitude of Italy, should a crisis arise, would depend on the individuals concerned. Barrère considered that the Italian government, which had "relied on a strong and often victorious Britain", had been taken aback. For the Italian government, however, in the context of rivalry and tension between Britain, Germany and France, it was a question of finding a happy medium.

One consequence of Italy's loss of confidence in Britain was its rapprochement with France, an unavoidable presence in the Mediterranean, and considered to be more conciliatory than Britain. Concluded in two stages, in

1900 and 1902, this rapprochement brought Italy into close relations, as regards both Mediterranean and European policy, with France. As a Mediterranean power itself, Britain was concerned about any such agreement, and Rome awaited signs of its disapproval. Instead, the British helped the rapprochement by giving it their blessing. On 4 July 1902, two members of parliament accused the British government of having ditched "the old alliance with Italy" by signing the agreement with France of March 1899, which had produced the Franco–Italian rapprochement. The under-secretary of state at the Foreign Office, Lord Cranborne, recognized that mistakes, such as the question of languages in Malta, had been made; he also denied that any Anglo–Italian treaty or agreement existed. Further questions were asked two weeks later. Gibson Bowles MP proposed a reduction in the salary of the British ambassador in Rome, Sir Phillip Currie, on the grounds of incompetence. A future foreign secretary, Sir Edward Grey, considered that Britain had lacked "tact and prudence" in respect of Italy as regards the Anglo–French agreement of 1899, but welcomed the Franco–Italian rapprochement. Cranborne, still in denial that Britain had thrown Italy into the arms of France, desired good relations with everyone. He wished the Franco–Italian rapprochement well, and hinted that it was time that Britain did the same with France. [34]

Tensions between Italy and Austria-Hungary, and the Franco–Italian rapprochement, plus the discontent provoked by the measures imposed on Malta by Britain, were part of an awakening of "latinity". The fact that Britain emerged only with difficulty as the victor in a guerrilla war in Africa produced, in Europe but especially in Italy, a lasting disenchantment. In June 1902, at the time of the signing of the Franco–Italian agreement, which opened the doors of Tripoli to Italy, a new Italian ambassador to London, Pansa, expressed his anxiety about the growth of nationalism and the development of British imperialism, which he dated from the Fashoda crisis.[35] In this climate France became, for Italy, a serious alternative to Great Britain.

Notes

1. T. Filesi, "L'Italia e gli Italiani nella guerra ango-boera" in *Africa* (1987); G. Sarri, "Voluntari e emigrati taliani nella guerra anglo-boera", *Affari Sociali Internazionali* 3, 165–73 (1983).
2. See F. Chabod, *Storia della politica estera italiana 1870–1896* (Bari, 1951).
3. Archives du Ministère des Affaires Etrangères, Paris (hereafter AMAE), NS Italie, vol. 2, dep. 353, Geoffray to Delcassé, 25 June 1898.
4. See M. Michel, *La Mission Marchand 1895–1899* (Paris, 1972).
5. AMAE, NS Italie, vol. 14, tel. 110, Blondel to Delcassé, 1 April 1899.
6. Archivio storico del Ministero degli Affari Esteri (hereafter ASMAE), P1891/1916, pac. 489, de Renzis to Canevaro, 31 March 1899.
7. *Ibid.*, pac. 488, Grande to Canevaro, 29 March 1899.
8. *Ibid.*, Costa to Visconti Venosta, 10 November 1900.

9. AMAE, NS Italie, vol. 58, tel. 155, Barrère to Delcassé, 15 November 1900.
10. ASMAE, P1891/1916, pac. 488, Costa to Visconti Venosta, 11 December 1900.
11. *Ibid.*, pac. 489, Grande to Prinetti, 6 May 1901.
12. *Ibid.*, Grande to Prinetti, 18 November 1901.
13. *Ibid.*, pac. 490, Grande to Morin, 6 July 1903.
14. C. Lombroso, "Gli stati uniti d'Africa e d'America", *Nuova Antologia*, 16 March (1900).
15. Filesi, "L'Italia e gli Italiani".
16. E. Serra, "Il Re diplomatico" *Nuova Antologia*, December (1952).
17. Filesi, "L'Italia e gli Italiani", p. 70.
18. ASMAE, P1891/1916, bust. 607, Morpurgo to Visconti Venosta, 2 October 1899.
19. *Ibid.*, pac. 489, de Renzis to Visconti-Venosta, 28 February 1900.
20. *Ibid.*, pac. 488, Costa to Viscont-Venosta, 25 November 1899.
21. AMAE, NS Italie, vol. 10, dep. 179, Barrère to Delcassé, 20 December 1899.
22. F. Nobili Vitelleschi, "la questione del Transvaal", *Nuova Antologia* **167**, 16 September (1899).
23. General Dal Verme, "Tre mesi di guerra fra Inglesi e Boeri", *Nuova Antologia* **169**, 16 January (1900), and *Nuova Antologia* **170**, 16 March (1900).
24. ASMAE, P1891/1916, pac. 488, de Renzis to Visconti Venosta, 6 and 23 October 1899.
25. *Ibid.*, Costa to Visconti Venosta, 12 and 19 December 1899.
26. *Ibid.*, pac. 489, Costa to Visconti Venosta, 7 February 1900.
27. *Ibid.*, Tornielli to Visconti Venosta, 13 January 1900
28. *Ibid.*, de Renzis to Visconti Venosta, 10 February 1900.
29. *Ibid.*, de Renzis to Visconti Venosta, 12 March 1900.
30. *Documenti Diplomatici Italiani*, 3rd series, vol. 3, no. 353 (Rome, 1962), Visconti Venosta to Lanza, 14 January 1900.
31. ASMAE, P1891/1916, pac. 489, de Renzis to Visconti Venosta, 22 May 1900.
32. AMAE, NS Italie, vol. 58, dep. 148, Barrère to Delcassé, 9 November 1899.
33. *Ibid.*, dep. 185, Barrère to Delcassé, 31 December 1899.
34. ASMAE, P1891/1916, pac. 490, Pansa to Prinetti, 4 and 19 July 1902.
35. *Ibid.*, Pansa to Prinetti, 22 June 1902.

CHAPTER SEVEN

The United States and the Boer War

William N. Tilchin

Most Americans have never heard of the Boer War. Even very serious young students of US history – those who attend all lectures and do all the assigned reading in their undergraduate-level courses – are likely to know little or nothing about this long turn-of-the-century war in which the mighty British Empire was compelled to expend vast resources to subdue the South African Republic (the Transvaal) and the Orange Free State.[1]

Although perhaps understandable, this state of affairs is regrettable, for the Boer War did engage the attention of contemporary Americans and did become an issue of contention in American politics, particularly during the presidential election year of 1900. Much more important, the Boer War was a pivotal event in the history of American foreign relations. By conducting a decidedly pro-British neutrality policy throughout the war, the US government bolstered the fledgling Anglo–American friendship and prepared the way for the emergence under President Theodore Roosevelt of the uniquely special relationship that would play such a crucial role in twentieth-century international history.

I. The backdrop

For well over a century following the American Revolution, Anglo–American relations were marked by conflict and a great deal of mutual antipathy. A turn for the better occurred during the mid-1890s. One important stimulus was Kaiser Wilhelm's telegram of 3 January 1896 congratulating President Paul Kruger on beating back the Jameson Raid and preserving the Transvaal's independence. Increasingly perceiving Germany as a threatening rival, and recognizing the strong and growing anti-British feeling of the governments

and citizens of the other continental European powers as well, the government of Lord Salisbury began to grasp the obsolescence of the long-revered
policy of "splendid isolation" and decided to conciliate and to seek the friendship of the United States. Thus, England moved rapidly early in 1896 to
defuse a dangerous Anglo–American dispute over the Venezuela–British
Guiana boundary by agreeing to the US demand for arbitration.

What Bradford Perkins has called "the great rapprochement" of 1895–
1914[2] was advanced by a number of major events – very prominently including the Boer War, as this essay contends – but perhaps the single most critical
episode was the Spanish–American War of April–August 1898. While joining
the continental powers in encouraging peace, Britain was extremely solicitous
of US concerns in its prewar diplomacy; and during the war Britain carried
out an unmistakably pro-American neutrality policy. In sharp contrast to the
governments of the continental powers – all of whom favored Spain – British
leaders demonstrated during this war their great determination to cultivate
American goodwill. Correspondingly, Britain's conduct opened American
eyes to some of the benefits the United States could derive from a friendship
with its old foe. And Americans were appreciative that British public opinion,
like government policy, was manifestly partial to the United States – again, in
sharp contrast to the hostility prevailing on the continent.

The momentum carried over into 1899. In March America and Britain
collaborated against Germany during a struggle for control of Samoa. At the
Hague conference of May to July, they cooperated in the establishment of an
arbitral court. In September US Secretary of State John Hay issued the first Open
Door notes – a call for equality of commercial opportunity in China – clearly
displaying the commonality of Anglo–American interests in the most perilous
international hot spot of the time. With regard to South Africa, where US
interests were minimal, the US stood quietly on the sidelines as Britain prepared
to go to war against the Boer republics during the summer and early fall. Once
the fighting began, the US provided its good offices to represent British interests in the Boer republics, reciprocating what Britain had done in Spain during
the Spanish–American War. Meanwhile, the British government worked
purposefully to find compromise solutions to Anglo–American disagreements
over a future isthmian canal and over the boundary between Alaska and British
Columbia. In neither of these two western hemispheric matters were vital
British interests at stake; so the cultivation of American friendship could be and
was accorded a high priority as Britain endeavoured to resolve them.

II. Central players: John Hay and Theodore Roosevelt

The sentiment of the American public and Congress during the Boer War
was "overwhelmingly" favourable to the underdog Boers.[3] Purely from a

domestic political standpoint, the most advantageous course for the presidential administration in power to pursue would have been a policy reflecting this sentiment. But because pro-Boer feeling in the US was significantly less passionate than it was in continental European countries,[4] American political leaders did have some room to manoeuvre (how much depending on their skills) in devising US policy toward the war.

Making the most of this flexibility, American leaders forsook the path of least resistance and instead conducted a distinctly pro-British neutrality policy throughout the Boer War. Two individuals were primarily responsible for this policy. Of foremost importance was John Hay, secretary of state from 1898 until his death in 1905 under Presidents William McKinley and Theodore Roosevelt. The second most influential player was Roosevelt, who assumed the presidency upon McKinley's assassination in September 1901.

"As regards foreign policy", writes Charles S. Campbell, Jr., "it was Secretary Hay's opinion that counted as long as McKinley occupied the White House".[5] Specifically concerning the Anglo–Boer confrontation in South Africa, contends Stuart Anderson, "McKinley left the formulation of American policy toward the war almost entirely in the hands of his secretary of state".[6] (In carrying out foreign policy under McKinley, Hay was ably assisted by the clear-thinking and experienced second assistant secretary of state, Alvey A. Adee.[7])

John Hay had served as US ambassador to Great Britain from the onset of the McKinley administration until his appointment as secretary of state following the Spanish–American War. As has often been argued, Secretary Hay was an Anglophile and an Anglo-Saxonist who felt great affection for England, believed in the superiority of Anglo–American civilization and perceived British and American interests to be fundamentally in harmony.[8] These views underpinned both Hay's own strong partisan interest in the Boer War and the American government's unvaryingly pro-British (even while officially neutral) wartime diplomacy. On the eve of the outbreak of the war, in a letter to the first secretary at the American embassy in London, Henry White, Hay declared: "The one indispensable feature of our foreign policy should be a friendly understanding with England".[9] In November 1900 Hay inadvertently and embarrassingly disclosed his identification with the British cause in South Africa when he reacted to news of British military gains by telling the Dutch minister to the United States (according to the minister): "At last we have had a success".[10] To the like-minded White, Hay had written these revealing words earlier that year: "The fight of England is the fight of civilization and progress and all our interests are bound up in her success".[11] Even the most widely condemned of Britain's wartime policies – the system of concentration camps (established at the beginning of 1901), which exacted an enormous death toll among Boer civilians, particularly children[12] – was dismissively attributed by Hay to the stubborn unwillingness of the Boers to give up their fight.[13]

Theodore Roosevelt, already an accomplished public servant and writer and a popular war hero, was governor of New York when the Boer War began and then vice president of the United States for six months beginning in March 1901. Throughout the nearly two years of warfare that preceded his accession to the presidency, Roosevelt followed the Anglo–Boer contest with great attention. Despite the deep Dutch roots of his paternal family, Roosevelt's outlook on the war and his policy once he became president were consistently favourable to Britain. This point is especially important because, unlike McKinley, Roosevelt was a hands-on presidential diplomatist who both charted the broad course of his administration's foreign policy and attended personally to the significant details of its execution. Roosevelt retained Hay as secretary of state, and Hay served Roosevelt effectively, but the secretary's autonomy was now substantially diminished.

It is true that, unlike Hay, Roosevelt developed genuine sympathy for the Boers and great admiration for their fighting ability. Initially considering the Boers to be primarily to blame for the war, by early 1900 Roosevelt had come to believe that "both sides . . . were, from their different standpoints, in the right".[14] As time went on, Roosevelt became increasingly dissatisfied with official British explanations for the war and increasingly disenchanted with British setbacks on the battlefield. In a letter of April 1901 to his oldest son, Roosevelt declared "that the English had no right whatever to go into this task as they did, for their capacity and the justice of their cause did not warrant their position".[15] In the meantime Roosevelt's respect for the spirited Boers steadily grew; in March 1901 he observed in a letter to his English friend Arthur Lee that "the eighteen months' warfare has given many people a strong feeling that the Boers must possess altogether exceptional qualities".[16] Indeed, in the aforementioned letter to his son, Roosevelt went so far as to call the Boer military effort against the British Empire "as gallant a struggle as has ever been made".[17]

Yet when it came to the question of US policy, there were larger and more important considerations that completely overrode Roosevelt's sympathy and admiration for the hardy Boers. The two largest of these considerations pertained to what Roosevelt saw as the advance of civilization and to the security of the United States.

Theodore Roosevelt believed very firmly in the notion of a civilizing process whereby the less advanced peoples or races (the term "race" was very broadly and flexibly construed by Roosevelt[18]) could and did progress under the tutelage of the more advanced peoples or races. "The English-speaking peoples" were in the vanguard of this process. Notwithstanding the "many fine traits" of the Boers, Governor Roosevelt averred in a letter of 2 December 1899 to his British friend Cecil Spring Rice, "it would be for the advantage of mankind to have English spoken south of the Zambesi".[19] Nineteen months later Vice President Roosevelt reiterated this perspective in another letter to Spring Rice:

> A good many of the Boer leaders have called upon me, most of them with a certain dignified sorrow that though I was of Dutch blood, I seemed to have no sympathy with them . . . As a matter of fact, I had and have the warmest personal sympathy with them, and yet I have always felt that by far the best possible result would be to have South Africa all united, with English as its common speech.[20]

And in two letters written soon after the signing of the Treaty of Vereeniging, President Roosevelt urged upon the British editor John St. Loe Strachey "a universal amnesty" and expressed his confident expectation "that the Boer farmer" would "become part of an English-speaking, homogeneous population of mixed origins, . . . a very valuable addition to the English-speaking stock throughout the world".[21]

Probably of even greater importance, Roosevelt saw the international balance of power and vital US interests at stake in the Boer War. In Roosevelt's estimation, a British defeat in the war would be disastrous for the British Empire and also, as he wrote to Captain Richard Wainwright during the very difficult month of December 1899, would place the United States "in grave danger from the great European military and naval powers".[22] Should the Boers somehow prevail, Roosevelt more specifically told Arthur Lee the following month, "I believe in five years it will mean a war between us and some one of the great continental European nations" – here he clearly meant Germany – "unless we are content to abandon our Monroe Doctrine for South America".[23]

Indeed, in the event of European military intervention on the side of the Boers, Roosevelt would advocate American intervention on the side of the British Empire. In the immediate aftermath of Black Week (10–15 December 1899), Roosevelt wrote to Lee that "if the powers of continental Europe menace your people", he hoped and expected that America would "promptly give them notice of 'hands off'".[24] Four days later, in a letter to US Civil Service Commissioner John R. Proctor, Roosevelt was even more assertive: "I should very strongly favor this country taking a hand in the game if the European continent selected this opportunity to try to smash the British Empire".[25]

As the quotations presented in the three foregoing paragraphs demonstrate, Theodore Roosevelt believed that the English-speaking peoples were fulfilling a crucial civilizing mission and that Great Britain and the United States had compatible strategic interests and needed to be wary of the same potential enemies. But Roosevelt's thinking on and conduct toward the Boer War reflected a third factor as well. As noted previously, Britain's cultivation of American goodwill during the Spanish–American War had been quite effective; in Roosevelt's case it had been *extremely* effective.[26] Roosevelt explained to Wingate Sewall in April 1900 that he was greatly perturbed by people "howling" against Britain after the British had been so friendly to the

United States in 1898.[27] In November of the same year, Roosevelt privately stated his outlook somewhat more fully:

> I am not an Anglomaniac any more than I am an Anglophobe, . . . but I am keenly alive to the friendly countenance England gave us in 1898 . . . I have been uncomfortable about the Boer War, . . . but I [do not] wish to say anything publicly that would . . . excite feeling against a friendly nation for which I have a hearty admiration and respect.[28]

III. Obstacles overcome

During the Boer War, the actions of various private citizens, journalists, members of Congress and diplomats tested the political acumen and diplomatic agility of John Hay and Theodore Roosevelt. While a number of issues pertaining to US policy arose, the two most important centred around US wartime trade with Britain and the question of US support for international mediation to end the war.

Exports from the United States to the United Kingdom and British South Africa expanded considerably during the Boer War. The average annual value of these exports of about $577 million during 1899–1902 marked an increase of around $112 million over their average for 1895–98. The most significant wartime US exports were horses and mules. Over 100,000 of the former and over 80,000 of the latter were shipped from the United States to South Africa; about half of all the mules used in the war by British forces originated in America. Very large quantities of cartridges, hay, oats and preserved meat were also sold. In addition, loans from US bankers underwrote approximately 20 per cent of the costs of Britain's war.[29]

Of even greater consequence than wartime trade was the mediation question. As the months passed it became ever more obvious that the British government was prepared to commit enormous resources to its effort to conquer the Boer republics. (Eventually Britain fielded an army of nearly 500,000 men, a figure exceeding by tens of thousands the entire combined white population of the Transvaal and the Orange Free State.) Boer leaders thus realized that outside mediation offered the best and perhaps the only hope of an acceptable outcome. They also came to understand that the US was essential to the success of any mediation scheme. Because Britain perceived the continental powers as hostile and was endeavouring to counter this hostility by developing a partnership with the United States, the British government would certainly reject outright any European mediation proposal that lacked US support. For their part, unfriendly European governments were hesitant to propose mediation due to their grudging respect for the power of the British Empire. In this context, in the words of John H. Ferguson, only the United States "might successfully urge upon Great Britain an early settlement of the war upon terms more favorable to the republics than . . . destruction of their independence".[30]

The landscape of public opinion in the US gave the Boers reason to be hopeful. Americans siding with the Boers greatly outnumbered those favouring Britain. Organizations of Irish-Americans, Dutch-Americans and German-Americans were especially outspoken supporters of the Boers.[31] Leading pro-Boer activists included George Van Siclen, a New York lawyer; Cornelius Van Der Hoogt, an immigration commissioner in Baltimore; and James O'Beirne, a prominent Irish-American Republican.[32] Among the large number of noteworthy Americans who upheld the cause of the Boers were former President Benjamin Harrison, Andrew Carnegie, Carl Schurz, Henry Adams, David Starr Jordan and Clarence Darrow.[33]

Led by Joseph Pulitzer's *New York World* and by the *Philadelphia North American*, most American newspapers also sided with the Boers. Among the many US newspapers publishing pro-Boer editorials were the *New York Herald*, the *Washington Post*, the *Chicago Tribune*, the *Baltimore Sun* and the *Atlanta Constitution*. The Hearst press and the *New York Times* assumed more equivocal stances. Among the minority of US publications favouring Britain were the *New York Mail and Express*, *Harper's Weekly*, the *Philadelphia Press* and Whitelaw Reid's *New York Tribune*.[34]

The US Congress was another arena where pro-Boer sentiment predominated. In both houses of the new Congress that convened in December 1899, Republicans held more seats than Democrats, by counts of 50–26 in the Senate and 185–163 in the House of Representatives. Among Democratic congressmen pro-Boer feeling was particularly widespread. Secretary of State Hay regularly insisted – with some justification and to good effect – that Democratic pro-Boer agitation was motivated by partisan rivalry with the Republican McKinley and Roosevelt administrations. Still, partiality toward the Boers was plentiful among congressional Republicans as well. Indeed, some of the most vehement pro-Boers in Congress were Republicans. Foremost among them was Senator William Mason of Illinois, who in 1899 accused Britain of "criminal aggression" and offered a resolution of sympathy and praise for "the heroic battle of the South African Republic against cruelty and oppression".[35] Senator George Wellington of Maryland was another very outspoken pro-Boer Republican. "Their foe has been our foe", Wellington publicly declared, "and their battle for right is a repetition of our own".[36] Outside Congress, Webster Davis, McKinley's former assistant secretary of the interior, angrily renounced his Republican party affiliation at the Democratic convention in July 1900 and soon afterward published a book entitled *John Bull's Crime*.[37]

The work of pro-Boer citizens groups, newspapers and members of Congress was supported, naturally, by the diplomacy conducted by the South

African Republic and the Orange Free State. Based in the Netherlands, Willem Leyds was in charge of coordinating Boer diplomacy in Europe and America. Leyds assigned Montagu White, former Transvaal consul general in London, to traverse the Atlantic in order to spearhead the Boer diplomatic effort in the US. White arrived in America in January 1900 and performed his duties, by choice, without official status, preferring the flexibility afforded by such an arrangement. Ferguson describes Montagu White as "a quiet, cautious man" who "shunned publicity and fully understood the delicacies of diplomacy" and compliments "the reasonableness of his manner".[38] White was never deluded by the predominant American sympathy for the Boers; he soberly defined his objective as persuading the people *in power* to alter their positions, which, he recognized early on, would be very difficult to achieve. As it turned out, White's efforts in this direction were undermined (while John Hay's pursuit of a pro-British policy was abetted) by the ineptitude of an official three-man Boer delegation that came to the United States in May 1900.[39] Serious discord among American pro-Boer organizations – which White tried hard to resolve, but failed[40] – further weakened White's cause.

But even had Boer diplomacy in America been conducted with the cohesiveness and level-headedness desired by Montagu White, and even had pro-Boer groups in America been able to avoid feuds and coordinate their work effectively, the end result would probably have been much the same, for the fact is that despite a climate of broad public, journalistic and congressional displeasure with Britain and sympathy for the embattled Boers, Secretary Hay and, eventually, President Roosevelt never strayed – never came close to straying – from the path they had charted. Hay and Roosevelt did their best to frame US policy toward the Boer War as a partisan issue, were able to rely on well positioned Republican loyalists to thwart the designs of those opposing their policy[41] and made well considered decisions at various critical points.

The policy of permitting extensive wartime exports, including contraband, to the United Kingdom and British South Africa proved relatively easy for the McKinley and Roosevelt administrations to sustain. In the Boer War, as it happened, adherence to the traditionally liberal neutral trading policy of the United States coincided with the attainment of the US government's policy goals. Because Britain possessed immensely greater resources than the Boer republics and completely dominated the seas, "equal access" meant British access only. Protests against US trade policy emanated continually from Boer officials and from pro-Boer American organizations, newspapers and members of Congress. The particular focus of these protests was the large-scale open purchasing by uniformed British military personnel of mules and horses that were then shipped from New Orleans; indeed, the Boers and their American supporters charged repeatedly that Britain was illegally operating a military base in that city. Hay emphatically rejected such claims. "The right of trading in all munitions of war is absolutely incontestable", the secretary insisted in a letter of 3 July 1900 to Senator James McMillan of Michigan. "We are perfectly free to sell to both belligerents all they are able to pay for".[42] In 1901 a US district court upheld Hay's position by ruling against accusations that New Orleans was a British military base and that Americans were illegally selling munitions to Britain.[43] And in March 1902 President Roosevelt told two Boer envoys he could find "no evidence which would indicate that the United States had permitted the violation of its neutrality" and "made it clear that no action could be taken".[44]

A more challenging and more important test for the US government was administered in the form of an official appeal by the Transvaal and the Orange Free State for outside mediation. Issued to the European powers and the United States in March 1900, this appeal was especially well received by the government of Russia, which immediately embarked on an attempt to orchestrate a collective call for joint action.

But subtle yet bold diplomacy by Hay masterfully pre-empted the Russian initiative, protected England from embarrassment (then or afterward) and affirmed the thoroughly pro-British character of US neutrality. To ignore the Boer appeal, Hay recognized right away, would facilitate European mischief-making and would likely produce an "offensive and injurious" congressional resolution.[45] So without delay he dispatched the following telegram to Henry White at the American embassy in London:

> By way of friendly good offices, you will inform Lord Salisbury that I am today in receipt of a telegram from the United States Consul at Pretoria, reporting that the governments of the two African Republics request the President's intervention with a view to cessation of hostilities, and that a similar request is made of the representatives of European Powers. In communicating this request, I am directed by the President to express his earnest hope that a way to bring about peace may be found, and to say that he would be glad to aid in any friendly manner to promote so happy a result.[46]

Three days later, on 13 March, White telegraphed to Hay the anticipated (and hoped-for) negative reply: "His Lordship . . . requested me to thank the President for the friendly interest shown by him, and added that Her Majesty's Government cannot accept the intervention of any other power".[47]

Unofficial reports of the American offer of mediation stirred much excitement in Britain and in the US. Both the US Senate and the British House of Commons requested detailed information. Hay then proceeded to coordinate with the Salisbury government the simultaneous release of the key telegrams. As a result, the Russian initiative was stillborn. As for the Boers, they well understood Hay's purposes and therefore expressed no gratitude.

Although many in England were slow to appreciate the entirely pro-British nature of Hay's telegram, most thinking Britons apprehended this reality before long. For Hay had given Britain, in Ferguson's words, "an opportunity to make an announcement which precluded later overtures for collective action". At the same time, the secretary had established "a useful talking point" for the upcoming US encounters with Boer envoys and had placed the administration "in a more favorable position to offset criticism in Congress and in the presidential campaign then just beginning".[48] While Boer officials and their American friends would continue until the end of the war to lobby for American mediation, Hay and Roosevelt would readily reply that the United States could not become involved unless both warring sides were in favour of such involvement, that the US had put forward a sincere offer to mediate in March 1900 and that in response to the US offer the British had made clear their absolute unwillingness to countenance any such mediation.

The presidential election campaign of 1900 further tested Hay's mettle. The Democrats, whose national convention was set for early July in Kansas City, were certain to adopt a vigorously pro-Boer platform plank, and – in light of the state of public opinion – the Republicans, meeting in Philadelphia two weeks earlier, felt some pressure to do likewise. With pro-Boer letters pouring in and numerous Republican delegates advocating a pro-Boer plank, Hay and his loyalists "had great difficulty to prevent the Convention from declaring in favor of the Boers".[49]

A deliberately well timed speech in London by Colonial Secretary Joseph Chamberlain may have reinforced Hay's steadfastness. After minimizing the significance of European criticism, Chamberlain declared that, on the other hand, "there are quarters whence even a note of disapproval would be a matter of serious concern", specifically identifying "our colonies and the United States". Chamberlain indirectly reminded Americans of Britain's consistently supportive policy during the Spanish–American War, stressed the imperative of Anglo-Saxon solidarity and expressed confidence "that in the long run we shall gain the final seal of their approval".[50]

In any case, in the end the administration forces did prevail in Philadelphia. They won an ambiguous plank that praised McKinley for the US mediation offer of March 1900, asserted the need to uphold "the policy prescribed by Washington and affirmed by every succeeding President . . . of non-intervention in European controversies", and finished by declaring innocuously: "The American people earnestly hope that a way may soon be found, honorable alike to both contending parties, to terminate the strife between them".[51]

For their part, the Democrats – led by their staunchly anti-imperialist nominee, William Jennings Bryan, who for months had been assailing the administration's approach to the Boer War[52] – did as expected. Professing "indignation" toward Britain and blasting "the ill concealed Republican alliance with England", the Democrats' plank extended on behalf of "the entire American Nation, except its Republican office holders, . . . our sympathy to the heroic burghers in their unequal struggle to maintain their liberty and independence".[53]

Any Republican worries that the parties' divergent positions on the Boer War might affect the outcome of the November election proved unfounded. Although most American voters sympathized with the Boers, this sympathy apparently did not translate into many votes for the Democrats. McKinley defeated Bryan even more decisively in 1900 than in 1896, and many pro-Boer senators failed in their bids for re-election.[54] The goodwill England had gained by its conduct during the Spanish–American War unquestionably rendered American pro-Boer sentiment less passionate. Economic prosperity and other issues, including the hotly debated question of US imperialism and specifically the ongoing war to secure the annexation of the Philippines, were of far greater concern to most of the electorate; besides, by the time of the election (which took place after Britain had achieved many important battlefield successes and had formally annexed both Boer republics), eventual British victory appeared to be inevitable. In any event, after November 1900 Hay and Roosevelt could pursue their policy with less concern about possible domestic political repercussions.

The Americans assigned to represent the United States in South Africa constituted a final problem to which Secretary of State Hay had to apply his diplomatic talents. The US consular service in that part of the world was, to borrow a description used by Robert L. Beisner, "distinctly amateurish".[55] While this problem was more a sideshow than a central issue, Hay nonetheless (and appropriately) took it seriously and handled it ably.

The principal US consular officials in this mini-drama were James Stowe, Charles Macrum, Stanley Hollis and Adelbert Hay. Stowe, consul general at Cape Town before and during the war, was unpolished and indiscreet, but he was a strong partisan of the British side. Secretary Hay, therefore, was largely untroubled by Stowe's clumsiness.

In contrast, the pro-Boer conduct of Macrum, consul general at Pretoria at the beginning of the war, did create difficulties for the secretary. After repeatedly insisting during November 1899, against the explicit wishes of the State Department, that on returning to America for personal reasons, he was instructed in December to "come home", whereupon he was informed that he had been relieved permanently of his duties. Embittered, Macrum publicly charged in February 1900 that there existed a secret Anglo–American alliance and that British censors had read his mail (which they had), throwing Hay on the defensive and compelling a coordinated US–British effort at damage control diplomacy, which featured a publicized British apology.

More openly and avidly pro-Boer than Macrum was Hollis, who represented the US in Portuguese East Africa throughout the war and was, as Ferguson puts it, "a constant annoyance to his government".[56] Hollis's various escapades brought admonishment from the State Department, and in one instance his behaviour induced the following private message to Hay from Assistant Secretary Thomas Cridler: "Hollis needs a guardian; he is almost insane".[57] Nevertheless, Hollis was not removed from his position.

The Macrum case had been painful for Hay, who wanted very much to avoid provoking a second such uproar; besides, Hollis's continuing presence in South Africa lent some credibility to the claims of the McKinley and Roosevelt administrations that they were genuinely impartial toward the Boer War.

Meanwhile, to help sustain on the ground the United States' pro-British neutrality policy, 22-year-old Adelbert Hay, the secretary's son, was appointed to replace Macrum in Pretoria. After a controversial stopover in London, where he was greeted enthusiastically, the new consul arrived in Pretoria, where he was received reluctantly but properly by the Transvaal's leaders, at the beginning of February 1900. While carefully avoiding, on the instructions of his father, any overt displays of favouritism, young Hay did remain in Pretoria after the city fell to the British in June; he and the secretary of state both apparently believed that rather than following the retreating Transvaal government to Machadodorp, it was preferable for him to be in regular contact with the British occupation forces. Months later, having vindicated his father's confidence by upholding US policy effectively during the most crucial year of the war, the young diplomat was offered the opportunity to return home, which he did, via London, in March 1901.[58]

IV. The Hay–Roosevelt policy in broad perspective

The policy toward the Boer War carried out by John Hay and Theodore Roosevelt was well conceived and well executed. It served US interests in both the short and the long term, winning tangible immediate benefits for the US and paving the way for Roosevelt to construct successfully an Anglo–American special relationship, the cornerstone of his presidential statecraft.

The British government attached enormous importance to a friendly US policy during the Boer War. Although Hay and Roosevelt were in any case predisposed – for strategic and philosophical reasons previously discussed – to pursue such a policy, they did not hesitate to take advantage of England's need for US benevolence. Most notably, early in the war the US was able to prevail on Britain to separate negotiations for an isthmian canal treaty from negotiations over the Alaska–British Columbia border. Canada had been insisting adamantly on keeping the two matters linked (believing that linkage strengthened its hand in the boundary dispute), but the British government succumbed to pressure from Hay, whose efforts were abetted by Sir Julian Pauncefote, Britain's ambassador to the United States. In a letter to Lord Salisbury of 19 January 1900, Pauncefote emphasized the intensity of American opinion on the canal question, contrasted the "world-wide" significance of the canal issue with the "purely local character" of the boundary dispute, and declared: "America seems to be our only friend just now & it would be unfortunate to quarrel with her".[59] Britain then leaned heavily on the self-governing Dominion of Canada, which was left with no viable option other than to acquiesce. Later, when the Hay–Pauncefote canal treaty of February 1900 proved unacceptable to the US Senate, Britain agreed to renegotiate the terms, and a revised treaty was completed successfully in November 1901.

During the years between the end of the Boer War in 1902 and the conclusion of his presidency in 1909, Theodore Roosevelt laboured assiduously to establish and then to fortify a genuinely special relationship between the British Empire and the US. The biggest obstacle, the Alaskan boundary quarrel, was overcome in 1903 when, in essence, Britain yielded on the fundamental issues while Roosevelt made concessions on less important aspects of the dispute. Other, less difficult, impediments included: Britain's reluctance to support more actively Roosevelt's mediation of the Russo–Japanese War; Britain's confusion regarding the purposes of Roosevelt's diplomacy during the first phase of the Moroccan crisis in 1905; the Newfoundland fisheries controversy, where Roosevelt was very understanding of the British predicament; the Jamaica incident of 1907, where Roosevelt and the British government engaged cooperatively in damage control diplomacy following an extraordinarily offensive anti-American outburst by the British governor of Jamaica; and Britain's unwillingness to pursue a joint Anglo–American policy on the Japanese immigration question. These and other difficulties notwithstanding, Roosevelt constantly kept his primary objective, Anglo-American unity, sharply in focus.

Meanwhile, throughout Roosevelt's presidency, the United States was consolidating its hegemony in the Caribbean region and was rapidly strengthening its navy. Both of these developments were viewed with favour by authorities in London – just as Roosevelt repeatedly encouraged Britain to preserve its own naval pre-eminence. The informal Anglo–American naval alliance that emerged and matured during the Roosevelt years (and that encompassed Roosevelt's wholehearted private backing for the formal Anglo–Japanese alliance) operated as a potent force for the protection of British interests, the protection of American interests, and, more generally, the maintenance of international stability and peace.[60]

The formidable, mutually beneficial Anglo–American partnership that first took centre stage during the opening decade of the twentieth century – and that would later extricate the world from the clutches of Nazi tyranny and, later still, attain victory over the Soviet Union in the Cold War[61] – was partly anchored in the pro-British neutrality policy conducted during the Boer War by John Hay and Theodore Roosevelt. A pro-Boer US policy or even a truly impartial US approach would have dismayed and discredited those in the British government who had been advocating a pro-American policy since 1896. The Boer War was the big test, and the American performance on that test unambiguously bore out the British courtship of the United States. In the aftermath of the war, with this anchor securely in place, the two English-speaking powers could, and did, proceed to build the remarkable special relationship on which so much would ultimately depend.

Notes

1. Even some of the most thorough and well-structured US history textbooks – notably including John A. Garraty, *The American Nation: A History of the United States* (seventh edn, New York, 1991) – neglect altogether to mention the Boer War.
2. Bradford Perkins, *The Great Rapprochement: England and the United States, 1895–1914* (New York, 1968).
3. John H. Ferguson, *American Diplomacy and the Boer War* (Philadelphia, 1939), p. 192; Stuart Anderson, "Racial Anglo-Saxonism and the American Response to the Boer War", *Diplomatic History* 2(3), Summer, 219–36 (1978), p. 220. See also Richard B. Mulanax, *The Boer War in American Politics and Diplomacy* (Lanham, MD, 1994), p. 81.
4. See Perkins, *Great Rapprochement*, p. 92; and Mulanax, *Boer War in American Politics*, pp. 108–9.
5. Charles S. Campbell, Jr., *Anglo-American Understanding, 1898–1903* (Baltimore, 1957), p. 172.
6. Anderson, "Racial Anglo-Saxonism", p. 223.
7. A good brief account of Adee's long diplomatic career is provided by Peter Bridges, "An Appreciation of Alvey A. Adee", *Diplomacy & Statecraft* 10(1), March, 31–49 (1999).
8. Hay's "Anglo-Saxonist convictions" as "a major determinant of American policy during the Boer War" (p. 235) is a prominent theme in Anderson, "Racial Anglo-Saxonism", p. 235.
9. John Hay to Henry White, 24 September 1899, quoted in David Dimbleby and David Reynolds, *An Ocean Apart: The Relationship between Britain and America in the Twentieth Century* (New York, 1988), p. 48.
10. Memorandum of 9 November 1900, quoted in Anderson, "Racial Anglo-Saxonism", p. 231.
11. John Hay to Henry White, 18 March 1900, quoted in Mulanax, *Boer War in American Politics*, p. 83.
12. For example, official British government figures indicated 5,963 total camp deaths during the two-month period October–November 1901, with the annual death rate in October for children only a staggering 572 per thousand. *Manchester Guardian*, 16 December, 7 (1901).
13. See John Hay to Henry Cabot Lodge, 19 February 1902, in Anderson, "Racial Anglo-Saxonism", p. 235.
14. Anderson, "Racial Anglo-Saxonism", p. 232.
15. Theodore Roosevelt to Theodore Roosevelt, Jr., 9 April 1901, quoted in Ferguson, *American Diplomacy*, p. 212.
16. Elting E. Morison, John M. Blum, and Alfred D. Chandler (eds), *The Letters of Theodore Roosevelt* (8 vols, Cambridge, Mass., 1951–54), vol. 3, p. 20, Roosevelt to Arthur Lee, 18 March 1901.
17. Roosevelt to Theodore Roosevelt, Jr., 9 April 1901, quoted in Ferguson, *American Diplomacy*, p. 213.
18. See William N. Tilchin, *Theodore Roosevelt and the British Empire: A Study in Presidential Statecraft* (New York, 1997), pp. 19–20.
19. Roosevelt to Cecil Spring Rice, 2 December 1899, quoted in Anderson, "Racial Anglo-Saxonism", p. 223. A victory for England, Roosevelt explained to another British correspondent in February 1900, would bring about a mutually beneficial fusion of Britons and Boers, with the latter gaining the "freedom and order and material and moral prosperity" characteristic of English-speaking civilization. Roosevelt to Frederick C. Selous, 7 February 1900, quoted in Anderson, "Racial Anglo-Saxonism", p. 232.
20. Morison *et al.*, *Letters*, vol. 3, p. 109, Roosevelt to Spring Rice, 3 July 1901.
21. Roosevelt to John St. Loe Strachey, 20 June 1902, and 18 July 1902, quoted in David H. Burton, "Theodore Roosevelt and His English Correspondents: A Special Relationship of Friends", *Transactions of the American Philosophical Society* 63(2), March, 3–70 (1973), p. 39.
22. Roosevelt to Captain Richard Wainwright, 16 December 1899, quoted in Ferguson, *American Diplomacy*, p. 208.
23. Roosevelt to Lee, 30 January 1900, quoted in Burton, "Theodore Roosevelt", p. 39.
24. Roosevelt to Lee, 19 December 1899, quoted in Ferguson, *American Diplomacy*, p. 209.
25. Roosevelt to John R. Proctor, 23 December 1899, quoted in Anderson, "Racial Anglo-Saxonism", p. 227.

26. To Arthur Lee in July 1900 Roosevelt offered this revealing, if overstated, observation: "The attitude of England in 1898 worked a complete revolution in my feelings and the attitude of the continent at that time opened my eyes to the other side of the question". Roosevelt to Lee, 25 July 1900, quoted in Howard K. Beale, *Theodore Roosevelt and the Rise of America to World Power* (Baltimore, 1956), p. 93.

27. Roosevelt to Wingate Sewall, 24 April 1900, quoted in Ferguson, *American Diplomacy*, p. 210. See also Mulanax, *Boer War in American Politics*, p. 99.

28. Quoted in Byron Farwell, "Taking Sides in the Boer War", *American Heritage* 27(3), April, 20–25, 92–7 (1976), p. 24.

29. See Ferguson, *American Diplomacy*, pp. 49–51; Farwell, "Taking Sides", p. 22; and Anderson, "Racial Anglo-Saxonism", p. 221.

30. Ferguson, *American Diplomacy*, p. 176. John H. Ferguson's *American Diplomacy and the Boer War* is one of two published monographs exploring US policy toward the Boer War in depth. Despite various shortcomings, each has been helpful in the preparation of this essay. Actually, Ferguson's book, although predating Richard B. Mulanax's *The Boer War in American Politics and Diplomacy* by 55 years, is by far the better and more useful of the pair. On the whole, Ferguson's book offers a well researched, well organized, coherent narrative account (although it rather curiously surveys prewar US–Boer relations but not prewar US–British relations). Yet Ferguson's study is legalistic and time-bound, and its interpretations lack insight and imagination. The possible importance of an Anglo–American special relationship simply is not on Ferguson's radar screen; thus, without any reference to US interests, he attributes Hay's decision to stay on as secretary of state in 1900 to a determination "to prevent England from being embarrassed" (pp. 191–2). Six years into the Hitler regime, on the eve of World War II, Ferguson is focused on "problems yet to be solved if the United States is to remain neutral in future wars" and declares: "How to keep officials unbiased in their opinions is one of the unsolved problems confronting neutral states" (pp. 176, 125). Nevertheless, the weaknesses of Ferguson's monograph pale in comparison to those found in Mulanax's. The inadequacies of *The Boer War in American Politics and Diplomacy* are so large in quantity and so fundamental in nature – for the author proves incapable of organizing his impressively extensive research and of coherent narrative writing (and in addition there are well over 100 printing and proofreading errors, invariably irritating and sometimes, as in the numerous cases of incorrect dates and identifications, misleading and confusing) – that the book's value is ultimately very limited. Actually, Stuart Anderson's "Racial Anglo-Saxonism and the American Response to the Boer War" is superior in quality to either book just discussed; it is not only carefully researched but also crisply and elegantly written: an exemplary specimen of historical scholarship. (Anderson, however, does attribute somewhat too much significance to the Anglo-Saxonism factor in explaining US policy, particularly where Theodore Roosevelt is concerned.) Clearly there is a need for a good new book on US policy toward the Boer War, one that both effectively presents key developments and properly places its narrative in a broader context.

31. It is of interest (if not of much historical consequence) that some Americans actually took part directly in the Boer War. About 300 fought on the side of the Boers, and a somewhat larger, but uncertain, number joined the British army. In "Taking Sides in the Boer War", Byron Farwell tells some fascinating individual stories – most notably those of John Blake (who daringly commanded a force of mostly Irish-American volunteers, some of whom had slipped into the Transvaal as an ambulance unit) and George Labram (a personable and brilliant engineer whose ingenious creations were of real value to the British, especially during the siege of Kimberley). Farwell, "Taking Sides", pp. 25, 92–3, 95, 97.

32. See Ferguson, *American Diplomacy*, p. 179.

33. See *ibid.*, pp. 182–3, 205; Mulanax, *Boer War in American Politics*, pp. 119, 136–7, 148–9; and Perkins, *Great Rapprochement*, p. 92.

34. See Farwell, "Taking Sides", p. 25; Mulanax, *Boer War in American Politics*, pp. 117–18, 121; Ferguson, *American Diplomacy*, pp. 180–81; and Anderson, "Racial Anglo-Saxonism", pp. 227–8. For example, the *Philadelphia North American* – which at one point delivered to President Kruger a handsome book of clippings and a memorial (containing the signatures of about 29,000 schoolboys) expressing sympathy for the Boers – asserted that "England's triumph will not be a gain for civilization, but a victory of might over right, of monarchy over republicanism". In

contrast, *Harper's Weekly* urged Americans not to "lose sight of the stupendous fact that British prestige is in mortal danger; nor can we fail, if we have a proper pride of race, or a decent sense of gratitude, or a consciousness of what the English have accomplished in the homes of the savage races, to mourn over these disasters [a reference to events of December 1899]".

35. Quoted in Ferguson, *American Diplomacy*, pp. 187–8.
36. Quoted in Mulanax, *Boer War in American Politics*, p. 133.
37. See Ferguson, *American Diplomacy*, pp. 196–7.
38. *Ibid.*, pp. 184–5.
39. See *ibid.*, pp. 143–56; and Mulanax, *Boer War in American Politics*, pp. 149–55.
40. See Mulanax, *Boer War in American Politics*, pp. 162–7.
41. In the Senate, Hay's two most effective operatives were Henry Cabot Lodge and Cushman Davis, the latter holding the position of chair of the Foreign Relations Committee, to which all pro-Boer resolutions were referred and where they all died. In the House of Representatives, similarly, pro-Boer resolutions were sent to and killed by the Foreign Affairs Committee, which was chaired by another administration ally, Robert Hitt. See Ferguson, *American Diplomacy*, pp. 188, 191. Finally, in the closing weeks of the war in May 1902, the House Foreign Affairs Committee went through the rather meaningless exercise of holding hearings on the sale to Britain of large numbers of American horses and mules.
42. John Hay to James McMillan, 3 July 1900, quoted in Ferguson, *American Diplomacy*, p. 51.
43. See Ferguson, *American Diplomacy*, pp. 53–5.
44. *Ibid.*, p. 219. Roosevelt did agree to commission an investigation. Headed by Colonel E. H. Crowder, it discovered no military base and no illegal commerce. See *ibid.*, pp. 219, 56–60.
45. *Ibid.*, p. 139.
46. John Hay to Henry White, telegram, 10 March 1900, quoted in *ibid.*, p. 139.
47. Henry White to John Hay, telegram, 13 March 1900, quoted in Ferguson, *American Diplomacy*, p. 139.
48. Ferguson, *American Diplomacy*, p. 142.
49. John Hay to John W. Foster, 23 June 1900, quoted in *ibid.*, p. 195.
50. Joseph Chamberlain, speech of 19 June 1900, quoted in Anderson, "Racial Anglo-Saxonism", p. 234.
51. Quoted in Ferguson, *American Diplomacy*, pp. 195–6.
52. Interestingly, Bryan had refused to sign a petition organized by the *New York World* in October 1899 urging President McKinley to resolve through mediation the Anglo–Boer conflict. Bryan equated the plight of the Boers with that of the Filipino independence fighters then at war with the US; a US mediation offer, Bryan argued, would therefore be hypocritical and embarrassing. See Ferguson, *American Diplomacy*, pp. 179–83; and Farwell, "Taking Sides", p. 25.
53. Quoted in Ferguson, *American Diplomacy*, p. 197.
54. See *ibid.*, pp. 197–8; and Anderson, "Racial Anglo-Saxonism", p. 234.
55. Robert L. Beisner, *From the Old Diplomacy to the New, 1865–1900* (New York, 1975), p. 83.
56. Ferguson, *American Diplomacy*, p. 105.
57. Thomas Cridler to John Hay, 9 November 1900, quoted in Mulanax, *Boer War in American Politics*, p. 191.
58. Both Ferguson, *American Diplomacy*, and Mulanax, *Boer War in American Politics*, discuss Stowe, Macrum, Hollis and Adelbert Hay, as well as a few less important US diplomats, at some length. The two authors' most noteworthy disagreement in this area is over the appointment of young Hay; here Ferguson is quite critical, whereas Mulanax, more convincingly, sees "a brilliant diplomatic stroke". Ferguson, *American Diplomacy*, pp. 116–17; Mulanax, *Boer War in American Politics*, p. 177. (Sadly, Adelbert Hay died as the result of an accident in 1901 shortly after returning to the United States.)
59. Sir Julian Pauncefote to Lord Salisbury, 19 January 1900, quoted in Campbell, *Anglo-American Understanding*, p. 190.
60. The events and issues identified in this and the preceding paragraph are treated in depth in Tilchin, *Theodore Roosevelt and the British Empire*.
61. Between 1909 and 1939, the Anglo–American partnership was frayed at times; indeed, it effectively ceased to function in the 1930s.

CHAPTER EIGHT

The Netherlands and the Boer War[1]

Their Wildest Dreams: The Representation of South African Culture, Imperialism and Nationalism at the Turn of the Century

Martin Bossenbroek

Her Majesty was troubled. Perhaps she could overcome her personal antipathy for the man vying to form a new government, but she could not conceal her distrust of his political agenda. As a member of the opposition in parliament, Abraham Kuyper had always prided himself on being a man of principles. At the same time, this leader of the orthodox Protestants had proven to be a talented opportunist. What were his intentions? This is what Queen Wilhelmina wished to know for certain before asking him to form a new government, after the confessional parties' election victory in June 1901. During Kuyper's first audience with her, on 11 July, the monarch demanded sure-fire guarantees about the future of South Africa and the Dutch East Indies colony. With regard to East Indies policy, Queen Wilhelmina wanted the new government to continue the war against the implacable sultanate of Aceh. Furthermore, the queen wished "the Netherlands to remain a neutral power concerning the events in South Africa". Wilhelmina received these promises two days later. Kuyper assured her in writing that he would seek no change of policy in either area. True, he had spoken out against the declaration of war on Aceh, but that was nearly 30 years earlier, in 1873. In the years since, he had become an outspoken advocate of a policy of "perseverance". On South Africa, he stressed that "however painful it was to the hearts of all Dutch people to see the rights of our kinsmen trampled by violence and dominance, to my mind our powerlessness required us to maintain strict neutrality". With these assurances in hand, Her Majesty could rest at ease. She officially ordered Abraham Kuyper to form a government and within just a few days the Kuyper cabinet was a fact.[2]

   This constitutional *pas de deux* between the monarch and Kuyper was not unprecedented. Four years earlier, Queen Regent Emma had made her wishes known to Liberal party leader N. G. Pierson before he appointed his cabinet. These overt interventions in the political process were indicative of the monarchs' personal involvement with the East Indies and South Africa policies. The monarchs made no secret of their preferred strategies: full commitment to expansion in the East Indies, regretful restraint towards the war in South Africa.

The Dutch presence in South Africa dates back to the seventeenth century. It began when the Dutch East Indies Trading Company (the VOC) established a staging post at the Cape of Good Hope on 6 April 1652. The post grew into a colony under the leadership of its first commander, Jan van Riebeeck, when civil servants of the VOC received permits to settle there. From 1657, the number of these so-called *vrijburgers* (free citizens) increased rapidly. The spread of the population throughout the region was not only due to natural growth, but also to the arrival of more *vrijburgers* and immigrants – among whom were Huguenots of different nationalities. In the next 50 years the call for self-rule grew steadily louder, but the VOC refused to relinquish power. In 1795, a number of districts adopted a kind of independent constitution under the direct rule of the Dutch Republic. This situation was ended by the first British occupation of the Cape. From that moment on, the battle between the Boers and the British would repeatedly flare up. In 1837, the Boers colonized Transvaal, which the British 15 years later recognized as an independent state called the South African Republic. Similarly, they recognized Orange Free State in 1854. Thus, two republics emerged alongside the existing British colonies. But this did not put a stop to the unrest. Economic motives – the discovery of diamonds in south-west Transvaal and, later, gold mines in east Transvaal – revived the struggle for control. The conflict was not resolved until the Treaty of Vereeniging was signed in 1902.

A remarkable aspect of this game of musical chairs was the position of the Netherlands. As the smallest European power, with a disproportionately large overseas empire, the Dutch were up against the world's greatest colonial power; their mighty neighbour Britain. This predicament was most evident in the Dutch colonies. The Dutch East Indies did not include the entire Indonesian Archipelago until the beginning of the twentieth century. The Dutch were confronted by "Mighty England" time and again because of Britain's position in the region. For instance, the British had once controlled northern Borneo and were becoming interested in regaining control over the territory. The Dutch forces' inability to subdue Aceh became an especially serious problem after the Suez Canal was opened in 1869. From then on the most important shipping route to south-east Asia was no longer around the Cape of Good Hope and through Sunda Strait, but through the Strait of Malacca and thus along the Acehnese coast. The Dutch feared it would now be all too easy for another Western power to seize control where they were failing to do so. Another problem for the Dutch was the imperial policy implemented by Tory Prime Minister Benjamin Disraeli in the 1880s. This British doctrine of active engagement was yet another reason why the Dutch were feeling quite threatened.

Towards the end of the nineteenth century, the people of the Netherlands felt a growing concern about developments in South Africa. There was a budding commitment to this colony of dreams, and at its vanguard was Abraham Kuyper, although he did make some strange moves along the way. The only principle regarding the issue of Transvaal that he never discarded was its usefulness in furthering his own political ambitions; not that he failed to admire and appreciate South Africa's Boers, whom he embraced as his kinsmen and kindred spirits. Kuyper had discovered these strong ties thanks to Protestant minister Frans Lion Cachet, his chief contact in South Africa. The Boers, Kuyper felt, resembled the freedom-loving, wholesome, devoutly Christian Dutch of the past, precisely because "*they* have managed to preserve the old spirit of our nation more truly than we", while "*we* have become more cosmopolitan". The Boers embodied the idyllic, pastoral life the Dutch longed for.[3] Nor was it the English annexation of the South African Republic in 1877 that prevented Kuyper from passionately defending the republic; he simply realized that English domination of the territory was inevitable. It was not until the end of 1880, when the Boers revolted, that he threw his full weight behind their struggle for independence. By that time, however, the Boers had made many friends – in politics too.

In parliament, liberals and orthodox Protestant "anti-revolutionaries" were demanding Dutch mediation in the conflict. This position was not shared by Foreign Affairs Minister C. T. Van Lynden Van Sandenburg. To his mind, "the position of the Netherlands was, just like that of any other power . . . the position of a third party, that is to say a state uninvolved in the dispute".[4] It had become clear to him through cautious probing that Britain would not appreciate a Dutch offer to arbitrate, and so the Dutch government did nothing for the Boers. "Must they be crushed?" asked Kuyper, not without a touch of melodrama. As it happened, the Boers held their own without Dutch support, forcing the English to accept a truce and, in 1881, sign the Pretoria Convention. Their independence was reinstated, albeit under English suzerainty. The Dutch government may have declared itself neutral, but the hearts of the nation were clearly lifted by the results of the First Boer War. Many felt it a kind of poetic justice that it was their "distant cousins" who punished the British for their "imperialistic greed".

In the last decade of the nineteenth century, Dutch politicians abandoned their misgivings about waging war in Aceh. When it came to South Africa, however, they remained apprehensive. Particularly in government circles it was widely felt that the Netherlands could not afford to make an enemy out of England – an opinion that had already been proven justified in the years 1880–81, and that was borne out once again at the turn of the century. After the Boers had fended off Jameson's raid in January 1896, the Dutch government again proceeded with great caution, watching developments carefully at first and then sending a telegram. "Express sympathy with the Boers, without crossing the British" was the credo of Dutch government policy towards the escalating conflict in South Africa, and continued to be in the years to follow.

It was not an easy position to take. During the Second Boer War, the deeply sympathetic Queen Wilhelmina had great trouble respecting the policy of strict neutrality. She personally appealed to German Kaiser Wilhelm II to mediate in the conflict, but he declined. In 1900, Dutch Foreign Affairs Minister W. H. De Beaufort barely managed to prevent her from making a similar appeal to the Russian tsar.[5] In the course of that year, De Beaufort faced increasing difficulty maintaining the neutrality policy. Emotions were heating up, even in liberal circles that supported the government, partly because of several incidents in which the British mistreated Dutch people still present in Transvaal. Liberal party leader Pierson and De Beaufort agreed that something had to be done to release the tension. The answer came from their colleague, navy minister J. A. Röell. He advised them to send the warship *De Gelderlander* to the Portuguese colony of Mozambique to pick up Boer president Paul Kruger, who had fled there to avoid capture by the British. It was a narrow escape. The British saw the operation for what it was: a gesture for public consumption in the Netherlands. Just like the Dutch government, they were pleased to see that the situation was no longer at boiling point. Even opposition leader Kuyper expressed satisfaction with the government decision.

The orthodox Protestant leader had basically accepted the inevitable. Except for a propagandistic sneer in his article entitled "La crise de sud-africaine", in which he called the blacks a "race inférieure" destined for bondage, he had not got personally involved in any of the numerous pro-Boer initiatives. This contrasted sharply with his own constituency, whose fiery pro-Boer sentiments he felt he needed to temper rather than encourage. Despite his criticism of De Beaufort's passivity, Kuyper believed parliamentary initiatives to aid the Boers were a lost cause: "A solitary action by the Netherlands would accomplish nothing whatsoever and would only cause bad blood".[6] Prayer and protest in the press were the only courses that remained.

In other parties too, emotions and cool rationality battled for the upper hand. The emotional Liberal party leader, Prime Minister Pierson, sometimes had trouble containing his feelings of sympathy for the Boers, just like the liberal faction in parliament. Liberal Lower House speaker J. G. Gleichmann did all he could to keep heads cool, which he believed was necessary "with an eye to our relations with England".[7]

Initially, the Catholics were hesitant to stake out a position with regard to the Boer issue. They ultimately decided to act on their principle of fighting injustice at all times. They believed it would also be "in the interests of our national conscience and the strength of our nation" to cooperate with compatriots regardless of their religion. "The Transvalers are, after all, as much *our* kinsmen as they are the kinsmen of the Anti-revolutionaries and the Liberals", wrote Catholic newspaper *De Tijd*.[8] Such sentiments of heartfelt kinship would become commonplace in Catholic opinion, both in print and from the pulpit.

The Boer issue also cost the socialists a fair amount of dialectics. In day-to-day politics, they dealt with the same phenomenon as the orthodox Protestants. The socialist constituency was much more taken with the Boer cause than the party leadership. The official party line became, "Rationally opposed to English capitalism, in favour of peaceful reform in Transvaal".[9] The socialists ridiculed the whipped up, chauvinistic indignation of the bourgeoisie. Even among the socialists' own constituency, however, solidarity with the Boers sometimes prevailed over party doctrine. The party leadership was unpleasantly surprised when, in 1901, a few dockers' unions announced a short-lived boycott of British ships. The board of the Social Democratic Workers Party (SDAP) could not openly distance itself from the boycott. Behind closed doors, however, leader Pieter Jelles Troelstra and his close associates were not exactly displeased to hear that the wildcat action never really got off the ground.[10]

In short, there was a groundswell of morally inspired expansionism in the 1890s. The combination of the East Indies and the House of Orange proved to be a particularly powerful catalyst of the nationalism that rose in Dutch society and eventually engulfed undecided politicians as well. This nationalism was reinforced by the unexpected successes of the Royal Dutch East Indies Army in quelling revolts in Lombok and Aceh. However, South Africa was a different story. It was not part of the Dutch sphere of influence, after all. Nothing could change this fact, not even the passionate ties of kinship felt across the political spectrum. The Dutch could not afford to pursue their aggressive East Indies policy in South Africa because this might upset the delicate balance between the Dutch and the British in the East Indies. This was a risk the Dutch could not afford to take. The British and Dutch governments were both keenly aware of this. In their hearts, Dutch parliamentarians knew this too. Retrieving Paul Kruger with a warship was enough to release the tension in Dutch society, a fact that speaks volumes; for although it was no more than a symbolic act, it took little to please a nation so powerless.

At the end of the nineteenth century, a global revolution in communication technology radically altered human perceptions of time and distance. The ties between colonial powers and their overseas possessions were strengthened, but what is more, the outside world increasingly invaded European consciousness. Steam cruisers, railways and telegraph connections stepped up the circulation of capital, goods, information and people. Improvements in printing and reproduction also broadened horizons. The growing interaction between western and non-western societies, although not on an equal footing, also affected the Netherlands, the East Indies colony and the African colony of dreams.

All the same, there was a great difference between the East Indies and South Africa. While Dutch ties with the colony in Asia were lined with gold,

Dutch capital specifically invested in South Africa was limited. The only big investment was the Dutch South African Railway Company. Even that project got started with great difficulty and never flourished. Characteristically, it was half owned by German investors. In terms of emigration, too, South Africa was of modest significance.[11] There were three main reasons for this: inter-nal divisions among Boer sympathizers; resistance in Transvaal to too much Dutch immigration; and a deterioration of the overall economic and politi-cal outlook. All in all, no more than 6,500 Dutch nationals emigrated to South Africa before the outbreak of the First Boer War. Once the fighting began, a third of these returned home.[12]

In any case, the prospect of doing business in South Africa was no motive for Dutch imperialist ambitions. So what motive did they have? To grasp a concept as complicated as imperialism, one must understand not only the motives but also the means. Both were present, but the question is: to what extent was persuasion used to convince others successfully of the imperialist mission? There was an effort to popularize and promote the East Indies and South Africa. Queen Wilhelmina's public gestures were among the most remarkable elements of this campaign. They strongly resemble "propaganda" as defined by the *Encyclopedia of the Social Sciences*: "The relatively deliber-ate manipulation by means of symbols (words, gestures, flags, images, monu-ments, music, etcetera), of other people's thoughts or actions with respect to beliefs, values and behaviours which these people . . . regard as controver-sial".[13] The deliberate attempt to influence thinking, the use of symbols, the controversial subject matter – Queen Wilhelmina's acts display all the characteristics of propaganda. In the pomp and circumstance surrounding the crown, one also immediately recognizes George Mosse's "creation of myths and their symbols", Eric Hobsbawm's "invention of tradition" and John MacKenzie's "the monarch's imperial role".[14] Once ritually cleansed, the colony, the colony of dreams and their defenders were embraced by the royal house and paraded before the people at appropriate times.

The central government, by contrast, kept a low profile. Aside from the recruitment of European soldiers for the overseas army, they allowed others to promote the East Indies. Towards Africa, it was felt, the government's job was not to encourage but to dissuade. Popularization and propaganda only came into play at the local level. Municipal leaders could afford to be more candid, even if their expressions of sympathy were equally symbolic. Town mayors and council members used petitions and street names as their means of resisting the British and honouring the Boers. Particularly urban city coun-cil members in the Protestant Belt – a narrow band that stretches from the south-western part of the Netherlands to the north-east – enlivened their municipalities by naming streets after Boer heroes.

Politicians and royalty were not the only ones to promote South Africa. When the first official club – the Dutch-South African Association (NZAV) – was established, it was a miracle of national unity. Bankers and reverends, entrepreneurs and academics all gathered to celebrate the founding of the association on 12 May 1881. Their unanimity, however, proved to be short-lived. When the fighting began in the autumn of that year, gestures of sympathy from the Netherlands showed signs of a fraying alliance, as they did elsewhere in Europe. NZAV secretary and Amsterdam philosopher C. B. Spruyt felt encouraged to shift the association away from economic and towards more social, cultural and nationalistic aims. More specifically, he strove for "an independent development of Afrikanerdom", where the Dutch colonist would to a great extent rediscover his language and national morals.[15] Not that there was a huge interest in this ideal; the association's membership in the Netherlands peaked at 6,259 in 1900.

Other large associations were the Christian National Boer Committee and the General Dutch Union, which had 4,000 and 1,400 members respectively in the Netherlands around 1900.[16] Despite the limited availability of membership data (only liberal Boer support has been quantified) – the strongest response appears to have come from predominantly Protestant parts of the Netherlands.[17] This was true in the early 1880s, and was still the case 20 years later. The provinces of Gelderland and Zuid-Holland showed greatest loyalty to the cause. The South African cause had a greater and wider appeal than the élite East Indies. It managed to unite its supporters, although not for very long. Once the Boers lost the war, the various associations were left with little *raison d'être*.

Clearly, organizations whose activities were directed specifically at South Africa and the East Indies never had large memberships. Yet this does not mean that the excitement was limited to an élite group of interested and directly involved parties. Some organized protests had a measurably large grass roots response. During the first Boer War, for instance, thousands of people from all walks of life signed petitions addressed to Britain's queen, parliament and people. This paled in comparison with the 140,000 who signed the *To the People of Great Britain* petition published by the NZAV in the summer of 1899; or with the 200,000 signatures collected by the Dutch Women's Association for International Disarmament and Arbitrage on a petition presented to Tsar Nicholas II, initiator of the Hague Peace Conference of 1899.[18]

Another expression of genuine interest, enthusiasm and commitment to the Boer cause was honouring heroes. President Kruger was twice given a hero's welcome in the Netherlands. Everyone, from the monarch down to the commoner, fell for him. His first visit was in the spring of 1884, when he came on business as a member of the Transvaal delegation. Accompanied by General N. J. Smit and Education Superintendent S. J. du Toit, the president had departed for Europe in 1883. His mission was to end British suzerainty over Transvaal, and he was successful; the British relinquished nearly all their authority. They retained only the right to veto future treaties between Transvaal and foreign powers. After signing the Convention of London, on 27

February 1884, the Boer troika visited the Netherlands, mainly to request financial support for their railway plans. They received a warm welcome, but no monetary aid. Despite this disappointment, the visit won Kruger and his compatriots widespread fame and sympathy for their cause. For in addition to meeting King William III, political leaders and representatives of the pro-Boer movement, the threesome also toured many large, mainly Protestant cities.

President Kruger's second great tribute, around the new year 1900, once again demonstrated the warm sympathy felt for his cause. This time, the South African leader had come seeking a way to end the Second Boer War. By then, the Boer cause was already lost, and the ageing Kruger was but a shadow of his former self. Nevertheless, he was showered with attention – as he was in France, Belgium and Germany. The fact that the admiration was now mixed with a heavy dose of pity did not diminish his popularity. To the contrary; Kuyper's magazine *De Standaard* noted how poignant it was to see "the thousands of people so deeply moved at the sight of this powerful old man, who this time, too, calmly surveys the stormy sea of humanity before him". Dignitaries, too, showed their emotions at this event, a heady combination of pride, frustration, admiration and sadness. Some Dutch people must have sensed that a beautiful dream was coming to an end. Others, such as the young social democrat and later prime minister, Willem Drees, felt a "budding urge to fight injustice in general" and "imperialist aggression" in particular.[19] In any case, few were unmoved by Kruger's visit.

One of the areas where that was reflected most clearly was in print. The new medium, printed paper, was a miracle through which every layer of Dutch and other western societies could be reached. Print was adjustable in height, depth and width and therefore appealed to everyone from the professor to the farmhand, from the Catholic south to the liberal Protestant north. In word and image, print brought the outside world into the home. A perfect example is *De Katholieke Illustratie*, a Catholic weekly that landed on the doorstep of 60,000–70,000 homes, especially in the southern provinces. The number of readers must have run into the hundreds of thousands.[20] The magazine had a large and loyal readership to serve and influence. As an instrument of popularization and propaganda, this richly illustrated publication had an enormous potential.

Reports about South Africa often focussed on the dream. The respected high culture monthly *De Gids* dreamt, campaigned and suffered alongside the established intellectual elite on both issues: the East Indies and South Africa. The magazine made room for writers to approach themes from a variety of angles. The editorial policy was broad, allowing everything from a study of the Koran to an appeal for the "elimination" of Aceh; a celebration of the nationalist reactions to the Lombok expedition and Jameson's raid appearing next to an article about the Netherlands' "Debt of Honour". In any case, *De Gids* never questioned the legitimacy of Dutch overseas possessions. Many of the Netherlands' expansionist academics were either on the editorial board, where they outnumbered the literary types, or wrote provocative articles for *De Gids*.

De Nederlandse Spectator, although a close cousin to *De Gids*, took a more critical attitude.[21] It was just as liberal, but a touch more highbrow, aristocratic and increasingly conservative. The main difference was that, as a weekly, it was more of a news magazine. It reported on science, arts and social affairs and commented on issues in satirical editorials. Opinions about the colony and the colony of dreams were more divergent than in *De Gids*. The *Spectator* was proud of colonial achievements in the East Indies one moment, then critical of unbridled expansionism the next. On South Africa, the magazine was more straightforward. It followed the common liberal opinion of the day, non-committal in 1877 and gradually more admiring from 1880 onwards. Yet, on the Boer issue too, the *Spectator* could not resist the occasional pinprick. While most of their political cartoons lampooned the British and extolled the virtues of the Boers, the latter were sometimes ridiculed as well. A favourite target of derision were the – in the eyes of aristocratic, literary readers – uneducated cousins from Transvaal whose bookshelves held no more than the Holy Bible and some eighteenth-century sermons.[22]

At the other end of the liberal spectrum was *De Amsterdammer*, a cultural weekly that, because of its borderline social democratic bias, was generally considered "radical". It was sometimes called "the green weekly", a reference to the colour of its cover, in order to distinguish it from the daily newspaper of the same name. The green weekly gained notoriety from the direct and appealing style of its editor in chief, former clergyman Johannes de Koo. From the mid-1880s, this style found political expression mainly in Johan Braakensiek's cartoons.

Despite its reputation as a radical magazine, *De Amsterdammer* would sometimes take a decidedly nationalistic line in reaction to the Boer War. In early 1896, after Jameson's raid, an editorial called for the formation of a large and powerful Dutch union. This ambition became a reality a few months later when the General Dutch Union was founded. After the new outbreak of war in 1899, the magazine urged its readers to take action: "Netherlands, awaken! Your kinsmen and your own sons are dying on the battlefield of honour. Wake up! It is not enough to reach into your pocket. Put some effort and thought into the cause".[23] In his political cartoons Braakensiek captured the mood in images such as the Dutch maiden (a symbol for the Dutch nation), who, dressed as a mailman, delivers invitations to the Hague Peace conference, but passes the Boer Republic by. Another one of his cartoons shows President Kruger on horseback amid Boer soldiers, invoking the image of William the Silent.[24]

The weekly *De Kroniek* covered politics, arts and science. Editor in chief Pieter Lodewijk Tak expressed little appreciation for the colonial exploits of the Dutch in the East Indies. South Africa was a more complicated matter since it could not be dismissed as a hobbyhorse of the élite. The Boer cause was an issue of ideology and kinship that could not be simply endorsed or rejected. The courage of the Boers in Jameson's raid gained them Tak's unmitigated admiration: "Uncle Paul has set things straight. How strong and clever that man is".[25] That admiration was not enough to convince Tak to join the General Dutch Union, however. He saw little use in an effort to spread the Dutch language around the world, certainly in the case of South Africa, where it had "shrunk to the limited needs of nomadic life". He wryly compared the union to a sewing circle, stitching garments "for the bare bottoms of the inhabitants of Tierra del Fuego".[26] Tak continued vacillating between emotion and reason until the beginning of the Second Boer War. Then, his feelings gained the upper hand and he openly defended the Boer Republics' right to exist, but only for the duration of the war.

Aside from these general weeklies and monthlies, there were a number of publications that represented ideologies or interest groups in Dutch society, and that were therefore rather more specific and explicitly political. The three largest liberal newspapers, *Nieuwe Rotterdamsche Courant* (NRC), *Algemeen Handelsblad* and *Het Vaderland*, respectively conservative, moderate and progressive, represented the main strands of Dutch liberalism. All three reported on the overseas empire, and all three were sympathetic to the national cause. In the Second Boer War, *NRC* and *Het Vaderland* endorsed the restraint shown by Foreign Minister De Beaufort, albeit regretfully. By contrast, *Algemeen Handelsblad* editor Charles Boissevain showed himself to be a staunch supporter of the Boers. His editorials on the war bore headlines like "The courageous Dutchmen" and "Blood and thunder".[27] For over 20 years, he filled his daily column with heartfelt cries of jubilation and anguish. There could hardly have been a more passionate journalistic advocate of a Greater Netherlands.

One possible exception might be Abraham Kuyper, who during his political career was also an editor in chief, a competing opinion-maker equally receptive to dreams of an overseas empire. He often expressed this dream from his own personal pulpit, *De Standaard*, the mouthpiece of the orthodox Protestant party. Other leading members of the party also showed themselves to be deeply concerned with the fortunes of the colony and the colony of dreams. This helped to popularize and promote the issue, particularly among orthodox Protestants. Readers were bombarded with the idea of kinship. After Jameson's raid, *De Standaard* wrote: "We as a nation are not reluctant to pride ourselves on what our descendants in Transvaal have done. Our pride is akin to that of a father who basks in his son's glory".[28] Readers swallowed this whole.

Catholic papers had a harder time spicing up the issue. At the outbreak of the Second Boer War in 1899, *De Tijd* had great trouble justifying its support for the Boers. Although this mouthpiece of conservative Catholics had used phrases such as "Uncle Paul", or "Brave men, those Boers of Transvaal", the paper had refrained from using the term "kinship". This only started after the war broke out. On the issue of colonial warfare in the East Indies and South Africa, *De Tijd* was even more hard-line than some liberal papers, defending national rather than Catholic interests. This contrasted sharply with the arch-conservative *De Maasbode*, the second biggest Catholic newspaper. Remarkably, this paper did print the 1899 NZAV manifesto *To the People of Great Britain*. It was a suitable occasion to dredge up an old issue: the separation of church and state in Italy in 1870. As far as *De Maasbode* was concerned, this was the symbolic *leitmotif* in the conflict between the Boers and the British: Chamberlain as Victor Emmanuel, Kruger as the pope. This was a battle between worldly power and the authority of the church.

De Katholieke Illustratie was somewhere in between, but closer to *De Tijd*, certainly in times of strong nationalist sentiment. Before 1899, *De Katholieke Illustratie* had hardly given a thought to the Boers. Once the South African conflict turned violent, however, the magazine provided its readership with a warm and lengthy introduction to the Boers. This included a special edition, an 18-part serial called "Shepherds and Mercenaries", heroic tales about "Paul the Lion Killer" and many illustrations of Boer commanders. The magazine pulled out all the stops to instil in its readers a sense of kinship to the Boers and their wholesome life. Thanks to its wide circulation, especially in the southern Dutch provinces, the magazine brought some of the commotion about the colonies into the very homes of Catholics.

Until 1896, the social democratic press took the uncompromisingly anti-colonial stance exemplified by the anarchist publication *Recht voor Allen*. However, party leaders and the editors of social democratic publications found themselves increasingly uneasy, their loyalties conflicting. Their position towards Paul Kruger, on his arrival in the Netherlands in late 1900, was typical. After a lengthy discussion, the party executive decided not to send the Boer leader a letter of solidarity. However, SDAP parliamentarians Troelstra, Henri van Kol and J. H. Schaper did attend Kruger's reception, much to the surprise of both the bourgeois press and fellow party members. In *Het Volk*, Troelstra loftily defended the social democrats' "solemn obligation to respectfully pay homage to the voluntarily exiled Transvaler". As opponents of capitalism, he said, they "could appear without shame before this man, enfeebled by worries and age, this pilgrim who seeks the City of Justice that he will never see".[29] Weakened by such dissonance, the anarchists' and socialists' indignation had only limited effect. It could not match the enthusiasm of other papers, which painted the colony and the colony of dreams in nationalist colours, and not in the red of socialism.

While party publications were primarily interested in sending the rank and file a politically correct message, the popular press were more interested in selling advertising space and increasing their circulation. The supply side in publishing was driven by ambitious tycoons, technological innovation and groundbreaking journalism; on the demand side there was an increasingly literate and enfranchised public, and businesses seeking new advertising opportunities. These ingredients caused explosive growth in non-partisan dailies and weeklies in the last decades of the nineteenth century. Big head-lines, short sentences, catchy news, revealing illustrations and clear opinions – these were the new formula for success that today seems self-evident.

In the Netherlands, just as in other countries, war sold newspapers. With respect to the East Indies and South Africa, newspapers such as *De Telegraaf* and *De Courant* were strongly nationalistic. In coverage of Transvaal, the popular papers constantly referred to Kruger as "Uncle Paul." After Jameson's raid, *De Telegraaf* expressed "the good right of Transvalers" to "fend off the English freebooters in their republic with armed violence".[30] Naturally, press coverage of the conflict reached its peak during the Second Boer War. In addition to accurate and suitably biased reporting, readers were wooed with special inserts and features. *Het Nieuws van de Dag* included a full-colour topographic map of the South African front lines.

While the popular dailies made occasional use of pictures, the illustrated weeklies were based on them. Aimed at the general public, Dutch illustrated weeklies became increasingly common in the latter half of the nineteenth century, following the trend in Britain, Germany and France. Many of these magazines, particularly *Eigen Haard* (*De Katholieke Illustratie*'s Protestant counterpart), *De Wereldkroniek* and *Het Nieuws van de Dag*, parroted liberal dream interpreters. Every commercial publication that called itself neutral celebrated the deeds of the nation in the East Indies and South Africa, in prose as well as in nationalist, imperialist poetry with a mass appeal.

Such jingoistic language was not only directed at men. Popular magazines were intended for the entire family. Articles about the Dutch East Indies and South Africa also appeared in "young ladies' magazines". The military opera-tions in the East Indies did not, however. The Boer War, on the other hand, was covered in numerous reports, and with the usual nationalistic bias. *De Hollandsche Lelie*, for instance, promoted collections in support of the Boers, romanticized their life and struggles, and published a full-page farewell poem to Uncle Paul on his death in 1904.

In the end, this homage to Kruger proved to be no more than an aftershock of the earthquake that South Africa had caused in Dutch society. After the Treaty of Vereeniging, little more was written or said about Africa. The result of the Second Boer War was an anticlimax after all the moral agonizing and ideological conflict in Dutch politics. Despite his assurances to the queen be-fore forming a government, Abraham Kuyper became a successful mediator between the warring parties in late 1 901 and secured the Treaty of Vereeniging on 31 May 1902. It was an ironic achievement considering how often Kuyper had changed views during his political career. Many criticized him because they felt the peace "smacked of a capitulation",[31] but Kuyper, as always, felt sure of himself. He was at no risk politically; he was convinced the Boers would have lost the war anyway, and he knew he had won international approval.

The expressions of sympathy and intense interest in South Africa quite suddenly evaporated. Only the three large associations remained, and their membership fell drastically.[32] The last great expression of love for the Boers was when the NZAV had the corpse of former president Kruger brought from Switzerland to Pretoria. It was a symbolic gesture. The burial, on 16 December 1904, symbolized not only the Dutch farewell to "one of the greatest sons of the ancient Dutch tribe", but also their reluctant goodbyes to "the rich past that was lowered into the grave" along with Kruger's body, as it was put in a press release.[33]

The East Indies and South Africa experiences bolstered Dutch national confidence and enriched the national culture at the turn of the century. Unlike the East Indies, which had gradually captured the people's imagination, South Africa suddenly sparked Dutch interest in the late 1870s. The British annexation of the South African Republic attracted the attention of Kuyper's orthodox Protestants and of liberal scholars in Utrecht, Leiden and Amsterdam. The former recognized the Boers as oppressed co-religionists while the latter saw them as victims of a brutal political power struggle. There were protests from these sections of society, but they were mild and the plight of the Boers soon receded into obscurity. Dutch society as a whole awoke only when the Boers successfully revolted against the British authorities in 1880. The Dutch were excited to see that justifiable violence worked. This changed matters. Now those who had sympathized with the Boers from the very beginning called attention to another kind of bond between the Dutch and the Boers. The Boers, they argued with increasing fervour, were actually kinsmen, lagging behind somewhat in development perhaps, but true to traditional values. They had been out of sight, but not entirely out of mind, and now, since the First Boer War, they had emerged from the shadows of history as heroes. The Boers were promptly etched into the nation's collective memory as the "Beggars of the nineteenth century".

Kinship made the popularization of Transvaal relatively easy. The idea was much simpler to sell than the "foreign" East Indies. In any case, the Dutch "Protestant Belt" identified quite readily with the image of tough, uncomplicated men. It was a direct and positive identification; the people quickly took Transvaal into their hearts. The Protestant Belt was also the region where the three Boer leaders toured in 1884, (vainly) hoping to cash in on the enthusiasm and to secure material aid.

But Transvaal inspired more than a passing enthusiasm. Emotionally, it probably had a more immediate impact than the East Indies. The Boer cause had a way of appealing to all Dutch people. The social élite, the urban west, the Protestant Belt, the Catholic south and the liberal Protestant north all forgot their differences and felt a common kinship. This was a welcome side-effect at a time when a process known as "pillarization" was segregating Dutch society into distinct ideological streams. By emphasizing kinship more than citizenship, cultural nationalists provided the Netherlands with a concept of nationhood in which other-minded people, and even the lowest social classes, could share. Because every ideological "pillar" in Dutch society could identify with something in the Boer cause, the issue united rather than divided the nation. Only the government managed to stay rational, in the interest of relations with Britain and the East Indies. Wilhelmina wanted to help the Boers, but her hands were tied. The anarchists were opposed to anything and everything. All others gave their emotions free reign. If at first it appeared to be an isolated chapter, the response to later dramas such as the Second Boer War showed how quickly the flame could be rekindled. After the conflicts in Lombok and Aceh, it was names like Magersfontein and Spionkop that inspired sweeping emotions in the Dutch, gentlemen and commoners alike. Swept up in the march of progress, the Dutch indulged in their own delusions for a while. It was vicarious heroism, but this did not dampen the cheers that welcomed Paul Kruger.

At the same time, Kruger's arrival in December 1900 was the beginning of the end. The physical appearance of the toothless old lion moved onlookers, but more out of pity than admiration. Pure (and purifying) violence, as had been preached and successfully practised in the East Indies, proved addictive. In South Africa, however, it failed. There, the Boers' "just" revolt was simply unable to match the "brutal" violence of the British. In their hearts, people continued to believe in the struggle, but in their minds they already knew the dream was over. Drama overseas persuaded the people to take to the streets and reach into their purses. Whether it was heroism or tragedy was not so important. As long as the drama continued, so did the emotion. But it did not last forever. To keep momentum, mass enthusiasm needs new impetus. The Boer heroes were destined to live on only in street names and in boys' adventure stories.

While the East Indies experience left its mark on nearly all sectors of Dutch society, South Africa did not. Language and discipline were really the only permanent traces it left in Dutch culture. Still, lasting influence is not the only criterion by which to judge a historical period's significance. Temporary influences also have their merit. Popularization and promotion of the colony and the colony of dreams helped to open up Dutch society. As the Dutch East Indies grew more integrated and unified, the Dutch nation's enthusiasm for the colony and the colony of dreams grew, and vice versa. The overseas empire, real and imagined, added an extra dimension, which lent greater attractiveness to the teaching of culture and which was exploited by the (mass) media in particular: tragedy and heroism, heroes and villains, sadness and joy. In short, the colonies provided plenty of uncomplicated emotions, a sharp contrast between the strange and the familiar and an unambiguous identification with national symbols. Although this effect was only temporary in most of the country, it did play a role in the cultural homogenization of Dutch society.

Dutch imperialism did exist. This is clear in the case of South Africa. Some hard-liners in the Netherlands no doubt dreamt of territorial expansion and widening the Dutch sphere of influence. However, these notions were about as unrealistic as they were amusing. Orthodox Protestant and liberal sympathizers with the Boers had more serious aspirations: to increase the Netherlands' economic, political and cultural influence in South Africa. For a few years, this seemed to work. The Netherlands South African Railway Company, the Transvaal civil service and the teaching profession became Dutch strongholds. These seemed an ideal stepping stone for further expansion.

Things did not go as planned. The development of Dutch influence stagnated, and the fault lay with both the Dutch and the Boers. The Boers, isolated as they were by the powerful British Empire, were glad to accept Dutch notions of kinship and kindred faith. Still, they had values of their own that they were unwilling to compromise, especially their independence. This, after all, was exactly what they had gone to war for. Anti-Dutch sentiment (*Hollanderhaat*) became a common notion in Transvaal, particularly when the self-proclaimed cousins from the north failed to provide any financial support beyond emergency humanitarian aid. Ultimately, too little money and too few Dutch people flowed into South Africa to significantly increase their influence. And even if the money and people had come, the Dutch government would have kept the enthusiasm in check to preserve harmony with the British.

The colonies did enrich the Netherlands, however, in economic, political and cultural terms. They helped the fatherland catch up to the march of progress and gave the Dutch nation more cohesion. Not that this was part of a well thought out plan. There were motives and means,[34] there were people and institutions. There was an interaction. And yet, this combination alone could not have guaranteed successful popularization and propaganda if the message itself had not struck a chord with the public. A propagandist needs more than motives and means. In the words of Aldous Huxley, a propagandist "canalizes an already existing dream. In a land where there is no water, he digs in vain".[35] There was plenty of "water" among the Dutch urban élite. In the latter half of the nineteenth century, the élite drew on the Dutch Golden Age as inspiration for a new cultural nationalism. The East Indies and South Africa, and their respective "founders", J. P. Coen and Jan van Riebeeck, were already part of the nationalist self-image at that time and so they fit perfectly into this evocation of past glory. Around the turn of the century, the waters also started welling up in the rest of the Netherlands. Such dreams, such imagination! The Dutch people's wildest dreams seemed to come true. "All those who sail the cape must be men of dreams". A New Holland under the Southern Cross – it was a recurring dream, but one from which all were eventually rudely awoken.

Notes

1. This chapter is based on another publication by the author, entitled *Holland op zijn breedst: Indië en Zuid-Afrika in de Nederlandse cultuur omstreeks 1900* (Amsterdam, 1996). My thanks to Julika Vermolen.
2. Chris A. J. van Koppen, *De Geuzen van de negentiende eeuw: Abraham Kuyper en Zuid-Afrika* (Maarssen, 1992).
3. See *De Katholieke Illustratie* (1900), nos. 3, 5, 6/7, 18 (quotation), 35, 45; (1901) nos. 10 and 36; (1902) passim (serial).
4. See Van Koppen, *Geuzen* and M. Kuitenbrouwer, *Nederland en de opkomst van het moderne imperialisme. Koloniën en buitenlandse politiek 1870-1902* (Amsterdam/Dieren, 1985).
5. J. P. de Valk and M. van Faassen (eds), *Dagboeken en aantekeningen van Willem Hendrik de Beaufort 1874–1918*, 2 vols ('s-Gravenhage, 1993), p. 71.
6. Van Koppen, *Geuzen*, pp. 64, 175.
7. Henk te Velde, *Gemeenschapszin en plichtsbesef: Liberalisme en nationalisme in Nederland, 1870–1918* ('s-Gravenhage, 1992), p. 165. Cf. Kuitenbrouwer, *Nederland*, pp. 181–2, 186–7.
8. *De Tijd*, 25 August (1899).
9. See *De Sociaal-democraat*, 8 August (1899).
10. Archives of "Uitvoerend Comité en Landelijke Propaganda Komitee inzake den Internationalen Boycot van den Engelschen Scheepvaart", map I, algemene stukken, in SDAP-archives, IISG. For the enthusiasm the socialist constituency felt for the Boer cause, see the memoirs of the later P. M. W. Drees, in Kuitenbrouwer, *Nederland*, p. 199.
11. E. W. Hofstee, "Demografische ontwikkelingen van de Noordelijke Nederlanden circa 1800–circa 1975", in *Algemene Geschiedenis der Nederlanden X*, 63–93 (Bussum, 1981), esp. p. 91. For the Dutch East Indies, see Martin Bossenbroek, *Volk voor Indië: De werving van Europese militairen voor de Nederlandse koloniale dienst 1814–1909* (Amsterdam, 1992).
12. Van Koppen, *Geuzen*, 103–9; G. J. Schutte, *Nederland en de Afrikaners. Adhesie en aversie: over stamverwantschap, Boerenvrienden, Hollanderhaat, Calvinisme en apartheid* (Franeker, 1986), pp. 45-50, 101–41, 182–3. Most émigrés worked for the government, the railroad or the church or in education.
13. Quoted by J. A. Mangan, "'The Grit of Our Forefathers': Invented Traditions, Propaganda and Imperialism", in *Imperialism and Popular Culture*, J. M. MacKenzie (ed.), 113–39 (Manchester, 1986), esp. p. 113.
14. George L. Mosse, *The Nationalization of the Masses: Political Symbolism and Mass Movements in Germany from the Napoleonic Wars through the Third Reich* (New York, 1975), p. 2; Eric Hobsbawm, "Mass-Producing Traditions: Europe, 1870–1914", in *The Invention of Tradition*, E. Hobsbawm and T. Ranger (Cambridge, 1989), pp. 263–307; cf. also David Cannadine, "The Context, Performance and Meaning of Ritual: the British Monarchy and 'The Invented Tradition', c. 1820–1977", in *The Invention of Tradition*, Hobsbawm and Ranger (eds), pp. 101–64; J. M. MacKenzie, *Propaganda and Empire: The Manipulation of British Public Opinion 1880–1960* (Manchester, 1984), pp. 3–4.
15. Quoted in *Nederland – Zuid-Afrika: Gedenkboek uitgegeven door de Nederlandsch Zuid-Afrikaansche Vereeniging, bij gelegenheid van haar vijftig-jarig bestaan 1881–1913* (Amsterdam, 1931), pp. 104–5.
16. The membership data for the Christian National Boer Committee refer to the year 1902, those for the General Dutch Union concern 1899. See Tables 6, 8 and 9 in Bossenbroek, *Holland op zijn breedst*. These numbers refer to members in the Netherlands only; members in the Dutch East Indies, South Africa, Flanders or elsewhere are not included.
17. There are no data available from 1900 for the Christian National Boer Committee or the General Dutch Union. The only source of information for that year is the NZAV membership list. These data have been supplemented by the names of those who signed the *Address to the British Nation* from 1880 to 1881, again for lack of data concerning other petitions. See Table 9 Bossenbroek, *Holland op zijn breedst*, p. 259.
18. P. H. Kamphuis, *Het Algemeene Nederlandsche Vredebond 1871–1901: Een verkennend onderzoek over dertig jaar ijveren voor een vreedzame internationale samenwerking* (The Hague, 1982), pp. 162–8.

19. Kuitenbrouwer, *Nederland*, pp. 186–7, 199.
20. Estimate based on two known data: in 1871 the magazine had 50,000 subscriptions, in 1935 this number had doubled. Therefore, it is estimated that in 1900 the number of subscriptions was more or less halfway between these two numbers. Considering the size of these families and the fact that many people shared subscriptions, the number of readers would certainly have been four to five times higher. See J. Hemels and Vegt, *Het geïllustreerde tijdschrift: Bibliografie. Deel 1: 1840–1945* (Amsterdam, 1993), pp. 262–7. For more on the media, see J. Blokker, *De wond'ren werden woord Honderd jaar informatie in Nederland 1889–1989* (Amsterdam, 1989); Maarten Schneider and Joan Hemels, *De Nederlandse krant 1618–1978: Van "nieuwstydinghe" tot dagblad* (Baarn, 1979).
21. See Nop Maas, *De Nederlandsche Spectator: Schetsen uit het letterkundig leven van de tweede helft van de negentiende eeuw* (Utrecht/Antwerpen, 1986); G. Stuiveling, *De Nieuwe Gids als geestelijk brandpunt* (2nd edn, Amsterdam, 1965), pp. 15–17.
22. *De Nederlandse Spectator*, 28 March (1896). See Maas, *De Nederlandsche Spectator*, pp. 320–22; Cf. Schutte, *Nederland*, pp. 10, 33, 44.
23. *De Amsterdammer*, 12 January and 2 February (1896); quoted in Kuitenbrouwer, *Nederland*, pp. 177, 181.
24. *De Amsterdammer*, 16 April (1899) and 8 October (1899) respectively.
25. T., "Engelschen politiek", *De Kroniek*, 12 January (1896).
26. T., "Het Algemeen Nederlandsch Verbond", *De Kroniek*, 18 December (1898).
27. Quoted in Kuitenbrouwer, *Nederland*, p. 181. See also Te Velde, *Gemeenschapszin*, pp. 153–61 and passim.
28. *De Standaard*, 10 January (1896).
29. *Het Volk*, 15 December (1900).
30. *De Telegraaf*, 3 January (1896).
31. *Het Volk*, 7 June (1902). For a detailed description of Kuyper's mediation, see Van Koppen, *Geuzen*, pp. 182–201.
32. Aside from the Dutch South African Association (NZAV), these were the General Dutch Union (1896), which advocated and promoted a language union between the Netherlands, Flanders (Dutch-speaking part of Belgium) and South Africa, as well as the anti-revolutionary Christian National Boer Committee, founded in 1899.
33. Quoted in *Nederland – Zuid-Afrika*, p. 121.
34. Cf. Daniel R. Headrick, *The Tools of Empire: Technology and European Imperialism in the Nineteenth Century* (New York/Oxford, 1981), pp. 3–14.
35. Quoted in Thomas G. August, *The Selling of the Empire: British and French Imperialist Propaganda 1890–1940* (Westport/London, 1985), p. 107.

CHAPTER NINE

Portugal and the Boer War[1]

Pedro Lains & Fernando Costa

In spite of the differences that characterized Anglo–Portuguese relations in the nineteenth century, the African imperial interests of Great Britain and Portugal coincided in many important instances. This did not always appear to be the case, however. In fact, up to 1850, relations between the two countries were particularly troubled by Britain's insistence that Portugal should put an end to the slave trade from the Portuguese colonies in Africa to Brazil. Other minor differences placed Portugal and Great Britain at logger-heads in the nineteenth century. They disputed ownership of the small island of Bolama off the coast of Guinea, and of Delagoa Bay. These differences were, however, settled in Portugal's favour by international arbitration and left hardly a mark on diplomatic relations between the two countries.

Another dispute would leave much deeper marks, though. It arose from Britain's objections to the ambitious plans of Barros Gomes, Minister of the Colonies in 1886, who claimed possession of the land stretching between Angola and Mozambique, which would later become Rhodesia, the so-called Rose-Coloured Map. To put an end to his plans, the British government sent the Portuguese government an ultimatum in 1890, and Portugal was forced to back down. The main effect of this incident was to cast a shadow over Portuguese public opinion about the African colonies, and Britain loomed as the great enemy of Portuguese aspirations in Africa. Yet, Portugal's involve-ment in the question of British political and military power in South Africa shows that Britain was in fact Portugal's best ally. She may not have been an optimal ally but was certainly better than any other of the European nations with interests in the region. Portuguese interests had very little to do with those of the feared Boer republics, contrary to what the popular press wanted people to believe in Lisbon, in spite of some demonstrations of solidarity from either side. The concrete sign of the cooperation between Portugal and Britain in South Africa was the delimitation of the borders of Mozambique that resulted from the negotiations between the two countries about the southern border, in Delagoa Bay, in 1875, and the Gaza and Zambezi borders in 1891.[2] In exchange for its support in defining Portuguese territorial limits in Africa, Britain accepted the presence of a colonial power that did not have the military capacity to pose a threat to British interests in the region. This presence also meant a colonial administration, which spared the Treasury in London.

This result took a while to achieve, however. Portuguese diplomacy continued to pursue an alliance with the Transvaal as an alternative to an alliance with Britain. Portuguese freedom ended with the arrival of the gold from the Rand and Britain's need to make the Transvaal one of the self-administering British colonies in South Africa, like the Cape Colony and Natal. Portugal's cooperation in this process was less important than one would imagine from reading the Portuguese newspapers and proceedings of the debates in the Lisbon parliament. It is true that Mozambique had a seaport that was the gateway to the Transvaal. Moreover, the city of Beira was also the gateway to Northern Rhodesia, a territory that would be used for British incursions into the republic during the Boer War. But these ports were of very little strategic importance, which was later proved by how little they were actually used during the conflict.

This chapter begins with a study of diplomatic talks on the ownership of Delagoa Bay, on the rights of passage through the adjacent port and territory and finally on the construction of a railway between Lourenço Marques and Pretoria. This study shows us the attempt by the Transvaal and Portugal to form an alliance that placed both these two states and Mozambique outside the orbit of informal British imperialism. The study also shows that this alternative proved to be impossible. In the first decades following the creation of the Transvaal, British diplomacy was relatively conciliatory and was not too concerned about occasional agreements between Lisbon and Pretoria to build a railway to Lourenço Marques or to sign favourable trade agreements.[3] But Britain's passivity ended with the emergence of the Transvaal as an economic centre within South Africa when the gold fields were discovered in the Rand in 1886. After that, the problems between Britain and the Transvaal got progressively worse and culminated in the Jameson Raid in late 1895. Meanwhile, the Delagoa Bay line had been completed a year before, together with other lines to Cape Town and Durban. This basic railway network underscored Pretoria's political and military power, and the need for greater political integration in the region.

Jameson's military incursion intensified the problems in southern Africa and forced Britain to change its plans for the Transvaal. After the failed raid, Britain no longer allowed hesitations and fluctuations in Portuguese diplomacy's attitude towards Lourenço Marques. To strengthen its presence in the area, the British government first made an agreement with Germany, in 1898, concerning their areas of influence in Mozambique. This process is explained in part II of this chapter. Having obtained Berlin's consent, in the following year London reaffirmed its alliance with Lisbon, securing the unequivocal cooperation of the Portuguese authorities in Mozambique at a time when the problems with Pretoria already showed signs of developing into a war. Portugal would indeed be asked to cooperate, as part IV shows.[4] The conclusion underlines the advantages for Mozambique of the return to an alliance with Britain.

I. The Transvaal and the Lourenço Marques railway

The issues that linked Portugal most closely to the problems between Britain and the Transvaal were the decision to build a railway between Pretoria and Lourenço Marques, the way the undertaking was financed and the negotiation of the treaties on customs and railway tariffs. The decision to build the railway to the port of Delagoa Bay was important, as the British had no control over it, which was not the case with the alternative routes to Cape Town and Durban. The importance of these railways became obvious after the gold mining operations began in the Rand in 1886. Until then, the Transvaal's economic survival had not depended on its access to the Indian Ocean and more important still was the fact that it was part of the economies of the Cape Colony and Natal.[5]

Yet the circumstances of the Boers in the Transvaal were changing rapidly. The first sign came when Cecil Rhodes's Royal South African Company was granted the concession to exploit the diamond mines in Kimberley in the Cape Colony region in the late 1860s. As a result, the Cape Colony began to develop considerably. There was an influx of immigrants, most of them British, railways were built between the ports on the coast and the interior, and farming grew in response to this general trend towards development.[6] In addition to all this, the opening of the Suez Canal in 1869 brought the east coast of Africa closer to Europe and increased its economic and strategic importance, although the Cape route still remained more important.[7]

In the late 1860s and beyond, it was the southern region of Mozambique that received most attention in the race to define borders and areas of influence. In 1868, the Boers occupied a small strip of coast that Portugal considered part of its Mozambican colony. The dispute was quickly settled and in 1869 Pretoria and Lisbon signed an agreement guaranteeing the passage of goods to the Transvaal free of customs duties, although it forbade the passage of military supplies (and slaves). This agreement also defined Mozambique's southern border.[8] Soon after, in 1871, work began on building 80 kilometres of road between the Transvaal border and the sea. The Boers were among the few white colonists in Africa who were able to use roads, because they had cattle and had developed overland transport. Nevertheless, the road, which was only finished in 1874, proved to be of little use as the area was infested with tsetse flies, to which the cattle had no resistance.[9]

The failure of the road link to Lourenço Marques did nothing to conceal the importance of the diplomatic agreement that authorized its construction, which the British government did not recognize; they claimed ownership of the Delagoa Bay area. The British government was afraid of the greater economic and strategic independence that a direct outlet to the sea would give the Transvaal, making it more difficult to force the republic to join a South African federation.[10] Portugal and Britain chose to resort to arbitration by France in 1872. In 1875 President MacMahon approved Portugal's aspirations, which were implicit in the treaty with the Transvaal in 1869. The French arbitration was welcomed in Portugal and few people remembered that there had been a time when Portugal claimed a border further south.[11] In the early 1870s, Lourenço Marques had about 500 inhabitants, of whom around 100 were Portuguese.

While the dispute between Lisbon and London was being settled by international arbitration, the Portuguese and Transvaal governments continued their policy of diplomatic cooperation and resumed their plans to link Pretoria and Lourenço Marques, but this time by railway. In 1872, the Boer republic granted the concession to build the railway line as far as the border to a Dutch financial group with German capital. Two years later, in 1874, the Portuguese government granted the concession to build the railway from the border to Lourenço Marques to an American company. The fact that the line would be built by two different concessionaires would cause problems later. Moodie, the American concessionaire, had taken advantage of his position and fixed high prices in his contract with the Portuguese government. To solve the problem, in 1875, the president of the Transvaal offered to buy the concession from Moodie and tried to borrow money in the Netherlands in order to do so. About a year later, however, he had only managed to obtain less than a third of the capital he needed, £300,000, and the deal eventually fell through.

Also in 1875, following MacMahon's decision, Portugal and the Transvaal signed a friendship and trade treaty. This treaty fixed low customs barriers for products in transit to the Transvaal (a maximum of 6 per cent) and allowed the passage of arms and munitions to supply the Boer armies.[12] The treaty was only ratified by the Portuguese parliament several years later, however, in 1882. Meanwhile, in 1878, the British government toughened its policy in the area and formally annexed the Transvaal. London then suggested a treaty with Portugal. The treaty first authorized the free passage of British troops through the port of Delagoa Bay to fight the Zulus in the interior. The Zulus had received the consent of the Portuguese authorities to bring in arms the same way. Secondly, the treaty provided for the construction of a railway under British control. The clause allowing the passage of British troops was greeted with displeasure in Portugal's colonial circles. Moreover, the undertaking to use British capital to build the railway was no more than that, as the government in Whitehall, as usual, never involved itself directly in the project.

Despite the protests in Lisbon, the treaty was signed in May 1879, but the Portuguese government fell immediately after and the treaty was never ratified by parliament. On the insistence of the British ambassador in Lisbon the treaty was eventually submitted to the Portuguese parliament in January 1880, but the vote was postponed until the following year. Meanwhile, in December 1880, the Boers started the First Boer War by declaring their independence, causing even louder protests against the 1879 treaty in Portugal. The Boers were very popular in Lisbon, especially now that they were standing up to British colonial policy. Nevertheless, the treaty finally passed in the lower house of the Portuguese parliament in March 1881, but its passage to the upper house was postponed, which was tantamount to a *de facto* rejection of the treaty.[13]

The construction of the Delagoa Bay railway line became a matter of honour for those involved in colonial issues in Lisbon, as it seemed the best way to guarantee the prosperity of the economy of the area. Portuguese ownership of the line was also the best guarantee for the independence of Portuguese colonial policy in Mozambique.[14] Due to the reestablishment of Transvaal's independence, in 1881, the following year, the Portuguese parliament finally ratified the treaty with the Transvaal that had been signed in 1875. In the same year, the Banco Nacional Ultramarino offered to buy the concession to build the part of the line that ran through Mozambique territory. Their proposal was passed over in favour of another that was submitted in 1883 by an American financier. Unlike the other offer, his proposal had the apparent advantage of requiring neither monetary support from the Portuguese treasury nor interest guarantees, although the financier, whose name was MacMurdo, would be free to fix his own tariffs.[15] In the end, MacMurdo was unable to begin building the railway line and used his position to demand excessively high tariffs. In May 1884, the Lisbon government agreed with the Pretoria government on the possibility of building a tramline across Mozambique territory parallel to the line that the American was planning. When word of this agreement got out, it raised doubts as to the Portuguese government's good faith and complicated the financier's already considerable difficulties in raising the necessary capital to build the railway line.[16]

In 1884, the Pretoria government finally announced that it had raised the capital to build the stretch of railway between Pretoria and the border. The work did not get under way, however, because no agreement had been reached as to the tariffs for the part of the line going through Mozambique. The discovery of the gold fields in Witwatersrand in 1886 made the Rand the greatest gold producer in the world, with about a quarter of the production.[17] At the time, there was no railway in either the Orange Free State or the Transvaal and it became more and more important to build a railway line to the coast. The Portuguese government threatened to begin construction on its own account, but MacMurdo managed to play for more time. In May 1887, he succeeded in raising capital in Britain to begin, and complete in a matter of months, about 80 kilometres of railway track to a location near the border. In the same year, the Transvaal granted the Netherlands South African Railway Company, financed mainly by German capital, the monopoly for building railways in the Transvaal. The first line that this company built was to be the one to Lourenço Marques. However, the delay in building the Mozambique part of the line led to an agreement between the company and the Cape Colony authorities to build a railway to Cape Town and Port Elisabeth.

As no agreement had yet been reached as to tariffs, however, the Transvaal had not begun building the railway line on the other side of the border, using the excuse that the line laid by the MacMurdo consortium ended 8 kilometres from the border and that the Komatipoort bridge still had to be built. In June 1889, the Portuguese government decided to withdraw the concession and, in September, signed a tariff agreement with the Dutch company responsible for building railways in the Transvaal. Work finally got under way and the line was completed in March 1890.[18] It comes as no surprise that the minister who made the decision, Barros Gomes, was also the one who had been behind the publication of the Rose-Coloured Map and the decision to send troops to the Niassa region, which were the acts that provoked the British ultimatum in 1890. The Portuguese government's withdrawal of MacMurdo's concession helped to mark a turning point in relations between Portugal and Britain. The British reaction to the withdrawal of the concession was not particularly harsh and reflected London's policy of not directly defending British capital spread around the world. The British government presented a protest to the Portuguese government but only asked for due compensation to be paid for the funds invested.

Another consequence of the 1889 rescission was the prospect of having to compensate MacMurdo's company for the financial losses incurred by the withdrawal of the concession. MacMurdo's calculations of the compensation that Lisbon would have to pay were far from reality, as the amount eventually decreed a few years later by the arbitration tribunal set up for the purpose would show. Nevertheless, expectations as to the amount owed were such that the governments in London, Berlin and Paris were convinced that Portugal would not be able to bear the cost and would have to borrow money. Expectations as to Portugal's ability to pay the compensation were reflected in the Anglo–German treaty in 1898, which we will discuss below, and which provided for dividing up Portuguese territory in Africa if Lisbon's finances went under. The tribunal's decision obliging Portugal to pay five million dollars was finally published in 1900.[19]

The two railway lines from Pretoria to Cape Town and Port Elisabeth were completed in 1894 and for a year the Cape Colony held the monopoly for

Transvaal outward-going rail transport. The Delagoa Bay railway line was finally completed in late 1894 and the Natal line was finished a year later, in 1895.[20] The fact that Delagoa Bay was closer to Pretoria meant that rail traffic was diverted there from the Cape Colony and Natal. In 1895, the Pretoria–Lourenço Marques line managed to take over a quarter of the traffic from the Cape line and in 1898 trade from the Transvaal was divided almost equally between three lines; those of the Cape Colony, Natal and Lourenço Marques.[21] The history of Portugal's involvement in the region and especially its involvement in the difficult relations between the Transvaal and Britain would eventually revolve almost entirely around the construction of the railway line. It was of undeniable economic importance. To Portugal, it meant the fastest way of obtaining the resources it needed for developing and occupying Lourenço Marques. Some estimated the cost of building the line, plus the cost of building quays, as being lower than the same investment made for Durban. The advantage was the fact that Lourenço Marques had the best natural port in the region, that it was 45 kilometres closer than Durban and that the mountain range between Durban and Pretoria was very difficult to cross.[22]

II. The Jameson Raid and the 1898 Anglo–German agreement

The fact that the railway line from Pretoria and Johannesburg to the Indian Ocean via Lourenço Marques was finished at almost the same time as the lines through Durban and the Cape Colony detracted considerable strategic value from the line's potential. The Transvaal government used the existence of the three alternatives as a political weapon and decided to distribute traffic among the three lines by manipulating tariffs and customs duties.[23] The construction of the railway network demonstrated the Transvaal government's power in controlling its share of the South African economy. But the issue of rail traffic was probably not an essential problem, and neither were a whole series of economic measures implemented by the Boer government, like that by which it kept the monopoly for the production of dynamite. The essential issue was that the railway line placed in the hands of the Transvaal government perhaps the best means of military mobilization and the route for importing war material from abroad.[24]

When Jameson and his men tried to overthrow Kruger in December 1895, the Transvaal government proved to be invincible. In spite of its economic problems due to inadequate, inept administration, in spite of the problems caused by the exclusion of the Uitlanders and in spite of its relative international isolation, Jameson was not able to replace the Transvaal administration with one that favoured greater integration of the Boer Republic with the rest of South Africa under British influence. The failed attempt in 1895 had unfortunate consequences for those interested in integration. After the raid, Britain and its allies in the area, including the immigrants and British capitalists in the Transvaal and Bechuanaland, had less room for manoeuvre. The best illustration of this was the fact that the German government expressed its support for Kruger, but this reduction in Britain's room for manoeuvre is also illustrated by Cecil Rhodes's forced resignation as Prime Minister of the Cape Colony.[25]

In the next few years, between early 1896 and the outbreak of war, the Pretoria government exploited the possibility to increase its military arsenal. To do so, it imported arms and munitions via the three routes opened by the railways to the ports of Cape Town, Durban and Lourenço Marques. To isolate the Transvaal from the outside world, it would be necessary to neutralize these channels, and this raised diplomatic problems where the Lourenço Marques line was concerned. First, these problems involved the need to achieve the unquestionable support of the Lisbon government, which had so far been sitting on the fence between Boer and British interests. Secondly, neutralizing access to the Indian Ocean via Lourenço Marques meant clarifying the interests of other European powers in the area, particularly those of Germany. The understanding between London and Berlin was eventually consecrated in the agreement of August 1898, which defined the spheres of interest of the two powers with regard to the Portuguese colonies.[26] The agreement contained two conventions, which, in practice, defined the spheres of interest of the two countries where the Portuguese territories were concerned. The first convention established that each country would be obliged to inform the other if it wished to grant Portugal a loan guaranteed by income from the customs authorities of Angola, Mozambique or Timor. If the other country was interested in participating, the loan would be made jointly and the revenue would be divided on the basis of a certain territorial division. In Mozambique, the customs authorities south of the Zambezi would fall within the British sphere of interest. The second convention, which was supposed to be kept secret, defined the two powers' territorial right of preference if it was not possible to maintain the integrity of the Portuguese possessions or if Portugal renounced its rights of sovereignty over the territories. The origin of the Anglo–German agreement of 1898 lay in the suspicion that Portugal was in a shaky financial condition, which would be worsened by the need to cover the costs determined by the court's ruling on the withdrawal of the Lourenço Marques railway concession.[27] In 1898, the Portuguese government was in the middle of negotiating a loan from Britain, giving as a guarantee part of its colonial customs revenue and other privileges to British colonial interests in South Africa. In fact, London wanted to form a company with British and Portuguese capital to run the railway line between Lourenço Marques and Pretoria, in order to gain better control over the transport of goods between the two cities. In 1898, after hope of developing independent relations between Portugal and the Transvaal had died, the Portuguese government was more inclined to accept greater British intervention in the area and it agreed to the British terms for the loan.

Germany was displeased, however, and the Berlin government, concerned about a possible change in the status of Lourenço Marques and interested in expanding its sphere of influence in South Africa, informed Lord Salisbury's government that it wished to participate in the loan to Portugal. Britain was not at all interested in incurring the wrath of German diplomacy, especially as this wrath might cause Germany to join forces with France. The Berlin government warned the British government that any disagreement over the issue of granting the loan to Portugal might result in the "reassessment" of Germany's support of the French cause in Egypt.[28] Although Portugal's experience in the international financial markets had been less than brilliant throughout the nineteenth century, the truth was that Portugal was not exactly "the sick old man of the West" and, unlike other countries like Turkey or Greece, had never agreed to direct intervention by foreign authorities in managing its foreign debt. Moreover, Portugal's financial situation in 1898 had improved considerably since the partial suspension of payment of its foreign debt six years previously. Lord Salisbury was informed of the improvement in Portugal's financial situation.[29] This improvement was due to the contribution made by the revenue in gold and foreign currency from exports of goods from the colonies, which had risen dramatically since 1892.

The August 1898 agreement was particularly favourable to British strategy in South Africa. While Berlin undertook not to support the Boers, all London had to accept in return was that the implementation of the agreement would depend on a formal request for financial help from Portugal.[30] Portugal soon found out about the existence of an agreement between Britain and Germany on the Portuguese colonies, although its terms were not known, and this gave rise to speculation. The British government kept Portugal informed of Germany's initiatives in London, and Portugal informed Lord Salisbury that it was withdrawing its request for a loan, as a result of Germany's objections. At the same time, it began contacts in Paris with a view to borrowing money there.[31] However, the colonial circles in Lisbon were sure of one thing, and that was Germany's interest in Portuguese Africa. The obvious threat posed by Germany's ambitions opened the Portuguese government's eyes to the fact that the best policy for defending its interests in Africa was to resume friendly diplomatic relations with Britain. With the agreement of August 1898, Britain had not only excluded Germany from the dispute over control of the Transvaal and the Orange Free State, but had also regained Portuguese cooperation.

III. Portugal's cooperation

Although the lull in relations between Portugal and Britain was a significant development after the troubled times of the 1890 ultimatum, Portugal's authorities wanted to go even further. It seemed like a good opportunity to take advantage of the situation that the British were faced with in South Africa and make a favourable agreement that would commit Britain more clearly to defending the Portuguese colonies against German ambitions. For the Portuguese government it was basically a question of playing the trump of the Transvaal in neutralizing the Anglo–German agreement of 1898. Consistency was not one of Portuguese foreign policy's best qualities, which often used to exasperate British diplomacy. Where Africa was concerned, however, Portuguese diplomacy had one goal alone and that was to keep its colonies. The Lisbon governments were repeatedly reminded of this in the streets and they had the support of several organized interests, including the press. The main doubt was about the best way of achieving this desideratum. In the 1890s, however, Portuguese policy in relation to the African colonies became clearer. After the diplomatic setback brought about by the publication of the Rose-Coloured Map by the progressive minister of foreign affairs, Barros Gomes, in 1886, Portuguese diplomacy began to grow closer to Britain in 1891, while still under the progressive government but without that particular minister. Between 1891 and 1893, Portuguese diplomacy lived through troubled times, including some financial problems. However, in February 1893, Hintze Ribeiro's new government of the Partido Regenerador took office and was to last for four years. This government's foreign minister, the Marquis of Soveral, would be appointed ambassador in London and become the driving force behind restoring good relations between Portugal and Great Britain. Barros Gomes returned to the government with his Progressive Party in February 1897 and was appointed minister of the navy and overseas colonies, although he was replaced in August 1898.

In spite of closer relations with Britain, Portuguese colonial policy was somewhat hesitant at times because of the unpopularity of the alliance with Britain in many of the Lisbon newspapers. As a result, the moves made by Portuguese diplomats in London or other European capitals did not always coincide with the moves made by the Portuguese authorities in Lisbon and Mozambique. Thus, while the Portuguese ambassador in London, Luís de Soveral, intensified his contacts with the British government with a view to signing an agreement on the Portuguese colonies, the new government led by the left Partido Progressista of José Luciano de Castro tried unsuccessfully to pursue a policy of "effective neutrality" in the Transvaal question. First, the Portuguese government forbade the passage of arms and munitions to the Boer Republic via Lourenço Marques only to give in to pressure from the Transvaal secretary of state later and lift the embargo.[32] The Lisbon and Oporto republican newspapers were so vehement in their criticism of Britain that the British ambassador in Lisbon went as far as to comment on it.[33] These newspapers supported Portugal's declared neutrality in the conflict. The issue of neutrality was also raised in the House of Peers by the opposition leader, Hintze Ribeiro.[34]

The vagueness of Portuguese diplomatic policy was soon cleared up when Portugal finally chose to restore its alliance with Britain. Barros Gomes's exit from the government contributed considerably. The role of the Portuguese ambassador in London, Soveral, proved to be extremely important and in the end he was placed in direct charge of the negotiations with the British government.[35] Although Lisbon had originally declared that it was not in a position to submit a proposal, the fact is that on 3 October 1899, the minister of foreign affairs, Veiga Beirão, asked de Soveral to inform Lord Salisbury of Portugal's intention to reinstate both the secret article of the 1661 treaty on the defence of the territorial integrity of Portugal and its colonies and the article on the alliance between the two countries. Britain agreed to reinstate the secret article and, where the alliance was concerned, proposed the version of the 1642 treaty. After the rough edges had been smoothed out, such as not using Lourenço Marques as a British military base and not declaring war on the Transvaal, the two countries completed their negotiations on 6 October 1899. King D. Carlos had defended Portugal's direct involvement in the Anglo–Boer conflict in a meeting with the British ambassador in Lisbon, Hugh MacDonnell. The British government took advantage of the king's words to put pressure on Luciano de Castro's government to accept an agreement that suited British interests in South Africa.[36] Lord Salisbury and de Soveral signed the declaration at Windsor a week later. It contained the articles that had been discussed in early October. On the basis of the historic treaties of 1642 and 1661, Britain undertook to respect and defend Portuguese sovereignty, which included defending Portugal's historical territorial rights in Africa. In turn, Portugal expressly prohibited the passage of arms and munitions to the Transvaal, and, in case of war, would not declare itself neutral, which would open the door to cooperation with Britain.[37]

The Windsor treaty was kept secret however, because British diplomacy did not want to confront the Berlin government directly and wanted to leave open the possibility of returning to the 1898 agreement.[38] In spite of Portuguese diplomacy's efforts, Lisbon was not able to get the treaty announced during the visit to Lisbon by the Channel Fleet in December 1900. All that was said at the time was to reaffirm the validity of the seventeenth-century treaties, but neither side mentioned the secret Windsor declaration.[39] The British fleet's visit to Lisbon gave some pause to German diplomacy and the Berlin government questioned the British government about the feasibility of the Anglo–German convention of 1898. True to its strategy, the Foreign Office informed the German ambassador in London that the speeches in no way jeopardised Britain's understanding with the imperial government and referred only to the treaties that had already been signed with Portugal.[40] In spite of Britain's cautious game where Germany was concerned, the truth is that relations between Britain and Portugal entered a friendly phase.

The Windsor declaration obliged the Portuguese government to prevent the passage of goods and military materiel to the Transvaal via the Delagoa

Bay port and railway. The Portuguese government did not, however, completely fulfil this undertaking, claiming that it lacked the proper means to monitor shipping entering the port of Lourenço Marques.[41] Given Portugal's inability to control incoming ships, Britain offered to station a representative at the Lourenço Marques customs office. Although it first turned down the offer, the Portuguese government eventually consented to the unofficial presence of the former British consul and some other officers in Lourenço Marques. The control of goods to the Transvaal affected trade from Lourenço Marques to the republic and the local economy suffered, as it had profited from this trade.[42] It was important for the Portuguese authorities to make a list of prohibited products to avoid uncertainty and to prevent a total blockade of trade. After all, Lourenço Marques practically owed its existence to trade with the Transvaal and it was very difficult to tell which consignments were intended for the Boer troops. The Portuguese authorities tried to draw up a short list of goods that were not allowed through and gave the British consul a list of prohibited products. The British consul in Lourenço Marques welcomed this initiative on the part of the Mozambican authorities and sent the list to the Foreign Office on 8 March 1900. The version that the Foreign Office sent back was considerably longer, however.[43] On 15 May 1900, knowing nothing of these diplomatic manoeuvres, a deputy from the Partido Regenerador asked the Portuguese government whether this list existed and expressed his party's concern about the growing losses being suffered by Portuguese traders with businesses in Mozambique. In reply, Beirão said that Portuguese traders could send their goods as long as they were not for the Transvaal, but failed to mention that he had received a number of letters from Portuguese traders protesting against the seizure of their goods by the Royal Navy off the coast of Mozambique.[44]

The problems that arose around the control of goods to the Transvaal helped to mark Portugal's final position in the Boer War. In June 1900, Hintze Ribeiro's government, which had recently taken office, was obliged to settle a complaint from the British consul in Lourenço Marques about a wagon loaded with tins of corned beef bound for the Transvaal border and presumably intended for Pretoria's troops. At de Soveral's request, the new minister of foreign affairs, João Arroio, set up an enquiry to ascertain the part played by the customs authorities and the railway in this matter. The enquiry's findings confirmed the involvement of these two authorities in trying to smuggle military supplies to the Transvaal.[45] The case ended with the dismissal of the directors of the railway and of the customs authorities and with the transfer of several employees to other departments. As a result, the governor of Mozambique, Joaquim José Machado, tendered his resignation. Of all the episodes that occurred during the Boer War, this was certainly the most serious. It had been clearly proved that some Mozambican departments were working for the Boer cause in clear defiance of Portugal's commitments in the Windsor declaration.

In September 1900, Hintze Ribeiro expressly informed London of the Portuguese government's willingness to allow British troops and materiel through Lourenço Marques. His proposal was not accepted, however, and the British government suggested that the railway line should be closed to traffic instead.[46] At the time, the railway was being used as a supply line for Kruger's troops and the British army apparently had no plans to attack on that front. In reply to London's suggestion, Portugal said that any stoppage in rail traffic might provoke retaliation from the Boers and the entry of troops into Mozambique in search of food. The British subjects living in the city, who would be directly affected by this measure, also voiced their objections to the closure of the line. Faced with these arguments, London did not press the matter and, instead, reiterated its wish that Portugal should comply with its commitments to put a stop to the contraband of war supplies.[47] The close watch kept over the goods that arrived at Lourenço Marques and the checks carried out by the Royal Navy on the high seas had caused a substantial drop in trade with the Transvaal since the beginning of the Boer War. The deterioration in Mozambique's economy led Portugal to appeal to the British government to try to find a solution.

The possible solution suggested by the press and in some British and Portuguese political milieux in the first weeks of the war was to use Lourenço Marques as a military base for an attack on the Transvaal. The alternative plan was to send men and war materiel through the port of Beira. The idea of this contingency was to reinforce British troops in Rhodesia and help free the city of Mafeking, under siege by the Boers. On 2 December 1899, the Foreign Office informed the Marquis de Soveral that Britain needed to send 200 rifles and 500,000 cartridges through Beira to supply the troops near Salisbury in North Rhodesia. The request was made under the Anglo–Portuguese treaty of 1891, which had ended the dispute about the ultimatum of the previous year. Lisbon was obliged to consent.[48] On 31 January 1900, the British government informed its Portuguese counterparts that it had approved a proposal by the British South Africa Company whereby a military force would be sent to operate on the border between Rhodesia and the Transvaal.[49] The Portuguese government did not agree immediately and argued that there might be protests from the Transvaal and Germany. José Luciano de Castro was not at all convinced of the advantages that Portugal's involvement in the Boer War might bring Mozambique.[50] The British government did not accept Luciano de Castro's refusal and on 1 March it informed the Portuguese ambassador that the SS *Pondo*, loaded with animals and sundry military supplies, had sailed from the Cape bound for Beira.[51] Four days later, Lord Salisbury asked Hugh MacDonnell, British ambassador in Lisbon, to inform the Portuguese government of the need to instruct Luciano de Castro to facilitate the unloading of the goods and animals and their subsequent passage to Rhodesia. Luciano de Castro eventually agreed.[52]

On 17 March, just when everything seemed to have been settled, the British consul in Beira informed his government that the animals and supplies, which had arrived at the port at the beginning of the month, had been seized as contraband of war. Salisbury immediately informed the Portuguese ambassador of the situation and asked him to have the cargo released. De Soveral attributed the problem to the lack of coordination in the despatch of instructions to Mozambique, which must have led the Governor of Beira to confiscate the cargoes of the first ships to arrive at the port.[53] In view of the serious nature of the situation, de Soveral asked Veiga Beirão for permission to inform Lord Salisbury that the Mozambique authorities had been ordered to cooperate with the British consul without waiting for specific instructions from Lisbon.[54] If his request was denied, de Soveral was prepared to tender his resignation. Faced with de Soveral's threat to quit, Lisbon agreed and authorized the ambassador to inform the Foreign Office that instructions had been sent to Mozambique to clear up the misunderstanding. Nevertheless, the Portuguese government held its ground in the matter of Anglo–Portuguese cooperation in Mozambique, and made it contingent on the despatch of specific instructions to the Portuguese colony.

After the problem had been solved, Lord Salisbury asked de Soveral, at the meeting they had on 31 March 1900, to inform Lisbon of the British government's decision to send several more military detachments to Rhodesia. The Portuguese government would be informed of their despatch to Beira well in advance. The contingents of the Rhodesian Field Force began arriving at the port of Beira on 11 April 1900 and a total of about 5,137 men had landed there by 24 June; 7,105 horses and 1,914 mules were disembarked along with the troops.[55] As it had with the passage of the first goods and animals to Rhodesia, the Transvaal once again protested to the Portuguese government about the arrival of Lord Carrington's troops.[56] Willem Ritz, Transvaal's secretary of state, found Lisbon's policy ambiguous, as the Portuguese government had accepted the secret notes to the treaty of 1891 as the legal basis for allowing the troops through in detriment to its formal agreements with the Boer Republic in the 1875 treaty. In spite of their protests, the Boers were aware that the Portuguese had very little room for manoeuvre in South Africa.[57] What still remained to be seen for a while was what kind of support they would give Britain after war broke out. When the Transvaal found out about Portugal's concessions, it tried to take maximum advantage of the situation. As Pretoria was unable to prevent British troops from going through to Rhodesia, it tried to keep the Lourenço Marques corridor open, as it transported goods that were considered vital to its survival. This explains the moderation of the Transvaal protests.

The news of the passage of British military contingents through Beira caused a wave of alarm in the republican press in Portugal. Luciano de Castro's government was accused of complicity with Britain and of being unable to remain neutral in the conflict. References to the 1891 treaty as legitimizing this measure only served to further incense anti-British opinion, as the British ultimatum of 1890 was still fresh in the Portuguese collective memory. In the House of Deputies, the most violent criticism came from the leader of the Republican Party, Afonso Costa. On 3 April 1900, he asked the progressive government about the applicability and contents of the articles legitimizing the use of Beira by British military forces.[58] Luciano de Castro's government adopted the same strategy in both houses. It only informed parliament of that which it thought was probably already known. The aim was to try and prevent the debate on these issues from going too far and jeopardizing the difficult diplomatic negotiations with Britain.

The strategic importance of the British forces that came in via Beira turned out to be negligible, as the expedition did not achieve its objectives.[59] Their failure was due to a lack of coordination in the planning, constant delays in the disembarkation and despatch of men and animals to their quarters, the weather conditions and the tropical diseases that attacked the British contingent in Mozambique.[60] Lord Carrington's force arrived in Rhodesia physically exhausted and had to wait several weeks before it was fit enough to advance and fight. As a result, the British military command was unable to use the men who were supposed to free the city of Mafeking.[61] In the end, their contribution was to reinforce the border between Rhodesia and the Transvaal.

IV. Conclusion

Portugal's involvement in the Boer War helped to reinforce the strategic alliance between Portuguese and British interests in southern Africa. The signature of the Windsor Declaration in October 1899 was the culmination of the process that brought the two countries closer together again and ended the drift in their relations that had started after the publication of the Rose-Coloured Map in 1886, which resulted in Britain's ultimatum to Portugal in 1890.

The cooperation that the Portuguese authorities gave the British troops during the war, both by preventing the contraband of war supplies via Lourenço Marques and by allowing troops to use the port of Beira, was probably not vital to the outcome of the war. In fact, there were hardly any military operations on the border between the Transvaal and Mozambique or even on the border between the Transvaal and Rhodesia. Mozambique benefited from the new lease of life given to the alliance between Portugal and Britain. When the conflict reduced to guerrilla warfare, Hintze Ribeiro's government warned Lord Salisbury's government of the need to restore rail traffic between Pretoria and Lourenço Marques and to think about the basic terms of an agreement to regulate trade between Mozambique and the British colonies.[62] The fact that the new British colonies depended on Mozambican labour to work in their mines helped the Portuguese government to get what it wanted.

In August 1900, the Portuguese Consul in Pretoria said that it was necessary to sign a *modus vivendi* to safeguard the interests of the two countries and their colonies during the transition, and replace the suspended treaty of 1875, which would expire on 7 October 1902. Britain wanted to revive the Transvaal mines, as the exodus of Mozambican workers when war broke out had affected production. Lisbon gave in where the labour force was concerned and, in exchange, obtained a promise to maintain the pre-war tariffs on the railway lines between Pretoria and Johannesburg, which placed the Lourenço Marques line on an equal footing with the Cape and Durban lines. Portugal was also given the guarantee that, if there were any changes, they would be in proportion to the readjustments applied to the railway lines in the new British colonies. In December 1901, Lisbon and London signed a *modus vivendi* temporarily regulating trade relations between the Transvaal and Mozambique. In June 1902, however, Natal and the Cape Colony reacted and managed to get the British government to alter the agreement and limit the tariff benefits for imports from Lourenço Marques only to goods coming from the colony itself. This new rule did, however, enable Mozambican sugar exports to grow.[63] In spite of the partial setback where the tariffs were concerned, the agreement was welcomed by most of the Portuguese press, which saw it as providing an opportunity to revive the Mozambican economy. The *modus vivendi* meant that trade from Lourenço Marques could get back on its feet and opened the door to the integration of the southern Mozambique economy in the group formed by the British colonies of the future South African Union.

In spite of the difficulty that Portugal had in enforcing the provisions of the Windsor Declaration of 1899 and the negative effect that the Boer War had on the Mozambican economy, it managed to pass this test of its ability to mobilize its diplomacy in defence of its colonial empire in Africa. By granting Britain facilities in Mozambique, Portugal got Britain to publicly recognize the Anglo–Portuguese alliance, safeguard its African empire and include Mozambique in the new South African economy. Yet, within the unstable imperial policy in Africa, the agreement was doomed to last only a few years. In fact, in 1913, Britain and Germany signed a new agreement concerning the partition of Portuguese colonies. This did not have further consequences because of the war that was to break out the following year.

Notes

1. The authors would like to thank useful comments from Valentim Alexandre and Nuno Severiano Teixeira. The usual caveat applies.
2. Malyn Newitt, *A History of Mozambique* (Bloomington, Ind., 1995), cap. 15.
3. Valentim Alexandre, "Nação e Império", in *História da expansão portuguesa: Do Brasil para África, 1808–1930*, F. Bettencourt and K. Chadhuri (eds), vol. 4, 90–142 (Lisbon, 1998).
4. See further developments in Fernando Costa, *Portugal e a guerra anglo-boer: Política externa e opinião pública, 1899–1902* (Lisbon, 1998).

5. Tiyambe Zeleza, *A Modern Economic History of Africa: Vol 1, The Nineteenth Century* (Codesria, 1993), pp. 159–67 and 335–8.
6. Iain R. Smith, *The Origins of the South African War, 1899–1902* (London, 1996), p. 22.
7. P. J. Cain and A. G. Hopkins, *British Imperialism: Innovation and Expansion, 1688–1914* (London, 1993), p. 370.
8. Eric Axelson, *Portugal and the Scramble for Africa, 1875–1891* (Johannesburg, 1967), p. 12.
9. Valentim Alexandre, *Origens do colonialismo português moderno, 1822–1891* (Lisbon, 1979), pp. 179 et seq.
10. Axelson, *Portugal and the Scramble*, p. 15.
11. Axelson, *Portugal and the Scramble*, p. 13; and António Telo, *Lourenço Marques na política externa portuguesa, 1875–1900* (Lisbon, 1991) p. 28.
12. Ângela Guimarães, *Uma corrente do colonialismo português: A Sociedade de Geografia de Lisboa, 1875–1895* (Lisbon, 1984), p. 112.
13. Axelson, *Portugal and the Scramble*, pp. 27ff.; and Alexandre, *Origens do colonialismo*, pp. 176–7.
14. Guimarães, *Uma corrente do colonialismo*, pp. 115 et seq.
15. Axelson, *Portugal and the Scramble*, pp. 110–11; and Newitt, *A History of Mozambique*, p. 486.
16. Axelson, *Portugal and the Scramble*, pp. 111–13.
17. Cain and Hopkins, *British Imperialism*, p. 373.
18. Newitt, *A History of Mozambique*, p. 487.
19. James Duffy, *Portuguese Africa* (Cambridge, Mass., 1961), p. 222.
20. Smith, *The Origins*, pp. 55–6.
21. Telo, *Lourenço Marques*, pp. 130–31.
22. Guimarães, *Uma corrente do colonialismo*, pp. 122–4.
23. Smith, *The Origins*, pp. 62–6.
24. See, for example, Thomas Pakenham, *The Boer War* (New York, 1992), pp. 446–7, regarding the supply of the British troops.
25. Smith, *The Origins*.
26. On the first Anglo–German agreement of 1898 and that of 1913, mentioned below, see Nuno S. Teixeira, *O poder e a guerra, 1914–1918: Objectivos nacionais e estratégias políticas na entrada de Portugal na Grande Guerra* (Lisboa, 1996), pp. 112–36.
27. F. M. da Costa Lobo, *O conselheiro José Luciano de Castro e o segundo período constitucional monárquico* (Coimbra, 1941), p. 175.
28. R. Robinson and J. Gallagher, *Africa and the Victorians: The Official Mind of Imperialism* (London, 1992).
29. Costa Lobo, *O conselheiro José Luciano de Castro*, p. 189.
30. Bernard Porter, *The Lion's Share: A Short History of British Imperialism, 1850–1995* (London, 1996); and D. K. Fieldhouse, *Economics and Empire, 1830–1914* (London, 1984), pp. 360–62.
31. Costa Lobo, *O conselheiro José Luciano de Castro*, pp. 183–5.
32. *Report from Demétrio Cinatti, Portuguese consul in Pretoria, 10 August 1900*, Ministério dos Negócios Estrangeiros, Arquivo Histórico Diplomático (hereafter MNE/AHD), Secretaria de Estado, Consulado Geral de Portugal em Pretória (hereafter SE, CGPP) (Guerra Anglo-Boer), Box 971.
33. Public Record Office (PRO) Foreign Office (FO) 179, vol. 346, Africa, Sir Hugh MacDonell to Lord Salisbury, 8 November 1899.
34. *Diário da Câmara dos Dignos Pares do Reino,* 3 January 1900, p. 7.
35. PRO FO 179, vol. 342, Africa, p. 306, Lord Salisbury to Sir Hugh MacDonell, 13 September 1899.
36. MNE/AHD, Gabinete do Ministro, Livro de Registo de Correspondência (hereafter Gab. Min., Liv. Reg. Corr.), no. 493-E, telegram to London, 3 October 1899.
37. MNE/AHD, Gab. Min., Liv. Reg. Corr., no. 493-E. , telegram from London, 14 October 1899. PRO FO 179, vol. 342, Africa, p. 293, Lord Salisbury to Sir Hugh MacDonell, 16 October 1899.
38. In fact, in 1913, Great Britain and Germany signed a second treaty concerning the partition of African colonies in South Africa. See Teixeira, *O poder e a guerra.*
39. Luís Vieira de Castro, *D. Carlos I* (Lisbon, 1943), pp. 202–3.

40. PRO FO 179, vol. 355, p. 7, Marquis of Lansdowne to Viscount of Gough, 20 December 1900.
41. PRO FO 179, vol. 346, Africa, Report on the Anglo–Boer War and the Portuguese Government, Sir Hugh MacDonell to Lord Salisbury, 28 December 1899.
42. Newitt, *A History of Mozambique*, pp. 487–8.
43. PRO War Office (hereafter WO) 32, vol. 8343, telegram from the Foreign Office to the War Office, 9 March 1900.
44. *Diário da Câmara dos Senhores Deputados,* 15 May 1900, pp. 12–13.
45. MNE/AHD, Gab. Min., Liv. Reg. Corr., no. 497-B, telegrams to London, 22 July and 2 August 1900.
46. PRO WO 32, vol. 7908, secret telegram from Francis Bertie to the War Office, 7 September 1900; MNE/AHD, Gab. Min., Liv. Reg. Corr., 497-B, telegrams from London, 15 and 16 September 1900.
47. MNE/AHD, Gab. Min., Liv. Reg. Corr., no. 497-B, telegrams from London, 15 and 17 September 1900.
48. Nuno S. Teixeira, "O *Ultimatum* inglês: política externa e política interna no Portugal de 1890", *Análise Social* 23, 687–719 (1987).
49. PRO WO 32, vol. 7937, telegram from Sir Alfred Milner to the Colonial Office, 11 September 1900.
50. Marcelo Caetano, *Portugal e a internacionalização dos problemas africanos* (Lisbon, 1971), pp. 176ff.
51. Telegram 185. Portuguese Ambassador to London, 1 March 1999, Secretaria de Estado, Telegramas recebidos (Guerra anglo-boer), Box 970.
52. PRO FO 179, vol. 342, Africa, pp. 440–42, Foreign Office to Sir Hugh MacDonell, 3 December 1899. MNE/AHD, Gab. Min., Liv. Reg. Corr., no. 493-E, telegram from London, 2 December 1899.
53. PRO FO 179, vol. 350, Africa, telegram 16, Lord Salisbury to Sir Hugh MacDonell, 17 March 1900.
54. MNE/AHD, Gab. Min., Liv. Reg. Corr., no. 493-E , telegram from London, 19 March 1900.
55. PRO WO 32, vol. 7941, report from J. E. McMaster to the Foreign Office, 11 June 1900.
56. MNE/AHD – SE, CGPP (Guerra Anglo-Boer), Box 971, Annex 1, Document 142, report from the Portuguese consul in Pretoria to Veiga Beirão, 17 May 1900.
57. MNE/AHD – SE, CGPP (Guerra Anglo-Boer), Box 971, Documents 111 and 142, reports from the Portuguese consul in Pretoria to Veiga Beirão, 9 March and 21 April 1900.
58. *Diário da Câmara dos Senhores Deputados,* 3 April 1900, p.8.
59. PRO FO 179, vol. 351, Africa, report of the passage of British troops and military stores through Beira, Portuguese East Africa and the action of Mozambique Company in same matter. December 1899–June 1900.
60. PRO WO 32, vol. 7940, from British South Africa Company to the War Office, 30 May 1900.
61. PRO WO 32, vol. 7944, p. 6, statement by H. Seton Karr, MP (Hon. Sec. Sharpshooters Committee) in reference to the breakdown of the Beira Railway transport in May 1900 and reasons and consequences thereof. PRO WO 32, vol. 7944, from Lieut-General Sir F. Carrington KCB, Commanding Rhodesian Field Force, to Field Marshal Lord Roberts VC, GCB, etc., Commanding-in-Chief, South Africa, 25 August 1900.
62. Diana Cammack, *The Rand at War, 1899–1902: The Witwater's Rand and the Anglo-Boer War* (London, 1990).
63. G. Clarence-Smith, *The Third Portuguese Empire, 1825–1975: A Study in Economic Imperialism* (Manchester, 1985), pp. 108–9; Costa, *Portugal e a guerra anglo-boer*, pp. 192–202; and J. C. Valente Perfeito, *Lourenço Marques e o Transval* (Porto, 1909).

CHAPTER TEN

The Boer War in the Context of Britain's Imperial Problems

Keith Wilson

I

The effects of "the new imperialism" of the last quarter of the nineteenth century were felt most acutely by the British. Their relative monopoly in several areas was challenged both in theory (by the setting of new ground rules in 1884 at the Berlin Conference) and in practice. In December 1886 a Royal Commission on the Depression of Trade and Industry reported that in addition to losing her advantage in production (primarily to Germany), Britain was "beginning to feel the effects of competition in quarters where her trade formerly enjoyed a practical monopoly".[1]

One such area was the Far East. Lord Salisbury had said in 1885 that "the Power that can establish the best footing in China will have the best part of the trade of the world".[2] This deserves to be known as "the China syndrome" and, of course, it still applies. A decade later, in November 1895, Salisbury told an audience at the Guildhall, "In China there is room for us all".[3] Several Great Powers took him at his word. In July 1895 a Russian loan had been made to China. This was countered, in March 1896, by a joint Anglo–German loan. These were just preliminaries.

Shortly after matters in the Balkans were put on ice by the agreement to maintain the status quo there arrived at by Russia and Austria-Hungary in May 1897, the Far Eastern question proper was posed. In November 1897, with Russian connivance, Germany seized the port of Kiao-Chow. This was a distinct challenge to Britain, whose position for 50 years as the principal trading power with China rested on the presence of the British China Squadron at Hong Kong. Muraviev, the Russian foreign minister, wrote in a memorandum of 23 November 1897 that "the time for maintaining the integrity of China" was over.[4] Salisbury immediately offered to conclude an agreement dividing China into spheres of influence in such a way as to protect the British

stake in the Yangtze region. Indeed, in what was an extension and development of his thinking on the partition of the Ottoman Empire between 1885
and 1896, he envisaged a more general Anglo–Russian agreement, including
the Black Sea, the Straits of the Bosphorus and the Dardanelles, Arabia and
Mesopotamia:

> It is evident that both in respect to Turkey and China there are large
> portions which interest Russia much more than England and *vice
> versa*. Merely as an illustration . . . I would say that the portion of
> Turkey which drains into the Black Sea, together with the drainage
> valley of the Euphrates as far as Bagdad, interest Russia much more
> than England: whereas Turkish Africa, Arabia, and the Valley of the
> Euphrates below Bagdad interest England much more than Russia. A
> similar distinction exists in China between the Valley of the Hoango
> with the territory north of it and the Valley of the Yangtze.[5]

The Russians did not respond. In March 1898 they took what they wanted:
the ice-free port of Port Arthur, which because of its strategic location constituted a standing menace to the Chinese capital Pekin and represented therefore a source of Russian pressure on the Chinese government. The British
immediately took a lease on the less well endowed port of Wei-hei-Wei, in
sheer self-defence.

This was still only the beginning. These early developments, however, were
enough to cause some British ministers to contemplate drastic measures. The
colonial secretary, Joseph Chamberlain, was among the first to do so. In
December 1897 he had written to the prime minister, "Talking about allies,
have you considered whether we might not draw closer to Japan?"[6] In February 1898 he wrote again, this time to Balfour, who was shortly to be deputiz-
ing at the Foreign Office for a convalescent Salisbury:

> If matters remain as they are our prestige will be gone and our trade
> will follow . . . I should propose:
> 1. To approach the United States officially, and to ask an immediate
>   reply from them to the question – will you stand in with us in our
>   Chinese policy?
> 2. To approach Germany at the same time with the same definite
>   questions.[7]

An overture to the US for an alliance as regards Far Eastern matters was made
in March 1898. The Americans rejected it. Chamberlain was moved to state,
publicly, in May, "If the policy of isolation, which has hitherto been the policy
of this country, is to be maintained in the future, then the fate of China will be
decided without reference to our wishes and in defiance of our interests".[8] In
1900 the Boxer rising, largely directed against western activities in China, took

place. The Russians took advantage of this to occupy Manchuria. When the rising was put down, the Russians remained in Manchuria.

So much, for the moment, for the very Far East. The repercussions on the position of the British Empire were increased by the overlapping outbreak of war between Britain and the Boer republics in South Africa in October 1899. During this conflict Joseph Chamberlain's pre-war appreciation of the necessity for allies became much more widely held. The secretary of state for India, Lord George Hamilton, wrote to the viceroy, Lord Curzon, on 11 October 1900, "Unless we are prepared to risk something ourselves or to throw in our lot with some of the great European Powers we cannot expect them to stand in with us or to assist us in protecting our own interests".[9]

The First Lord of the Admiralty, Lord Selborne, speculated in December 1900 that "a formal alliance with Germany"' might be "the only alternative to an ever-increasing Navy and ever-increasing Navy estimates".[10] The foreign secretary, Lord Lansdowne, wrote in March 1901:

> Our South African entanglements make it impossible for us to commit ourselves to a policy which might involve us in a war (e.g. an energetic one in the Persian Gulf) unless we can assure ourselves that any obligation which we might incur would be shared by another Power.[11]

Hamilton wrote to Curzon again in April 1901:

> I am gradually coming round to the opinion that we must alter our foreign policy, and throw our lot in, for good or bad, with some other Power . . . As we now stand, we are an object of envy and of greed to all the other Powers. Our interests are so vast and ramified that we touch, in some shape or other, the interests of almost every great country in every continent. Our interest being so extended makes it almost impossible for us to concentrate sufficiently, in any one direction, the pressure and power of the Empire so as to deter foreign nations from trying to encroach upon our interests in that particular quarter.[12]

In the opinion of several senior ministers, then, Britain's own strength was no longer enough to sustain its position in the world. This was despite the facts that since 1895–96 the Army Estimates had risen more than those of any other Great Power, and the Navy Estimates had risen more than those of Russia, Germany and France combined.[13] The security of the British Empire itself was perceived to rest on a forbearance on the part of other powers, which was clearly not forthcoming: the US had annexed the Philippines and Cuba from Spain and become a Great Power in south-east Asia and the Caribbean; the French were advancing in Morocco; the Russians had remained in Manchuria, had in 1900 put pressure on Persia by making a loan on the condition that Persia receive no money from any other source for ten years; Russia had also renewed its pressure on Afghanistan, and was advancing closer to the frontiers of India with the Orenburg–Tashkent railway, which it had started to build in 1899 and was expected to complete in 1904 or 1905.

The primary threat to the British Empire undoubtedly came from Russia. Lord George Hamilton had written to Curzon in 1899, "I do not believe our position in Persia or even on the Persian gulf is such as to enable us successfully to have recourse to force to prevent the further advance of Russia".[14] The point of an agreement made with Germany on 17 October 1900 was to deter further Russian encroachments towards the Yangtze region of China. Salisbury had been forced by his Cabinet colleagues to conclude this agreement, much against his own judgement and inclination. Indeed, on the day after it was signed he wrote to Curzon:

> As to Germany I have less confidence in her than you. She is in mortal terror on account of that long undefended frontier of hers on the Russian side. She will therefore never stand by us against Russia; but is always rather inclined to curry favour with Russia by throwing us over . . . my faith in her is infinitesimal.[15]

Appreciations of Russian strength and of British weakness mounted. Selborne wrote to Curzon in April 1901, "Compared to our Empire, [Russia's] is invulnerable. We must be on the defensive in a contest because there is . . . no part of her territory where we can hit her".[16] Salisbury, lamenting the financial impact of the Boer War, wrote in September 1901, also to Curzon:

> Our main interest in the East (after China) has been the movements of the Persian Question. In the main it is a question of money. In the last generation we did much what we liked in the East by force or threats – by squadrons and tall-talk . . . but the day of individual coercive action is almost passed by. For some years to come Eastern advance must largely depend on payment, and I fear that in that race England will seldom win.[17]

The Committee of Imperial Defence, which was getting into its stride at this time, reported, on 30 December 1902, "The military position of Russia grows stronger every day and the completion of the Orenburg–Tashkent railway in or about 1905 will add immensely to the danger to which India may be exposed".[18] The British Empire would soon be vulnerable in its greatest possession to an overland attack by a Great Power. In the following week, the first week of January 1903, Selborne followed up this Committee of Imperial Defence report with another letter to Curzon, writing:

The Middle Eastern Question is the question of the future, Persia and Afghanistan. Persia is much the more difficult. We have all the cards stacked against us there, partly owing to Beach [Sir Michael Hicks Beach, Chancellor of the Exchequer], partly to the fact that we have not the men to compete with Russia on Persian soil.

He went on:

I am sure that a day will come when a Cabinet will decide that the Army Estimates must decrease in order that the Navy estimates may increase. All this has a very real bearing on the Middle Eastern Question. We had three exceptions to our naval and insular character – in three continents we had military frontiers with great land powers – the United States is great in every sense in America and Canada joins frontiers; the Dutch Republics were locally great and militarily powerful in South Africa; Russia is Russia in Central Asia.

Our diplomacy ought to save us from war with the United States, the Dutch Republics are eliminated, but we remain with all the difficulties and responsibilities of a military Power in Asia. That is the crux for us. It is easy with compulsory military service to be a great military Power for home defence or European warfare. It is easy to be a great Naval Power of a natural and continuous growth such as ours. It is a terrific task to remain the greatest Naval Power when Naval Powers are year by year increasing in numbers and in naval strength, and at the same time to be a military Power strong enough to meet the greatest Military Power in Asia.[19]

Lord George Hamilton also wrote, in February, of how the work of the Committee of Imperial Defence had brought home, especially to Selborne, Brodrick, Lansdowne and Ritchie, "a fuller sense of Britain's liability in the event of war with Russia and the magnitude of the military assistance which India would undoubtedly require".[20] In the same month the Chancellor of the Exchequer, now C. T. Ritchie, reported to the Cabinet that since 1899 expenditure had gone up by 30 million pounds, and revenue by 42 millions, but that 34 of that 42 had been raised by special war taxes. Such a level of expenditure could not be continued, in Ritchie's view, without risking severe social unrest at home.[21]

II

In these circumstances, circumstances that accelerated from the mid-1890s and which grew worse through the period of the Boer War, the question for the British government was twofold: should Britain abandon what some described as "isolation", and, if so, to whom should it turn for help in the maintenance of the British Empire and of its world position? With considerable reluctance, Salisbury had allowed Balfour to approach the US in the first months of 1898. He could not prevent Chamberlain, and others, from considering the merits of a connection with the German Empire. He allowed himself to be pushed into making an agreement with Germany in October 1900 so far as a particular part of the Far East was concerned, with, as already remarked, no great enthusiasm. Salisbury's phlegmatism, his apparent disposition to try to ride out the storm of the Boer War, proved too much for his Cabinet colleagues. In November 1900 enough of them insisted that he hand over the Foreign Office, and the conduct of foreign policy, to Lord Lansdowne. As a result, Lansdowne as foreign secretary had something in the nature of a mandate to end the recent policy, which if not regarded as one of "isolation" was certainly regarded as one of "drift".

This proved easier said than done, but, from the commencement of his foreign secretaryship, Lansdowne was on the lookout for agreements with other Powers in order to ease Britain's position and reduce the burden carried by the British Empire. Behind everything he considered was the ultimate objective of reaching an accommodation with the chief threat to the British Empire; Russia.

Although no longer foreign secretary, Salisbury was still prime minister, and throughout 1901 fought a strong rearguard action that represented, in effect, one side to an ongoing debate as to the merits of a policy of "isolation". This debate, and its outcome, reveal that the disposition to change was rather more transient than many commentators have maintained. They also reveal that "isolation" was understood as consisting of no solid commitments on the part of Britain to *European* powers.

The debate may be illustrated by two sets of remarks, both made in connection with the proposition of joining the Triple Alliance, an invitation renewed by the Germans early in 1901. In May 1901 Salisbury maintained that isolation was "a danger in whose existence we have no historical reason for believing".[22] In the following November Lansdowne stated that, "We may push too far the argument that, because we have in the past survived in spite of our isolation, we need have no misgivings as to the effect of that isolation in the future".[23]

In logic, Lansdowne clearly won that particular point; but it was Salisbury who was among the majority at the end of the debate as a whole. By November 1901, Lansdowne had decided against a full-blown defensive alliance of the kind the Germans were insisting upon. He preferred "a much more limited understanding as to policy in regard to certain matters of interest to both Powers". Of course, by November the war in South Africa had been won, and the pressure had eased to that extent. There was, however, no escaping the force of the case put forward by Salisbury in May: "The liability of having to defend the German and Austrian frontiers against Russia is heavier than that of having to defend the British Isles against France". In other words, if the main objective of British policy was the reduction of obligations as well as of the number of disputes with Russia, an alliance with Germany and her allies would be counter productive, for it would increase both. As Francis Bertie, assistant under-secretary at the Foreign Office and an advocate of an arrangement with Japan, as regards which Lansdowne had opened negotiations in July 1901, put it:

> If once we bind ourselves by a formal defensive alliance and practically join the Triplice we shall never be on decent terms with France our neighbour in Europe and in many parts of the world, or with Russia whose frontiers are coterminous with ours or nearly so over a large portion of Asia.[24]

Lansdowne came to agree with this. In November 1901 one of the objections that he stated to an alliance with Germany was "the certainty of alienating France and Russia".

By this time the Germans had fully justified Salisbury's lack of confidence in them of October 1900, by refusing to interpret the agreement of that date in the sense that would have best suited the British. Moreover, by the autumn of 1901 the press of both Britain and Germany was full of articles that seemed to suggest that the populace of the two countries were on the worst possible terms. Lord George Hamilton revealed that he was more and more impressed with revelations of German antipathy towards Britain.[25] Public opinion, not hitherto a force to be reckoned with, was now beginning to penetrate the corridors of power.

Lansdowne made clear how close he was, at heart, to Salisbury's position, and how much of an isolationist he remained, when he concluded the specific, localized alliance with Japan instead of a general one with Germany. Bertie had written on 9 November 1901 that the result of a formal defensive alliance with the German Empire would be "the sacrifice of our liberty to pursue a British world policy". On 12 December Lansdowne defended his decision to ally with Japan rather than persevere with Germany in a letter to Balfour, writing, "the chances of the *casus foederis* arising are much fewer in the case of the Anglo–Japanese agreement than they would be in that of an Anglo–German agreement. The area of entanglement seems to me much more restricted under the former".[26]

As a postscript to this debate, how easy it was for isolationists to revert to type may be illustrated by the fact that the man originally responsible for diagnosing "the British condition", Joseph Chamberlain, extolled the virtues of "splendid isolation" in a speech at Birmingham on 6 January 1902. Lord Lansdowne's often quoted arguments in the House of Lords a month later in justification of the Anglo–Japanese Alliance should be seen as a riposte to this.

In the following September Chamberlain wrote, "If the worst comes to the worst we could hold out, as our ancestors did, against the whole of them".[27] By then, Chamberlain had discovered his remedy for the malaise, and his answer to Protectionism, in a scheme for Imperial Federation and Tariff Reform.[28] Others moved in the same direction. Selborne, who in April 1903 was still prepared to keep open the option of a German alliance – "it cannot in any way serve our interests to make the cleavage between England and Germany greater", he told Curzon – was in October writing that while "in the years to come the UK by itself will not be strong enough to hold its proper place alongside of the United States, or Russia, and probably not Germany . . . the British Empire could hold its own on terms of more than equality", and "from UK to Empire can only be done through the tariff".[29]

III

The Anglo–Japanese Alliance of February 1902 appeared to solve, or at least to reduce temporarily, Britain's problem in the Far East. In Japan the British had found, as the French put it, their "soldier" in the Far East, although, given the influence of the Admiralty on this matter,[30] "sailor" might have been more appropriate nomenclature. The Anglo–Japanese Alliance, however, did not mark a distinct and categorical change in British policy; it was merely a tactical device designed to enable Britain to continue to function as a world power. In this respect Britain's main opponents remained Russia, and, to a lesser extent, France. These were the powers against whom, as from 1901, the Two-Power Standard of naval building was directed, instead of against the combined battle fleets of whichever two powers possessed at any one time the largest fleets. (It was considered impossible for Britain to take into account the fleets, actual and potential, of the US, Germany, and Japan.) Despite overtures to the French early in 1902, overtures that included the idea of deploying the new king, Edward VII, on a state visit, the French foreign minister, Théophile Delcassé, remained adamantly opposed to any agreement with Britain that did not include the British evacuation of Egypt. Delcassé remained of this persuasion until after November 1902, when the internal collapse of Morocco concentrated the French mind on the support that Britain might afford in helping the French to achieve their own selfish objectives there.[31] The main goal of British policy, and what all the tactical devices that Lansdowne had resort to – including the alliances with Japan of 1902 and 1905, the commitment to Afghanistan of March 1905, and the declarations that Britain would consider the establishment of another Power within the Persian Gulf as an unfriendly act – were intended to help secure, namely an understanding with Russia, was secured only after Russia, in turn, had been brought round, and to the negotiating table, by its defeat in the Far East at the hands of Japan and by the internal disorders that ensued. It was thanks to the Moroccans and the Japanese that the British were able to escape the calling of their imperial bluff.

Notes

1. Final Report of the Royal Commission on the Depression of Trade and Industry, *Parliamentary Papers*, 1886 (C4893), p. xxiii.
2. H. Sutherland Edwards, *Sir William White: His Life and Correspondence* (London, 1902), p.11, Salisbury to White, 30 September 1885.
3. *The Times,* 11 November (1895).
4. A. Popov, "Pervia Shagi Russkogo Imperializma na Dal'nem Vostoke", *Krasnyi Arkhiv,* 52 (1932), pp.103ff.; W. L. Langer, *The Diplomacy of Imperialism 1890–1902* (New York, 1951), pp. 457–8.
5. G. P. Gooch and H. W. V. Temperley (eds), *British Documents on the Origins of the War, 1898–1914* (11 vols, London, 1926–38) vol. 1, no. 9, Salisbury to O'Conor, 25 January 1898.
6. J. L. Garvin, *Life of Joseph Chamberlain* (London, 1934) vol. 3, p. 249, Chamberlain to Salisbury, 31 December 1897.
7. Blanche E. C. Dugdale, *Arthur James Balfour* (London, 1936) vol. 1, pp. 252–3, Chamberlain to Balfour, 3 February 1898.
8. *The Times,* 14 May 1898.
9. G. M. Monger, *The End of Isolation* (London, 1963), p.19, Hamilton to Curzon, 11 October 1900.
10. D. George Boyce (ed.), *The Crisis of British Power: The Imperial and Naval Papers of the Second Earl of Selborne, 1895–1910* (London, 1990), p. 106, Selborne to Hicks Beach, 29 December 1900.
11. J. A. S. Grenville, "Lansdowne's abortive project of 12 March 1901 for a secret agreement with Germany", *Bulletin of the Institute of Historical Research* 27 (1954), pp. 211–12, Lansdowne to Lascelles, 18 March 1901.
12. Monger, *The End of Isolation*, pp. 36–7, Hamilton to Curzon, 25 April 1901.
13. *Ibid.*, pp. 8–9.
14. Lord Ronaldshay, *Life of Lord Curzon* (London, 1928) vol. 2, p. 100, Hamilton to Curzon, 2 November 1899.
15. Monger, *The End of Isolation*, p. 17, Salisbury to Curzon, 17 October 1900.
16. Boyce, *The Crisis of British Power*, p. 5, Selborne to Curzon, 19 April 1901.
17. Monger, *The End of Isolation*, p. 5, Salisbury to Curzon, 23 September 1901.
18. Second Report of a Committee to consider the military defence of India, 30 December 1902, PRO CAB 38/1/14.
19. Curzon MSS, India Office Library (hereafter IOL) MSS, Eur. F111/229, Selborne to Curzon, 4 January 1903.
20. Monger, *The End of Isolation*, p. 111, Hamilton to Curzon, 27 February 1903.
21. Memorandum by Ritchie, 21 February 1903, PRO CAB 37/64/15.
22. Gooch and Temperley, *British Documents*, vol. 2, no. 86, memorandum by Salisbury, 29 May 1901.
23. Gooch and Temperley, *British Documents*, vol. 2, no. 92, memorandum by Lansdowne, 11–21 November 1901.
24. Gooch and Temperley, *British Documents*, vol. 2, no. 91, memorandum by Bertie, 9 November 1901.
25. Monger, *The End of Isolation*, pp. 62–3, Hamilton to Curzon, 22, 29 November 1901.
26. Balfour MSS, British Library (hereafter BL) Add. MSS 49727, Lansdowne to Balfour, 12 December 1901.

27. Monger, *The End of Isolation*, p. 107, Chamberlain to Devonshire, 22 September 1902.
28. J. Darwin, "The Fear of Falling: British Politics and Imperial Decline since 1900", *Transactions of the Royal Historical Society* (1986), p. 31.
29. Curzon MSS, IOL, Eur. F111/229, Selborne to Curzon, 24 April, 21 October 1903.
30. Z. S. Steiner, "Great Britain and the Creation of the Anglo–Japanese Alliance", *Journal of Modern History* 31, 27–36 (1959).
31. C. Andrew, *Théophile Delcassé and the Making of the Entente Cordiale* (London, 1968), pp. 180–200.

CHAPTER ELEVEN

The British in Delagoa Bay
in the Aftermath of the Boer War
Annexation, Partition or Independence

Sandra Ferreira

I. Introduction

The British in Delagoa Bay (Lourenço Marques) were an economically influential community.[1] They formed the largest group of foreigners in Portuguese East Africa's capital city during the first half of the twentieth century. A London daily newspaper described them as "the most progressive and wealthy community at the port".[2] They were state contractors and comprised the comprador elite. Together with their Portuguese agents, they engaged in speculative activities, and dominated the economic sectors of shipping, handling agencies, insurance and large-scale importation.

Given Delagoa Bay's strategic position, in terms of trade, transport and labour links with the southern African region, the presence of British capital and enterprise was important, as a means of securing control – both economic and political – over the port. This was particularly the case after the end of the Boer War (1899–1902). No longer essential to the political and economic independence of a British-controlled Transvaal, Delagoa Bay was, nevertheless, still a crucial factor in maintaining the flow of manual labour for the mining industry. The impact of British capital penetration, and its role in the stimulation of systematic economic colonialism in Mozambique was evident in many sectors of the economy. The activities targeted included the chartered companies, wholesale and retail distribution, economic and supportive infrastructures, the import/export trade, plantation agriculture and, less successfully, mining. Although the promotion of British private enterprise in East Africa was part of a post-"scramble" Foreign Office policy aimed at British territories, the effects were nevertheless felt in Portuguese East Africa.

During the Boer War, the strategic value of Delagoa Bay was reiterated, as control of the port and railway proved essential for Britain's successful isolation of the Transvaal from outside aid.[3] Once the British hold over the gold fields and the Boer Republic was consolidated, British regional hegemony was established. Interest in Delagoa Bay persisted, however, as this corridor of access to British-controlled interior remained in Portuguese hands. Since the end of the Boer War, Delagoa Bay had suffered the administrative disorganization, economic crisis and metropolitan indifference to regional politics that characterized the last years of monarchical rule in the colony. Although the plea of both settlers and local administration for greater autonomy was supported by the British business community in Delagoa Bay, not all elements of the Portuguese population welcomed the foreign presence and influence.

The extent of British influence was visible in attempts to affect local politics. Events between 1902 and 1910, show how the town's relationship with this community conditioned responses both to economic pressure and to regional challenges. This is most evident during the events of 1910 in both the Portuguese colony (with the declaration of the Republic) and in South Africa (with the Act of Union). The advent of the new regime once more brought to the fore the international debate on the future of the Portuguese colonies in Africa. Rumours of a possible annexation by the recently formed Union of South Africa fuelled the unrest of the local Portuguese population. Republicanism was, for this population, synonymous with anti-British sentiment. The possibility of a local revolt to declare an autonomous state was regarded as a real alternative, desirable to the Union, if not to British and Portuguese authorities.

Britain's reaction to the events of 1910 and afterwards would be conditioned by the economic and political significance of the British community at Delagoa Bay. However, imperial authorities had to balance the protection of local interests with considerations of wider regional politics. These were the sometime problematic priorities of "greater union" within British southern Africa, in order to safeguard economic interests that included Delagoa Bay; and the delimitation of spheres of influence in the context of Anglo–German rivalry in the area, in the aftermath of the Boer War.

II. British presence in Delagoa Bay

Delagoa Bay had, since the eighteenth century, served as a trading port for the hinterland of the south-eastern region of Africa, extending west to the Transvaal and south to Natal and Zululand. A permanent Portuguese settlement was established in the 1790s. British interest in the port dated from the nineteenth century, when the opening of a British trading station at Port Natal created competition for a stake in the commerce of the southern hinterland of Delagoa Bay.[4] However, by its geographical logic, Delagoa Bay was the closest natural access to the coast for the Transvaal, providing the landlocked territory with a port "potentially free from British control".[5] In 1882 a treaty of commerce and friendship was concluded between that Boer Republic and Portugal. The resulting conflict of interests between Boers and British would lead both to repeatedly challenge Portuguese possession of the port.[6]

The British trading policy in southern Africa determined subsequent diplomatic and commercial efforts: to maintain paramountcy over the Boer Republic and trade, not through direct rule, but through control of the only seaport with access to the interior. The mineral revolution in South Africa during the 1870s and 1880s added another factor to the equation. The significance of Delagoa Bay grew as industrialization in South Africa created a regional economy, which encompassed southern Mozambique. The port's importance was strategic (given its potential as a commercial or military naval base), economic (both as a threat to British trade and investment in the Transvaal, and as a competitor to the Cape and Natal ports) and political (as a means of influencing events in the Transvaal).[7]

In 1900 Delagoa Bay had over 3,000 white inhabitants. The town's involvement in the Boer War as a port of refuge and armament for the British forces explains why the numbers of foreigners exceeded 1,000 for the first time in that year. The British formed the largest group, with a population of 1,186, making up almost half of the foreign residents.[8] In 1912, the town's foreign inhabitants numbered 1,299 out of a total white population of 5,324. The British were again the largest group, and, in many ways, Delagoa Bay catered specifically for the needs of this community. Apart from the English-language newspapers, the city also had its own British Club and Caledonian Society, as well as sporting facilities, such as the lawn tennis and cricket clubs.[9] There was an English library and two private schools.[10] Charity organization included the British Relief Fund and the Seaman's Institute. Both were administered by the British consul and run by commissions composed of representatives of the Wesleyan and English churches, and the port chaplain. The Fund, founded in 1912, aided British subjects in need.[11] The Institute organized a library and games room for the use of British sailors passing through Delagoa Bay.

III. Foreign capital in Portuguese East Africa

The presence of foreign capital in the Portuguese colony was in part the consequence of a metropolitan economy weakened by recession and threatened with bankruptcy in the last decades of the nineteenth century.[12] The generalized recession of the 1870s hit Portugal more severely than the leading industrial countries. With the growth of balance of payments deficits and the fall in public revenues, Portugal was unable to service its foreign debts and faced bankruptcy in the 1890s. The extension of protected markets by colonial expansion, as a response to the crisis, was seen as a motive for

Portugal's part in the "scramble for Africa". The costs of "effective occupation", (in the form of "pacification campaigns" and in investments on infrastructure in Portuguese East Africa) increased colonial deficits, thus contributing, if on a modest scale, to the financial crisis of the 1890s. The critical economic situation worsened political agitation, which was brought about by Portugal's losses at the Berlin Conference and the territorial rivalry that culminated in the 1890 Ultimatum.[13]

As Portugal's main financiers and creditors, Britain, France and Germany did not neglect the opportunity to exploit the Portuguese colonies, directly (through local investments) or indirectly (using migrant labour from the Portuguese territories).[14] Consequently, from 1890 onwards, large quantities of foreign capital entered the Portuguese Empire. By the late 1920s, British capital interests in the colony were estimated as totalling over £20,000,000.[15] Between 1870 and 1936, foreign investments in Portuguese East Africa totalled £35 million. Along with the £32 million invested in Angola, this amounted to 6 per cent of all international investments in sub-Saharan Africa during this period. In contrast, the Union of South Africa absorbed 43 per cent, due mainly to the mining industry. More than half of the foreign capital in Portuguese Africa was English (principally from London), with investments per capita averaging £10 – one quarter of that of the Rhodesias and one fifth of that in the Union of South Africa.[16] Portuguese reluctance to invest in the colonies was due to government policy that offered subsidies and monopolistic concessions in order to revitalize the domestic economy. Consequently, Portuguese East Africa's transport infrastructures, chartered company economy and banking establishments were largely built with foreign capital.

In 1909, the Portuguese administrator who would become the Lourenço Marques district governor, described British interests in the colony:

> Mozambique is infiltrated by English capital, the English language, English customs, and other influences of this nature, and Lourenço Marques, above all, in intimate contact with the southern colonies, has to live in harmony with them, to adjust itself, in a sense, to their way of life, and to accompany them in their process of government.[17]

In Delagoa Bay, British investments targeted banking, land and infrastructure development, and the port and rail commercial network.

IV. Banking

The use of British gold and silver was widespread throughout the coastal regions and particularly among the floating population of Delagoa Bay. Local commerce dealt in this currency despite the 1897 prohibition of the circulation of foreign silver. The advantages were such that the Lourenço Marques Commercial Association, whose members included both Portuguese and English traders, repeatedly petitioned the authorities with a view to obtaining the right to trade freely in English silver.[18] The only exception to the 1897 decree was made for African labourers returning from the Transvaal, who were encouraged by the authorities to pay their taxes in English gold.[19] Portuguese and English traders alike complained of the constantly varying rate of exchange, the scarcity of Portuguese silver, and the severity of the penalties set out in the 1897 decree, which made its application impracticable and therefore its abeyance generalized. Furthermore, the trading relationship with the Transvaal resulted in payments frequently being made in pounds. Faced with such difficulties, legal tender for English silver, or the adoption of gold as a common currency for the region south of the Save was proposed. For political reasons, the suggestion was not taken up.[20] In 1916 the circulation of foreign coins was, again, prohibited and the tolerance extended to English money withdrawn.[21]

When the banking monopoly held by the Banco Nacional Ultramarino throughout the Portuguese empire was revoked in Portuguese East Africa in 1891, British banks entered the territory.[22] By the 1920s, the Banco Nacional Ultramarino was the only Portuguese bank with an agency in Delagoa Bay. The others were of British and/or South African origin, namely the Bank of Africa Ltd., Standard Bank of South Africa Ltd., the National Bank of South Africa Ltd., and African Banking Corporation Ltd. Through them, British companies would finance land purchases, investments and development projects.[23]

V. Land and infra-structure development

Spurred by the mineral revolution in South Africa in the 1870s, Lourenço Marques became a rapidly expanding urban centre. Public works were undertaken and the city was equipped with basic amenities. Portuguese authorities raised the capital needed to develop infrastructures by granting monopoly concessions for the operations of services to British and South African companies between 1885 and 1902. The city's water supplies, telephone and public tramway systems came under the monopoly control of the English-financed Delagoa Bay Development Corporation. This same company had a substantial share in the electricity company and was proprietor of large tracts of land.[24] Both the Delagoa Bay Development Corporation and their interests, such as the local representatives of Wenela, the firm Breyner and Wirth, used Portuguese businessmen as agents.[25]

When analysing the capital of firms registered in Lourenço Marques's Commercial Court, the governor-general, Freire de Andrade, concluded, in

1907, that Portuguese investments represented only 3.5 per cent. Foreign capital, predominantly British, accounted for 86.3 per cent. Asian capital constituted the remaining 10.2 per cent.[26] In 1913, it was estimated that Britons or British Indians owned 70 per cent of all residences and business plots.[27] Union financial groups in control of Rand mines were among the property holders.[28]

English property owners, merchants, and industrialists were among the founders of the Câmara do Comércio de Lourenço Marques (Lourenço Marques Chamber of Commerce) and the Associação Comercial de Moçambique (Mozambican Commercial Association); they were allowed to vote and could be elected to the board of directors. These associations acted as pressure groups, lobbying the local authorities in an attempt to influence colonial politics.[29] The fear that Lourenço Marques would fall either directly or indirectly into British hands prompted Portuguese authorities to regain the controlling interest in the city's services. Consequently, port operations, electricity, water and communications were all state or municipality owned by the 1920s.[30]

VI. Railway and port commercial network

Linked to the neighbouring British-controlled territories by a dense rail and commercial network, Delagoa Bay was made part of the South African consumer nexus. This contributed to "increasing the prosperity of Lourenzo Marques, which became the most important port between Durban and Suez".[31] The railways of South Africa were, until 1890, confined to the British colonies, with the exception of the 89 kilometre line from Delagoa Bay to Ressano Garcia, on the border with the Transvaal. This line was of political significance as it was intended to lessen the Transvaal's dependence on the British colonial railway system.[32] English companies and capital were responsible, until 1910, for the expansion of Mozambique's railway: 60 kilometres from Delagoa Bay to Mailana on the Swaziland border; 16 kilometres of the Chai-Chai line; and 27 kilometres of the Maquival line. Two-thirds of the Portuguese colonial railway network was privately owned (by Portuguese and English entrepreneurs), while the remainder was nationalized. Questions of conflicting railway administration, rate adjustments and the amalgamation of South African railways were topics discussed during the negotiations of the 1909 Convention.[33] Railway interests were of paramount importance given the role of Delagoa Bay as a port primarily dependent on its transit traffic.

After 1902, the shipping companies operating in Delagoa Bay and the British ports obtained a monopoly of the carrying trade by entering a combine. It sought to prevent rate wars and guard against the intrusion of outside firms into the shipping trade of South Africa.[34] In order to handle the transit trade and shipping activities, British South Africa built and staffed a modern wharf complex.[35]

Furthermore, Portuguese East Africa was included in the South Africa Postal Union embracing Transvaal, the Cape, Natal, Orange Free State and Rhodesia. A post office savings bank (Caixa Económica Postal), established in 1911, allowed the reciprocal transfer of balances between the colony, Portugal, the Union of South Africa and Southern Rhodesia. Finally, the Eastern and South African Telegraph Company controlled cables services, with lines from Durban direct to Delagoa Bay and three other towns.[36]

VII. The Portuguese, foreigners and local politics

The British presence met with a mixed response among the local population, particularly in Delagoa Bay and Beira, where English was said to be spoken almost as much as Portuguese. An active settler press expressed these views. In 1908, there were 15 newspapers in Delagoa Bay.[37] Three of these were under English ownership and editorship, being published wholly in English and with offices in various South African towns.[38] A further two, under Portuguese editorship, were bilingual.[39] The tone of the journalism was personal and opinionated, with an ongoing rivalry between the writers of Portuguese and English-language newspapers. Great care was taken in scanning publications from the neighbouring – mainly South African – territories, as a source of information.

The colonial administration itself was aware of the division of the population in pro- and anti-British factions. Local administrators, such as the governor-general, Augusto Freire de Andrade, were adamant in the defence of the economic benefits derived from the British presence in Delagoa Bay. It was believed that the British "would not look at the flag that covers them, and will only unite themselves to tear it down when it no longer gives them the protection they justly deserve".[40] This sentiment was reciprocated, with a bilingual weekly stating that "the commercial element of this town has always found in the governor-general a ready helper and willing listener to their claims, exaggerated and contrary to the general interests of the place although these have often been".[41]

British supporters, among them the governor-general, viewed legal impediments to the settlement of foreigners as the practical effects of a xenophobic colonial administration and public opinion. Two of the main concerns were the land concession laws and Delagoa Bay's municipal regime. In the first instance, the plethora of land laws passed since the 1890s had in common the distinction between Portuguese and foreign purchasers, in contrast with the legislation in neighbouring territories.[42] This distinction, along with the instability of the laws, the costs of drawn-out bureaucratic processes, and the complexity of the colony's tax system, created obstacles to the organized development of Delagoa Bay. As the aims of the Portuguese in Delagoa Bay rarely included long-term dedication to agriculture, many sought easy fortunes through speculative land purchases and sales to foreigners, a process that was seen as harmful.[43] Delagoa Bay received its first municipal government in 1877. Since 1897 however, a commission (comissão municipal) of five members chosen by the governor-general had replaced the elected municipal body (câmara municipal). The opposition of officials, eager to retain all power in their hands, and the apathy of Portuguese colonialists were responsible for this alteration. Consequently, the municipal council was powerless for many years. There was little interest in local politics, as there was no Portuguese population of a significant size with a long-term economic stake in Delagoa Bay. Those who possessed such a stake – namely the British – were, by law, not eligible for election or appointment. During Freire de Andrade's tenure, the local press and commercial associations campaigned for a change in the regime. The demands included that a property and/or income qualification should be established, irrespective of nationality, in imitation of the South African colonies.[44] The desire was to transform the câmara into an active body of an economic nature.[45] The indigenous population was excluded from government.

The anti-British sectors condemned this attitude as favouritism resulting in denationalization. Rivals ridiculed English-language newspapers, such as the *Delagoa Bay Gazette* and the *Lourenço Marques Guardian*, for their constant praise of the governor-general.[46] Freire de Andrade was censured for "the scandalous protection given to the English workers and the monomania of filling our public offices with British employees".[47] The emotive language used suggests that the issue was used to whip-up great public indignation. Other situations came under attack by the anti-British faction of the local press. These included the foreign administration of the port and railway and the political power exercised through commercial and industrial associations where English businessmen constituted a majority. The monopoly of public services and labour recruitment was also criticized, as was the preferential treatment of English newspapers that received government subsidies. There were also irregularities in land concessions such as unauthorized purchases by the British consul.[48] The bitter tone of the criticism was extended to the Anglo–Portuguese Alliance, portrayed as the root of the unequal relationship in Britain's advantage, and visible in Delagoa Bay's commerce:

England antagonises us, desiring even our sources of wealth . . . In addition, the campaign of slander against our colonial administration is, in truth, in our sincerest opinion and with the purest of intentions, proofs of the ferocious egoism of English commerce and the hypocrisy of its processes! No! The English are not our friends. They are merely our allies.[49]

This ever-present tension would be aggravated by the problems afflicting Delagoa Bay prior to 1910.

VIII. Delagoa Bay to 1910: crisis and controversy

After the end of the Boer War in 1902, the prospects of profits offered by the resumption of mining caused a boom in capitalist construction in the Transvaal.[50] Given the importance of the mining industry in terms of labour supply and rail links, southern Mozambique benefited. Delagoa Bay's transit trade increased in volume, positively affecting the commercial sector, as the greater demand for consumer imports was created by higher social wages and an increase in workers' savings repatriated to Delagoa Bay.[51]

The prosperity was short-lived. In 1903 the European capital market for the South African gold mining industry collapsed. The economic crash, marked by the decrease of capital investments in the Transvaal, was echoed in the neighbouring colony. Consequently, the slump caused a decline in the transit trade and smaller amounts of savings entered the Delagoa Bay economy.[52] By 1905, a deep commercial depression began to be felt in Delagoa Bay. In order to remedy the situation, the governor-general wanted the freedom to promote development by altering land concession laws and municipal government. However, a 1908 decree withdrew the authorization of the provincial government to alter the colonial budget. To protest against the centrally dictated colonial budget and a new 25 per cent municipal tax, the Lourenço Marques Commercial Association – a pro-British lobby – sent a delegation to Lisbon. The commercial associations of the capital and Porto were also contacted, in the hope that they would lobby the central authorities on the colony's behalf.[53] No response was forthcoming.

By 1909, matters had deteriorated. When Freire de Andrade went to Portugal on leave, rumours of his imminent resignation spread, intensifying the antagonism between his supporters and detractors. The foreign community cabled Premier Campos Henriques requesting the governor-general's return. The new budget dictated a reduction in the port operation costs and workers were made redundant. Consequently, tension increased between Portuguese East Africa and the Transvaal as they negotiated a new rail port and labour convention.[54] With no workers, the port closed and the railway came to a standstill. Three hundred families were reported starving.

In January 1909, the majority of retail and wholesale stores closed in protest at the Lisbon government's refusal to see the delegation. Armed policemen patrolled the streets in anticipation of violent confrontation. A day later, members of the Lourenço Marques Commercial Association voted to reopen for business, but suspended all orders made to Portugal. The episode deepened the animosity towards the British community when certain businessmen refused to join the protest. The British consul complained to the Delagoa Bay authorities that English businessmen had been coerced into closing, from fear that they would suffer damage at the hands of the local population.[55] As complaints persisted, the high inflation rate and depreciating currency caused a decrease in settler purchasing power. As better management in neighbouring territories allowed prices to drop, Delagoa Bay became increasingly uncompetitive commercially. Although the port and railway resumed activity, and Freire de Andrade returned in May 1909, the crisis was not alleviated. If anything, local agitation had grown to proportions considered worrying by the British consul in Delagoa Bay.[56]

For the settlers, administrative disorganization and the perceived indifference of central government aggravated the plight of Delagoa Bay. The period in question saw the consolidation of political power in southern Mozambique, in the wake of military conquest. The tension between centralizing and decentralizing tendencies continued to characterize colonial policy, although central control was viewed as detrimental to colonial development, particularly after the 1890s. Portuguese colonial authorities gradually recognized that "either we organise our colonial dominion rapidly and solidly, or we shall see it, very shortly, reduced to fragments of territory without value and ports without trade".[57]

In Delagoa Bay, demands for autonomy increased. In Lisbon, parliamentarians and politicians received petitions urgently requesting reforms. Among the petitioners were elected members of the Portuguese East Africa government council, associations, companies, farmers, newspaper owners, property owners, European and Asian merchants, Portuguese and foreign industrialists, and ship owners and forwarding agents.[58] The tone of press agitation contained, not infrequently, ill disguised threats. [59] While politicians and law makers in Lisbon were vehemently described as "legions of parasites" and "egotistical and ambitious men ignorant of local circumstances",[60] the government systems of the neighbouring British colonies were praised for being "as progressive in the ideas they obey as they are prosperous in the results obtained".[61] Although an administrative reorganization was carried out in 1907, it failed to create organs of settler democracy, despite the governor-general's lobbying in favour of greater autonomy.

Added to the sense of abandonment felt by the population, was the fear of what the political evolution in the South African territories would entail for the future of Delagoa Bay. The relationship between the Transvaal and southern Mozambique had, since the late nineteenth century, consisted of the migration of Mozambican workers to the Transvaal gold and coal mines. In exchange, a sizeable proportion of Transvaal's seaborne import traffic passed through Delagoa Bay and Portuguese East African goods had a duty-free entry into the Transvaal. To regulate this relationship, a temporary *modus vivendi* was signed in 1901 between the Mozambican colonial government and the Transvaal (ZAR).

If, on the one hand, the constant supply of low-paid manual workers was profitable to the mines, the preferential customs treatment given to a foreign port was, on the other, viewed as detrimental to Cape and Natal commercial and agricultural interests.[62] Opposition from these colonies increased as, in the course of preparations for unification, a permanent Convention was negotiated in 1909. Questions were raised over the control of Delagoa Bay's port and railway, while in Delagoa Bay "profound apprehension has been awakened by the uncertainty as to what she stands to gain or loose by the outcome of the deliberations now proceeding".[63]

The implications of unification were, however, perceived differently by Portuguese East Africa and South Africa. In common they had the underlying belief, expressed in the Selborne Memorandum, that "it is not by promises but by mutual interests that communities are bound together",[64] although the resulting arguments were opposing.

Given southern Mozambique's economic dependence on the Transvaal, Portuguese East Africa's governor-general feared that the vocal opposition of Natal and the Cape to the renegotiations of the *modus vivendi* would lead to the total exclusion of southern Mozambique from talks on customs and railway unification. With regard to the political aspects of the proposed union, Freire de Andrade thought Transvaal participation unlikely due to economic factors:

> Governments may want it, but the people will only begrudgingly allow it. One has only to see what is happening with the Transvaal and Rhodesia, where both territories aspire to free themselves of the shackles of the southern ports, and have sought the cheapest road to the sea.[65]

This opinion was echoed in the Selborne Memorandum, maintaining that material consideration were often stronger than patriotism:

> Whatever conventions and arrangements are made, be the people of the various communities of South Africa ever so united by common blood, be the physical boundaries which divide them ever so slight, so long as the political arrangements are such that the Transvaal has materially more to gain by traffic with Portugal than with her sister Colonies, her sympathies will unite her with Delagoa Bay, and divide her from them . . . The material interests of the Transvaal will become so involved with Delagoa Bay that it may in the end prove impossible to unite British South Africa.[66]

While the Earl of Selborne used the spectre of this undesirable option to encourage a closer cooperation between South African territories, Freire de Andrade saw it as a chance to "frankly adhere to a truly grand policy, as is

South Africa's, and admit that the Portuguese colonies, whilst remaining Portuguese, may have an important role to play or even openly enter the South African federation".[67] His enthusiasm was not, however, shared by central government, which viewed the situation from a different angle.

Given the pressing domestic situation and its apparent reluctance to respond to local demands for reform, Lisbon authorities were criticized as "revealing a most complete incomprehension of the current political situation in southern Africa and of the risky diplomacy that we must adopt".[68] Nevertheless, inaction was not synonymous with ignorance. Since the 1890 Ultimatum, the Portuguese government was acutely aware of imperialist designs on and the penetration of foreign capital into the African empire, particularly after the existence of a secret Anglo–German agreement regarding Portuguese Africa was leaked. However, the reality of Portugal's dependence on the neighbouring economy dictated its stance in the customs, railway and labour negotiations with the southern African authorities prior to 1910. As customs duties and recruitment-related charges became the single largest source of colonial income, dependence was inevitable. Given the difficulties in kick-starting the local economy, government policy opted for making the most of the colony's geographic position by servicing production in the more developed inland territories. The relationship was regulated by convention. The control and exploitation of this sector of the state's revenue was in this way guaranteed. Hence the mining industry monopoly on labour recruitment in southern Mozambique, in exchange for a percentage of the Transvaal's trade through Delagoa Bay.

In South Africa, newspapers[69] such as Durban's *Natal Advertiser* argued that the leasing of Delagoa Bay from Portugal was the only means to "end this never-ending and intolerable struggle between egoisms and interests", although it recognized this option as "totally impractical".[70] British parliamentarians questioned the colonial authorities on the truth of lease rumours,[71] while in the rest of Europe, the possibility of the cession of Delagoa Bay to Britain was circulated by Reuter's agency.[72] Others, such as the Pretoria News, presented Portuguese East Africa's participation in unification as the solution to its budget problems.[73]

In Delagoa Bay newspapers, South African press comments were often discredited as "extraordinary rumours", "extraordinary statements" and "press agitation". Describing local apprehension about the possible participation of the Transvaal in the Union, the British consul reported that "the feeling now is that should that colony become a partner in an unassailable amalgamation of South African states, local interests have little to hope and all to fear from such a combination".[74] However, despite the patent distrust of foreigners in certain sectors, settler discontent expressed itself both as the desire to emulate the neighbouring territories, and as implicit threats to take events into their own hands, with the two often being synonymous.[75] If the entry of southern Mozambique were not to prove feasible, Freire de Andrade warned of the alternative. For unified South Africa, given the threat that Delagoa Bay posed, the options were "to try and neutralise us by taking charge of our ports, either through a lease . . . or through the use of force".[76]

IX. The Portuguese Republic and Britain

The Portuguese Revolution of 5 October 1910 aimed at overthrowing the monarchy and establishing a republic. Middle-class intellectuals and professionals, in response to a national crisis that involved a dysfunctional political system, economic and financial stagnation, and increasing social discontent, carried it out.[77] Once in power, the provisional government sought international recognition and aid, in order to guarantee the survival of the fledgling regime.

Britain officially recognized the new republic in late 1911.[78] When compared to the prompt diplomatic support offered by other countries,[79] the attitude of Portugal's oldest ally seems cautious. Furthermore, Britain's example in delaying recognition until a constitutional assembly had been elected and a constitution approved was followed by other European powers. However, prior to the revolution the Portuguese Republican Party had, in August 1910, dispatched a deputation to the British Foreign Office to determine whether a continuation of the Anglo–Portuguese alliance was desired.[80] Overall, the British government and British opinion wanted the Anglo–Portuguese alliance to continue, but more than ever on British terms. These appeared to include absolute freedom to criticize any and all aspects of Portugal's management of her affairs, and to apply any pressure to Portugal that not only British interests but vague ideas of international standards of conduct seemed to require. Few allowances were made for the republic's difficulties in establishing itself against irreconcilable opponents supported by a hostile neighbour, or for Lisbon's perennial problem of maintaining Portuguese authority in the colonies.[81]

The republicans had been assured of Britain's neutrality in the dispute over the regime. The question that worried the provisional government was whether the British guarantee of independence and overseas possessions, most recently reiterated by the 1899 Treaty of Windsor, would end.[82] In the British Foreign Office, opinions diverged between those who thought the misrule of the Portuguese colonies would hinder the alliance unless the republican government implemented the reforms desired by Britain, and those who believed that these reprehensible aspects were irrelevant to the essence of the alliance.[83] This consisted of the importance of the Portuguese Atlantic possessions for British trade routes and communications.[84]

The uncertainty regarding the maintenance of the alliance was relevant to Delagoa Bay in that the port's situation served as a pretext for speculation on the future of the Portuguese colonies as a whole. London newspapers, followed closely by the French and German press,[85] stirred public opinion with speculations that "if Portugal is unable to maintain its colonies, who knows what devil awaits to take them over, and the consequences for European peace will be devastating".[86] Although the Foreign Secretary publicly stated that "one does not make new friendships worth having by deserting old ones",[87] the Portuguese minister in London was aware that Mozambique's inefficient administration could, if Britain so desired, become a potentially serious issue in Anglo–Portuguese relations: "At the slightest news of disturbances in Lourenço Marques, all the English press proclaim with one voice that it is quite inadmissible that we should retain possession of that vital port, on which the prosperity of the Union depends".[88]

The alliance was, nevertheless, maintained as a whole. Despite this, Britain used the colonial issue as a basis for rapprochement with Germany,[89] and this would have implications for reaction to events in Delagoa Bay.

X. Change of regime and unrest in Portuguese East Africa

The republic's inherent instability, characterized by the rapid succession of short-lived coalitions, was reflected in Delagoa Bay. Although the legal framework for the financial and administrative autonomy was set down in the 1913 Organic Charter, the outbreak of the First World War limited its practical effects. The high turnover of governor-generals contributed to the difficulties in implementing coherent development policies based on increased infrastructure expenditure and capital investment in the field of transport. The fact that some of the highest posts in colonial bureaucracy remained ministerial appointments, despite the principle of colonial decentralization enshrined in the 1911 Constitution, revealed that settler control of local affairs was still rudimentary. This contrasted to the persistence of the chartered companies' regime, functioning as independent and private authorities.

Initially, the settler population welcomed the new regime, viewed as a panacea for the colony's ills. Republican ideas were firmly established in the colony, with active centres, newspapers[90] and secret societies such as the Carbonária and Freemasonry lodges.[91] However, when administrative and financial chaos persisted, settler agitation in Delagoa Bay continued. The result was unrest, marked by anti-foreign outbursts that once more brought to the fore divisive pro- and anti-British sentiments. Unrest was sparked by three causes: the conflict of opinion as to the desirability of the return of Freire de Andrade; the undisciplined and disaffected state of soldiery and police; and the growing feeling of hostility to foreigners and their interests.

Hostility towards foreigners was manifested by those members of the Portuguese community described by the British consul as consisting:

chiefly of coarse, uneducated wine-shopkeepers, unimportant trades-
men, and employees of the port and railway department, that,
encouraged by certain members of local priesthood, and having
friends in the ranks of the military and other forces, regard themselves as a power, insist upon making their voices heard.[92]

The pro-republican working class distinguished itself from "better class
merchants and higher officials".[93] Whereas the latter were sympathetic to
British interests, the former were the main source of agitation "as they cannot
be readily dealt with by the authorities".[94] Apart from diverse economic
circumstances, their difference of opinion derived from differing faith in the
new regime's ability to solve problems. These were clear class issues in which
the state was used as a vehicle for patronage, for it was among the working
class that the republican societies found their greatest audience. Leaders of the
societies attacked land concessions to foreign capitalists, and meetings turned
into anti-foreign manifestations, targeting the former governor-general with
death threats.[95] In early 1911, the offices of two Portuguese newspapers were
ransacked and a bomb exploded near the house of the South African Customs
Union agent (also the British vice-consul).[96] Authorities reacted by deporting
the leaders of the local Carbonária and other members, totalling seven, for
agitation and possession of dynamite, gunpowder and bomb fabricating
materials.[97] Members of the local garrison also acted against the disruptive
republican societies by aborting an attempt to deport officers of royalist
convictions.[98]

Although the local authorities reiterated to the British consul and foreign
residents their determination to maintain order this promise proved difficult
to fulfil.[99] The British Foreign Office remarked that "this situation, on the
very threshold of South Africa, threatens the peace".[100] Republican societies
pressured the governor-general for the replacement of high-ranking civil
servants on suspicion of royalist (synonymous with pro-British) sympathy.[101]
This caused alarm in the British community that was not subdued by either
the arrival of a new civil police, the Guarda Republicana,[102] or the presence
of a British gunboat in Delagoa Bay.[103] While the British consul queried
rumours of the expulsion of British citizens, republican societies denied insti-
gating anti-foreign protests.[104] The Portuguese minister of foreign affairs
attempted to reassure British authorities that unrest in no way threatened
foreign lives or property.[105]

However, the Foreign Office chose to view events in a different perspective, given the concurrent "rumours" of annexation, partition and independence, and the worrying fact that in 1912 the governor-general himself led
popular protest against bad administration.[106]

XI. Delagoa Bay in debate: annexation, partition or independence?

The republican administration's treatment of the British community in Delagoa Bay was the apparent motive for Foreign Office complaints. However, other considerations, arising from the role of Delagoa Bay in the international and regional context, conditioned London's reactions. Thus the British community itself, while fundamental in giving the port its strategic importance, was nevertheless secondary to treaty responsibilities binding Britain and the threat to these that renegade action by the Union of South Africa posed.

The need for a reaffirmation of the ancient Anglo–Portuguese alliance in 1899 arose from the exigencies of the Boer War, namely the need to secure Portuguese support of the British cause and to end the passage of arms to the Boer republics via Delagoa Bay. The financial crisis undergone by Portugal (which, it was thought, would be forced to seek a large loan on the security of its empire) and the need to define spheres of interest in southern Africa lay behind the Anglo–German secret convention a year earlier.[107] However, the conventions stipulated opposing obligations for Britain. While by the 1899 Convention Britain guaranteed all Portuguese territories, the 1898 Convention established Britain's right of pre-emption in southern Mozambique.[108] While the Anglo–Portuguese agreement, which became known as the Treaty of Windsor, remained secret,[109] the Anglo–German secret convention was frequently referred to by politicians and press alike as amounting to a partition agreement. Britain persistently denied Portuguese government queries as to the truth of such "rumours". When dealing with the unrest in Delagoa Bay, however, the two agreements were foremost in the mind of British diplomacy.

When Portugal overcame its economic difficulties without need for a loan, started on the road to recovery unhindered by Britain, and lived through the revolution without collapse, Germany felt it had been cheated. The advent of the republic was, therefore, met with dissatisfaction, seen by Germany as "a reason for inducing circumstances in which the agreement would be enacted".[110] Britain, on the other hand, strongly advised restraint and caution to her representatives in both Mozambique and the Union. All action that would bring into operation the secret treaty with Germany was discouraged, "especially action by our colonies for we are bound by treaty to protect the Portuguese colonies".[111]

What Britain feared was the possibility of unsanctioned Union action, rumours of which circulated in Delagoa Bay. A newspaper article in April 1909 mentioned a proposed assault on the port by 400 armed Boers during 1908, of which the Portuguese East African government was aware. The newspaper commented, "if it was not carried out, it was due to circumstances unknown to us today and a blessing as the then governor admitted that there were neither troops nor arms to defend us from such an invasion".[112]

In October 1910, the Union governor-general, Lord Gladstone, reported that Union ministers Botha and Smuts feared events in Portuguese East Africa and believed that "public feeling would require forcible occupation of Lourenço Marques for protection of interests provoked".[113] In November 1910, Lord Gladstone portrayed South African public opinion as "keenly interested in the course of events in Portugal, because of the large Union interests involved in Delagoa Bay" adding that the situation had, however, been:

> received with quietude and common sense. The Pretoria News, as far as I know, is the only paper that has indulged in exaggerated and improper language. More influential journals, like the Transvaal Leader and The Daily Mail have strongly repudiated the views of the Pretoria News.[114]

Although Lord Gladstone was of the opinion that the ministers would not act hastily (even if there were strong public feeling in favour of intervention), the Foreign Office would not take any chances. Any outbreak of violent unrest at Delagoa Bay was considered "a dangerous temptation".[115] Hence the deliberations to send a British gunboat to Delagoa Bay.[116]

In Delagoa Bay, as already seen, the threat of cession was used to awaken central authorities to the urgency of the need for reforms. In both Britain and the Union, the possibility that settlers in Portuguese East Africa would declare an independent republic was considered real, but the question as to who would take the initiative remained unanswered. In 1909, a South African paper commented that "if it be alive to its own interests and its own future, the province will decide otherwise and the Lisbon government should take care how it coerces or attempts to coerce the cosmopolitan community of Lourenço Marques. King Manuel's advisors at Lisbon should read the story of the Boston Tea Party".[117]

When news that the British gunboat HMS *Forte* arrived in Delagoa Bay, it immediately spread the rumour of an intended British annexation of the province and the presence of British troops on the border ready to advance.[118] At the same time, rumours of "partition" were circulating rapidly, revealing an apparently widespread knowledge of the spirit, if not the letter, of the Anglo–German agreement.

In April 1911, the British consul in Delagoa Bay, in defiance of Foreign Office orders to communicate the evolution of the political situation only with the governor-general of the Union and to refer all other questions from Union sources to Lord Gladstone,[119] sent the following telegram to General Smuts: "It seems to me that the present and immediate future may hold out possibilities of consolidation of British interests here".[120] Taking the telegram to mean that a revolution was probable, General Smuts requested information from Lord Gladstone. Smuts informed the governor-general that in the event of an outbreak a strong appeal from the British for protection was expected and that this appeal would be supported throughout the Union: "The Union will say they have no option but to send in a strong body of police to hold and protect railways and docks and to give protection to British subjects".[121]

The Foreign and Colonial Offices harshly reprimanded the British consul for his unauthorized communication with the Union as "the terms of his communications have amounted to an invitation to the Union government to interfere".[122] To dissuade Smuts from the intended police action "as most serious complications would at once follow",[123] it was decided that the Union minister should be informed of the contents of the secret convention.[124] In his interview with Lord Gladstone, Smuts had shown knowledge of the convention. It was reiterated that in no circumstances would the German occupation of Delagoa Bay be allowed.[125]

If Union intervention was condemned for the pretext it would afford Germany for enacting the 1898 Agreement, the prospect of the declaration of an independent republic provided Britain with a means of escaping the dilemma posed by the terms of that agreement and the Treaty of Windsor. Some settlers denied the existence of the former, as unthinkable, linking such "rumours" to ill will borne against the fledgling republic. [126]

XII. Conclusion

It can be argued that 1910 offered the best opportunity for fulfilling long-standing ambitions regarding Delagoa Bay, both to the local settler population and to its neighbours. Portugal's instability, prompting the republican revolution, made this moment one of great vulnerability. However, the international scene had changed since the 1890s.

Whereas in the late nineteenth century the regional balance of power had been foremost in British colonial policy, in the aftermath of the Boer War British regional hegemony was a fact. The colonial debate served a higher purpose; that of constructing a new international balance of power to avoid a world war. Therefore, between 1896 and 1899, Britain prevented the *de facto* division of the Portuguese empire, even if that implied concessions to Germany in the form of partition plans on paper. In contrast, between 1902 and 1914, as the division of Portuguese Africa no longer threatened domination in southern Africa, Britain accepted it as a possible means of pacifying Germany and the ideal topic for an attempted rapprochement.

However, it can be argued that only Foreign Office pressure on Union ministers forestalled the annexation of Delagoa Bay, an act that would have precipitated the division of Mozambique along the lines of the 1898 agreement, which Britain sought to revise. Had annexation occurred, one can only speculate as to whether settlers' threats of independence would have materialized into substantial action. For Portugal, nevertheless, the continued threat posed by the re-negotiation of the Anglo–German agreement led to the rejection of all proposals, including those from within government circles, that advocated an alteration of the empire. These ranged from the lease of Delagoa Bay to participation in a customs union with South Africa.

Although the First World War removed Germany from Africa, the southern African regional order was unchanged. Territorially, the Union's hopes of immediate northern expansion into Rhodesia were thwarted in the years after the war. When, contrary to British expectations, Delagoa Bay was not placed under international control, both the Union and Britain lost a pretext for intervention. By siding with the allies, Portugal had successfully thwarted the varied ambitions of partitioning Mozambique.

Nevertheless, Delagoa Bay retained its strategic importance and, in the post-war years, Britain reiterated what it viewed as Portugal's obligations towards its neighbours in East Africa. The ever-present intimidation was clear:

> There is a strong realisation in Portugal of the dangers, which would have threatened her sovereignty if her dominions had become an obstacle to the general development of South Africa. The position of Portuguese East Africa has wholly changed in the last quarter of a century. Instead of the semi-civilized fringe of an unknown hinterland, the province has become a gateway to British territories in the interior, which have been developed more rapidly. Portugal has thus acquired the responsibility of keeping the condition of the gateway she controls abreast of the requirements of the territory to which it gives access.[127]

Notes

1. This chapter is the result of research undertaken for a Masters dissertation at the School of Oriental and African Studies, University of London. While it focuses on the role of the British in a narrow diplomatic struggle, it in no way wishes to diminish the influence of other competing forces in the area. As indicated by my use of Delagoa Bay and Portuguese East Africa (rather than Lourenço Marques and Mozambique) I am looking at the city from the British/British South African viewpoint, and the distinction is not trivial. Further work is necessary to complement and frame the events I present: key Portuguese figures for this period must be introduced and the role of both Afrikaans and Germans interests must be examined.
2. "Future of Delagoa Bay", *The Daily Chronicle* (London), 6 May (1913). This article was reprinted in a Lisbon bilingual magazine dedicated to colonial issues, *Revista Colonial* (Lisbon), ano 1, no. 5, May, p. 34 (1913).
3. The 1899 Treaty of Windsor, whereby Britain guaranteed the security of Portugal's colonial possessions, regulated Portugal's alignment with Britain against the Transvaal. A. J. Telo, *Lourenço Marques na Política Externa Portuguesa 1895–1900* (Lisbon, 1991), pp. 159–66; and R. Pélissier, *História de Moçambique: Formação e Oposição 1854–1918* (Lisbon, 1988), pp. 228–33.
4. Port Natal was opened in 1824 and diverted trade coming from the Zulu monarchy. See M. Newitt, *History of Mozambique* (London, 1995), p. 268; and A. Lobato, *História da Fundação de Lourenço Marques* (Lisbon, 1948).

5. Previously, the Natal and Cape ports had served as Transvaal's commercial outlets but these were blocked by disease, international hostility and hostile Swazi, Pedi and Tsonga; Newitt, *History of Mozambique*, p. 327.

6. Newitt, *History of Mozambique*, pp. 328–33, and D. Hedges, A. Rocha, and C. Serra (eds), *História de Moçambique* (Maputo, 1983), pp. 68–76.

7. P. Henshaw, "The 'Key to South Africa': Delagoa Bay and the Origins of the South African War, 1890–1899", Institute of Commonwealth Studies Postgraduate Seminar, May 1997.

8. "Mapa estatístico da população de Lourenço Marques referido a 1 de Dezembro de 1900", table in *Boletim Económico e Estatístico*, série especial no. 6 (1929), p. 52.

9. *Anuário de Lourenço Marques*, 1922, pp. 109–13.

10. *Anuário de Lourenço Marques*, 1936–37, pp. 223–4.

11. *Anuário de Lourenço Marques*, 1922, p. 69.

12. G. Clarence-Smith, *The Third Portuguese Empire, 1825–1975* (Manchester, 1985), pp. 81–115.

13. See R. J. Hammond, *Portugal and Africa 1815–1910* (Stanford, 1966), pp. 283–5; Telo, *Lourenço Marques*, pp. 97–110; and A. H. Oliveira Marques, *History of Portugal* (New York, 1972), vol. 3, pp. 201–12.

14. Hedges *et al.*, *História de Moçambique*, p. 77.

15. Fifty per cent of this amount was invested in the territory of the Mozambique Company. Of the remainder, 60 per cent was invested in the district of Lourenço Marques; Department of Overseas Trade, *Economic Conditions in Portuguese East Africa* (London, 1929), p. 10.

16. S. Sideri, *Trade and Power: Informal Colonialism in Anglo–Portuguese Relations* (Rotterdam, 1980), p. 281; and Hedges *et al.*, *História de Moçambique*, pp. 78–9.

17. E. J. Vilhena, *Questões Coloniaes: Discursos e Artigos* (Lisbon, 1910), pp. 364–5.

18. A. Freire de Andrade, *Relatórios*? **(Lourenço Marques, 1909)**, vol. 2, pp. 450–51.

19. Recruitment charges, emigration receipts and revenue from the collection of the hut tax accounted for more than half of Mozambique's income between the years 1895 and 1906. Freire de Andrade, *Relatórios*, vol. 1, pp. 58–62. For details of labour negotiations up to 1909, see S. E. Katzenellenbogen, *South Africa and Southern Mozambique* (Manchester, 1982), pp. 43–54.

20. Freire de Andrade, *Relatórios*, vol. 2, p. 451.

21. British Admiralty Naval Intelligence Division, *A Manual of Portuguese East Africa* (London, 1920), p. 152; and Clarence-Smith, *The Third Portuguese Empire*, pp. 127–9.

22. Clarence-Smith, *The Third Portuguese Empire*, pp. 97–8.

23. Freire de Andrade, *Relatórios*, vol. 2, p. 453.

24. For the properties acquired in the Lourenço Marques city and district during the period from 1888 to 1914, see M. L. Abrantes *et al.*, *Concessão de Terrenos em Moçambique: Catálogo* (Lisbon, 1989).

25. S. Vieira, *Os Eléctricos de Lourenço Marques* (Maputo, 1997), pp. 7–13.

26. Freire de Andrade, *Relatórios*, vol. 2, p. 349. A. Isaacman and B. Isaacman, *Mozambique From Colonialism to Revolution, 1900–1982* (Boulder, Colo., 1983), pp. 31–2, state that only 27 per cent of investments in 1900 consisted of Portuguese capital.

27. See Newitt, *History of Mozambique*, p. 395.

28. The Rand mines with land holdings and other interests in Lourenço Marques were: Ekstein & Co.; Consolidated Goldfields of South Africa Ltd.; Barnato Brothers; Neumans & Co.; S. & L. Albu; A. Goerz & Co. Ltd.; and J. B. Robinson. See Freire de Andrade, *Relatórios*, vol. 1, pp. 120–21.

29. *Diário de Notícias* (Lourenço Marques), 6 January (1909) and 16 May (1909); *O Futuro* (Lourenço Marques), 27 March (1909); *Delagoa Bay Gazette* (Lourenço Marques) 2(4), May (1910).

30. M. C. Mendes, *Maputo Antes da Independência* (Lisbon, 1979), pp. 69–77.

31. British Admiralty, *A Manual of Portuguese East Africa*, p. 368.

32. *Ibid.*, p. 363.

33. Katzenellenbogen, *South Africa and Southern Mozambique*, pp. 79–100.

34. British Admiralty, *A Manual of Portuguese East Africa*, p. 319.

35. Freire de Andrade, *Relatórios*, vol. 4, pp. 103–5.

36. British Admiralty, *A Manual of Portuguese East Africa*, pp. 437–9.

37. R. D. Neves, *A Imprensa Periódica de Moçambique, 1854–1954* (Lourenço Marques, 1956), pp.

15–17.

38. These were *The Delagoa Bay Gazette of Shipping and Commercial Intelligence*, the *Lourenço Marques Guardian*, and the *Lourenço Marques Advertiser*. *The Delagoa Gazette* was the town's first daily, starting publication in 1903 and had offices in Pretoria, Johannesburg, Cape Town, London and Glasgow. The weekly *Lourenço Marques Guardian*, founded in 1905, was property of A. W. Bayly & Co., the bookshop and printing office that owned the *Gold Field News* and *Barberton Herald*. Of the weekly *Lourenço Marques Advertiser* little is known except that it was founded in 1898, printed at the Crossley Brothers Printing Office in Barberton, and freely distributed; Neves, *A Imprensa Periódica*, pp. 65–70.

39. These were *O Futuro*, a weekly started in 1898, and the *Gazeta de Moçambique*, the 1913 version of the *Delagoa Bay Gazette*; Neves, *A Imprensa Periódica*, p. 65.

40. Freire de Andrade, *Relatórios*, vol. 1, p. 70.

41. *O Futuro*, 9 January (1909).

42. Freire de Andrade analyses Transvaal's Ordinance no. 45 (1902) and Ordinance no. 57 (1903), and the Cape's Crown Lands Disposal Act of 1887 and Act to Amend the Laws regulating the Disposal of Crown Lands of 1895; Freire de Andrade, *Relatórios*, vol. 1, pp. 67–8.

43. Freire de Andrade, *Relatórios*, vol. 1, p. 69.

44. *Ibid.*, vol. 2, pp. 337–49. Articles in the local press, relating to the issue, are transcribed, and, once again, a comparative study of South African legislation included, namely the Cape Town Municipal Act (1893); Natal's Municipal Corporation Law (1872); and Transvaal's Municipalities Elections Ordinance (1903).

45. *Ibid.* p. 349.

46. For criticism of *Delagoa Bay Gazette*, see, for example, *Diário de Notícias*, 24 October (1908). Attacks on the *Lourenço Marques Guardian* can be found in *O Incondicional* (Lourenço Marques), 29 November (1910). Curiously, the *Guardian* is equally criticized for its cynicism towards local issues by *O Futuro*, a newspaper that supported the governor-general. See *O Futuro*, 16 January (1909).

47. *Diário de Notícias*, 16 November (1908).

48. *Diário de Notícias*, 16 May (1909). The Portuguese authorities protested against the British consul's possession of property bequeathed by British citizens. For details of the process, see Minsitério de Negócios Estrangeiros (Ministry of Foreign Affairs), "Denúncia do tratado com a Grã-Bretanha de 3 de Julho de 1842 relativo à arrecadeção de heranças pelos cônsules de Inglaterra em Moçambique, 1908/1909", (Depósito do Palácio Velho, caixa de assuntos diversos, no. 1089).

49. *Diário de Notícias*, 5 November (1908).

50. G. P. Pirio, "Commerce, Industry and Empire: The Making of Modern Portuguese Imperialism in Angola and Mozambique 1890–1914", unpublished PhD thesis, California, 1982, p. 188.

51. This resulted from a rise in the number of migrant workers from southern Mozambique in the Transvaal. With the shortfall of labour during the post-war boom, African wages in the mining industry were on the rise, contributing to the growing demand for consumer goods. See Pirio, "Commerce, Industry and Empire", pp. 188–9.

52. The shortage of capital led the mining industry to seek increased profit rates through the lowering of African wages, the adoption of labour intensive techniques to expand output and the importation of Chinese workers to stem the labour shortage. The fall in African wages reduced consumer demand in Delagoa Bay. See Pirio, "Commerce, Industry and Empire", pp. 189–90.

53. The wine and textile crisis that had metropolitan associations lobbying for protectionist tariffs was detrimental to local trade and agriculture. As the colonial markets were a means of draining excess production, competition from locally produced goods was frowned on. This was in keeping with over-all economic policy whereby the function of the colonies was to balance the central budget. For details see Pirio, "Commerce, Industry and Empire", pp. 205–94; Clarence-Smith, *The Third Portuguese Empire*, pp. 89–93; and M. H. Pereira, *Política e Economia: Portugal nos Séculos XIX e XX* (Lisbon, 1979), pp. 56–67.

54. Katzenellenbogen, *South Africa and Southern Mozambique*, pp. 89–98.

55. See the weekly *O Futuro* and the daily *Diário de Notícias*, between January and May 1909.

56. Public Record Office (hereafter PRO) Foreign Office (hereafter FO) 371/723, "Unrest in Mozambique", Consul R. C. F. Maugham to FO, 14 January 1909. See also PRO FO 369/401 and

PRO FO 369/402, consular records, Portugal Files – 1911.

57. Eduardo da Costa, a Portuguese colonial administrator, writing in 1903, in Hammond, *Portugal and Africa*, p. 278.
58. *O Futuro*, 27 March (1909).
59. *Diário de Notícias*, 6 January (1909).
60. *Ibid.*
61. Vilhena, *Questões Coloniaes*, p. 348.
62. For details of the negotiations, contents and reactions to the *modus vivendi* and the 1909 Convention see Katzenellenbogen, *South Africa and Southern Mozambique*, pp. 45–54 and 79–100.
63. PRO FO 371/723, "Unrest in Mozambique", Consul R. C. F. Maugham to FO, 14 January 1909.
64. A. P. Newton, *Select Documents Relating to the Unification of South Africa* (London, 1924), p. 169.
65. Freire de Andrade, *Relatórios*, vol. 2, p. 39.
66. Newton, *Select Documents*, p. 169.
67. Freire de Andrade, *Relatórios*, vol. 2, p. 40.
68. Vilhena, *Questões Coloniaes*, p. 364.
69. The South African press reports on the situation were closely followed by Delagoa Bay's newspapers. These frequently transcribed whole articles from such diverse sources as *The Pretoria Chronicle*, *Pretoria News*, *Volkstem*, *Sunday Times*, *The Transvaal Chronicle*, *Natal Advertiser*, and the *Times of Natal*.
70. *Natal Advertiser*, 14 June (1907), in Freire de Andrade, *Relatórios*, vol. 2, p. 41.
71. PRO FO 367/142, "Parliamentary Questions" to the Under Secretary of State for the Colonies, Col. Seely, 11 March 1909.
72. *Ibid.*, "Port and Railway of Lourenço Marques", Sir F. Villiers to FO, 23 March 1909 (Lisbon).
73. *Pretoria News*, January (1909), in *O Futuro*, 19 January (1909).
74. PRO FO 367/723, "Unrest in Mozambique", Consul R. C. F. Maugham to FO, 14 January 1909 (Lourenço Marques).
75. *Diário de Notícias*, 8 March (1909).
76. Freire de Andrade, *Relatórios*, vol. 2, p. 40.
77. D. Wheeler, "The Portuguese Revolution of 1910", *Journal of Modern History* **44**, (1972), p. 189. See also, D. Wheeler, *Republican Portugal: A Political History, 1920–1926* (Madison, 1978); and A. H. de Oliveira Marques, *História da Primeira República Portuguesa* (Lisbon, 1978).
78. PRO FO 371/1463, no. 41, confidential, "General Report on Portugal for 1911", Sir A. Hardinge to FO, 16 March 1912 (Lisbon).
79. Both Argentina and Brazil established official diplomatic ties with the new regime in October 1910. Although official US recognition was delayed until May 1911, unofficial support was given. Wheeler, *Republican Portugal*, pp. 79–80. Britain's late recognition, almost a year after the revolution, was due largely to independent action by France. See J. D. Vincent-Smith, "The Portuguese Republic and Britain 1910–1914", *Journal of Contemporary History*, **10**, (1975), p. 713.
80. Wheeler, "The Portuguese Revolution of 1910", p. 189.
81. Vincent-Smith, "The Portuguese Republic and Britain", pp. 707–8.
82. *Ibid.*, p. 710.
83. The foreign secretary, Sir Edward Grey, believed that the reprimandable aspects of Portuguese domestic and foreign affairs "could only bring Britain into disrepute when she was in effect asked to associate herself with them". The rest of the Foreign Office was, in general, in disagreement with this view; Vincent-Smith, "The Portuguese Republic and Britain", pp. 717–19. Sir Edward Grey was British foreign secretary for eleven years, from 1905 to 1916.
84. See PRO FO 371/2105 and FO 367/342, "Remarks on the Anglo–Portuguese Alliance and the Strategic Value of the Portuguese Colonies", Admiralty War Staff, December 1912 (London).
85. The Portuguese diplomatic representatives in various European capitals, namely London, Paris, Berlin, Rome, Brussels, Bern and Vienna supplied the Ministry of Foreign Affairs with fortnightly summaries and clippings from the leading newspapers in each country. These articles revealed the general state of public opinion and journalistic/political debate regarding Portuguese affairs.

86. *The Standard*, in *O Incondicional*, 8 November (1910).
87. "Anglo–German Relations: Sir Edward Grey's Statement", *The Standard*, 28 November (1911). The article transcribed the foreign secretary's speech in the House of Commons on foreign policy and Anglo–German relations. The Portuguese minister in London, Teixeira Gomes, interpreted "old friendships" as referring to the Anglo–Portuguese alliance; MNE, Correspondência I, 24–5, "Teixeira Gomes to Vasconcellos", 28 November 1911 (London).
88. *Ibid.*, "Teixeira Gomes to Vasconcellos", 2 May 1911 (London),.
89. R. Langhorne, "Anglo–German Negotiations Concerning the Future of the Portuguese Colonies, 1911–1914", *The Historical Journal* 16(2), 361–87 (1973).
90. Prior to 1910, newspapers such as *O Portuguez*, *Imparcial*, *O Incondicional* and *Era Nova* were republican in orientation. Between 1911 and 1920, there were 22 new newspapers in Delagoa Bay, of which half were republican. See Neves, *A Imprensa Periódica*, pp. 71–8.
91. National Colonial Archive, Lisbon, Gabinete do Ministro, Telegramas, Moçambique, 1911–1912, Governor-General to Ministry of Colonial Affairs, 3 July 1911 (Lourenço Marques); *ibid.*, Governor-General to Ministry of Colonial Affairs, 8 July 1911 (Lourenço Marques). The number of freemasonary lodges, identified with republican radicalism in Portugal, grew from five in 1909 to eight in 1913; Oliveira Marques, *História da Primeira República*, pp. 648–51.
92. PRO FO 367/236, no. 5, Africa, "Disturbances at Lourenço Marques", Consul R. C. F. Maugham to Sir E. Grey, 24 February 1911 (Lourenço Marques).
93. PRO FO 367/291, no. 24, Africa, confidential, "Unrest at Lourenço Marques", Consul-general E. MacDonnell to FO, 1 June 1912 (Lourenço Marques).
94. PRO FO 367/236, no. 5, Africa, "Disturbances at Lourenço Marques", Consul R. C. F. Maugham to Sir E. Grey, 24 February 1911 (Lourenço Marques).
95. *Delagoa Bay Gazette* 3(7), July (1911); and National Colonial Archive, Lisbon, Gabinete do Ministro, Telegramas, Moçambique, 1911–1912, Governor-General to Ministry of Colonial Affairs, 24 June 1911 (Lourenço Marques).
96. These were *O Progresso* and *Vida Nova*. PRO FO 367/236, no. 5, Africa, "Disturbances at Lourenço Marques", Consul R. C. F. Maugham to FO, 24 February 1911 (Lourenço Marques). The bomb caused no damage. See *ibid.*, no. 6, Africa, "Disturbances at Lourenço Marques", Consul R. C. F. Maugham to FO, 10 April 1911 (Lourenço Marques).
97. National Colonial Archive, Lisbon, Gabinete do Ministro, Telegramas, Moçambique, 1911–1912, Governor-General to Ministry of Colonial Affairs, 5 July 1911 (Lourenço Marques).
98. PRO FO 367/236, no. 8, Africa, "State of Unrest at Lourenço Marques", Maugham to FO, 15 April 1911.
99. National Colonial Archive, Lisbon, Gabinete do Ministro, Telegramas, Moçambique, 1911–1912, Governor-General to Ministry of Colonial Affairs, 6 July 1911 (Lourenço Marques). The telegram continues, "have received compliments from foreign business men and South African press".
100. PRO FO 367/236, no. 6, Africa, minute of "Disturbances at Lourenço Marques", Consul R. C. F. Maugham to FO, 10 April 1911 (Lourenço Marques).
101. PRO FO 367/236, no. 7, Africa, "State of Unrest at Lourenço Marques", Consul R. C. F. Maugham to FO, 6 May 1911 (Lourenço Marques).
102. National Colonial Archive, Lisbon, Gabinete do Ministro, Telegramas, Moçambique, 1911–1912, Governor-General to Ministry of Colonial Affairs, 29 May 1911 (Lourenço Marques).
103. PRO FO 371/973, "Visit of HMS *Forte* to Lourenço Marques", acting-consul Richards to FO, 16 October 1910 (Lourenço Marques); and PRO FO 367/236, "Situation at Lourenço Marques. Report of Rear Admiral Paul Bush on the visit of HMS *Hermes* to Lourenço Marques", Admiralty to FO, 6 June 1911 (London).
104. *Ibid.*, no. 6, Africa, "Disturbances at Lourenço Marques", Consul R. C. F. Maugham to FO, 10 April 1911 (Lourenço Marques).
105. *Ibid.*, Bernardino Machado to Sir F. Villiers, 23 February 1911 (Lisbon), included in "Disturbances at Lourenço Marques", Sir F. Villiers to Sir E. Grey, 1 March 1911 (Lisbon).
106. "Future of Delagoa Bay", *The Daily Chronicle* (London), 6 May (1913), transcribed in *Revista Colonial* (Lisbon), ano 1, no. 5, May (1913), p. 34.
107. See Langhorne, "Anglo-German Negotiations", pp. 363–7, for details of the negotiation of these two secret conventions.

108. *Ibid.*, p. 365. The 1898 Agreement contained three parts. The Convention established that should Portugal seek a loan from foreign powers on the security of its empire, Britain and Germany would operate a joint loan. The Secret Convention established that should Portugal default on the loan, the two countries would oppose the intervention of any other powers in Mozambique, Angola and Portuguese Timor, territories in which they defined spheres of interest. Finally, the Secret Note established that each party would help to obtain equal privileges or cessions for the other as obtained for itself, or else forfeit the advantage gained. The agreement was the centre of internal controversy in the Foreign Office, as its negotiation had been undertaken against the wishes of the foreign secretary, Lord Salisbury, and concluded during his absence by his Germanophile substitute, Balfour.

109. Langhorne states that "even in 1913–1914 the Germans seem only to have had an inkling of it", "Anglo-German Negotiations", pp. 366–7.

110. *Ibid.*, p. 366.

111. PRO FO 371/972, "Delagoa Bay: Telegram of Governor-General of the Union to Secretary of State for Colonies", Colonial Office (hereafter CO) to FO, 5 October 1910 (London); and the reply, *ibid.*, "Delagoa Bay", FO to Gladstone, 7 October 1910.

112. *Diário de Notícias*, 13 April (1909). No mention could be found of this proposed invasion in either FO or Portuguese government documents reporting to that year. The other newspaper in publication at that time also makes no reference to such an event.

113. PRO FO 371/972, "Delagoa Bay: Telegram of Governor-General of the Union to Secretary of State for Colonies", CO to FO, 5 October 1910 (London). The interest in question was the 70 per cent of Transvaal trade taken by Delagoa Bay, mentioned by the Union ministers.

114. PRO FO 371/972, "The Portuguese Republic: Dispatch from the Governor of Union respecting the situation in Mozambique and South Africa", CO to FO, 7 November 1910 (London).

115. PRO FO 367/236, confidential, "Situation at Lourenço Marques", Admiralty to FO, 24 February 1911 (London).

116. PRO FO 371/973, "Visit of HMS *Forte* to Lourenço Marques", acting-consul Richards to FO, 16 October 1910 (Lourenço Marques).

117. *Pretoria News* article in *O Futuro*, 19 January (1909).

118. PRO FO 371/973, "Visit of HMS *Forte* to Lourenço Marques", acting-consul Richards to FO, 16 October 1910 (Lourenço Marques).

119. PRO FO 367/236, "Disturbances at Lourenço Marques", draft of memo to CO and Maugham, 13 April 1911 (London).

120. *Ibid.*, "Disturbances at Lourenço Marques. Copies of further correspondence between Harcourt and Gladstone on possibility of Union government action on own responsibility", CO to FO, 15 April 1911 (London).

121. *Ibid.*

122. *Ibid.*, "Disturbances at Lourenço Marques", Maugham to FO, 18 April 1911 (Lourenço Marques), minute requesting a full explanation of the proceedings. In his reply, Maugham stated that General Smuts was "a personal friend of mine of several years" and the telegram had been "dictated solely by my anxiety that vacancies in the higher posts of this administration should be filled as far as possible by British subjects, to the increase of general efficiency and of British interests in this place". Minutes to the consul's report doubted the explanation offered for being "an action so ill-judged and calculated to mislead authorities of the Union". It was further noted that "what he may do as a private friend he could not very well do in his official capacity of HM Consul". Outrage at the incident was such that it was advocated "that this in itself would be a sufficient reason for removing Mr. Maugham from a post, where his incompetence is a public danger". See PRO FO 367/236, "State of Unrest at Lourenço Marques. Reasons for dispatch of a private and confidential telegram to the Minister of the Interior of the Union", Consul R. C. F. Maugham to FO, 15 May 1911 (Lourenço Marques).

123. *Ibid.*, "Disturbances at Lourenço Marques. Copies of further correspondence between Harcourt and Gladstone on possibility of Union government action on own responsibility", CO to FO, 15 April 1911 (London).

124. *Ibid.*, secret to CO, "Disturbances at Lourenço Marques: Telegrams from Lord Gladstone", CO to FO, 19 April 1911 (London). In contrast, the Union governor-general, unaware thereof, requested full information in a private and personal note to the Colonial Office.

125. At the Foreign Office, it was later warned, "We must in future be extra cautious in acting upon the suggestions of our consul at Lourenço Marques". See *ibid.*, "Disturbances at Lourenço Marques", minute from German chargé d'affaires to FO, 20 April 1911 (London).
126. *Delagoa Bay Gazette*, 2(9), October (1910).
127. British Admiralty, *A Manual of Portuguese East Africa*, p. 515.

CHAPTER TWELVE

Colmar Freiherr von der Goltz and the Boer War

Feroz Yasamee

I

Colmar Freiherr von der Goltz was one of the leading military figures in Wilhelmine Germany.[1] Described by *The Times*'s correspondent, Colonel Repington, as perhaps Germany's most important general, he rose in 1911 to the rank of field-marshal, retiring two years later.[2] At the outbreak of the Boer War in October 1899, he was a relative newcomer to Germany's military leadership, having exercised the functions of chief of the corps of engineers and pioneers and inspector of fortifications only since May 1898, with the rank of lieutenant-general.[3] For the preceding two years he had served as commander of the 5th division at Frankfurt an der Oder, and for the 12 years before that he had served abroad, as an adviser and instructor in the army of the Ottoman Sultan. He was not to remain in his new post for long, soon provoking controversy with his proposals for a thorough reorganization of the corps of engineers and pioneers, and a change in fortifications policy, and in January 1902 he was abruptly transferred to command of the 1st army corps in East Prussia. Meanwhile he had also expressed controversial views on the subject of German foreign policy, and the Boer War in particular; it is not clear whether these opinions contributed to his eventual removal from Berlin, though Goltz appears to have believed that they had, and henceforth regarded himself as something of an outsider and dissident.

Goltz also enjoyed a considerable reputation as a military writer, in particular as the author of two original works of military theory, *Leon Gambetta and his Armies*, and *The Nation in Arms*, in which he had expounded his fundamental views on contemporary warfare.[4] In these works he argued that the era of short cabinet wars was over, and that future armed conflicts between civilized or developed states would be truly national trials of strength in which each side would seek to deploy the totality of its moral and material resources, as the French had done in 1870, when they had refused to bow to the capitulation of their regular army at Sedan and Metz, and instead raised fresh volunteer armies, which had enabled them to continue their struggle against Prussia for another four months. It was not simply that modern governments, endowed with a complex organization, and resting on the principle of nationality, could exercise an unprecedented command over the human and material resources of their countries; there was a strong strain of social Darwinism in Goltz's thinking, and he predicted that future wars, unlike those of the mid-century, would not be fought for limited territorial or political goals, but would be true "struggles for existence". It followed that future conflicts were likely to be protracted; Goltz, at least, was never prey to the "short war illusion".[5]

Goltz placed a corresponding emphasis on the moral dimensions of warfare. It was not just that he insisted that character, guts and bravura would continue to count on the battlefield, regardless of advances in military technique. More originally, he held that mass conscript armies, as the "nation in arms", would inevitably reflect the character and capacities of the civil populations from which they were recruited. Further, given that future wars were likely to be protracted, a great deal would depend on the willingness of the civil population, in the rear, to withstand the privations and dangers to which it, too, would be exposed. For both of these reasons, the moral health of the civil population, in peacetime as in war, was a matter of direct military concern, that moral health being construed in terms of patriotism, national solidarity, physical fitness and habituation to the hardships of military life. This concern was reinforced by Goltz's belief that conditions of life in prosperous, industrial societies, like Germany, tended to undermine those moral and physical characteristics that made for good soldiers. A large part of his striking admiration for the Turks stemmed from his belief that their martial virtues reflected their pre-industrial way of life; he was to take a similar view of the Boers. Finally, Goltz held that military organization, strategy and tactics must take account of national character and capacities. He had often warned his Turkish pupils against the blind acceptance of recipes drawn from European military experience, and noted that the Turkish army's performance against Russia in 1877 had shown how the Turks' national gifts for improvisation and endurance had made up for conventional deficiencies in organization.[6] This theme, too, would recur in his assessment of the Boers.

II

From the start, Goltz saw the Boer War of 1899–1902 as an event of political significance on a world scale. It was, he believed, the harbinger of a new era, in which competition between Great Powers would increasingly shift away from the European continent to the wider colonial world; in which the competition would be joined by new powers like the US and Japan, and perhaps, eventually, by revived Chinese and Ottoman Empires; and in which competition would no longer be waged over limited goals, as in the German and Italian wars of unification, but would assume the form of a Darwinian "struggle for existence". Germany herself must participate in this struggle, for she "can no longer sufficiently employ her innate forces on home territory. Her expansion over the world seas, the 'greater Germany' of which the younger generation dreams, has become a requirement of iron necessity".[7] In the process, Germany would inevitably come into conflict with other states, above all with Britain, a power bent on "world conquest".

These views were of recent origin. Until the mid-1890s, despite his long Turkish experience, Goltz's view of Germany's interests had remained resolutely Eurocentric, focused on the potential military threat posed by the Franco–Russian Alliance, and latterly on the implications of a possible breakup of the Austro-Hungarian Empire. Thereafter his attitude began to change, under the influence of a series of extra-European crises: the Sino–Japanese war of 1894–95, Germany's own seizure of Kiao-Chow in 1897, and the Spanish–American war in 1898. To Goltz, these were not isolated episodes, but heralds of a world war that would be fought over the domination of the non-European world. Already in May 1898, in a private letter to one of his former Turkish pupils, Major Pertev, he noted:

> Political complications are becoming ever more serious. The, in my view, rash occupation of Kiao-Chow has set things in motion in East Asia. The partition of China has begun, as has the plundering of Spain by North America. The quarrel over the booty will in the end provoke war.

He added that the Turks, too, must develop their military strength, if they wished to avoid the fate of Spain or China.[8]

Although new, this shift of focus was not unusual. It reflected the German government's own proclamation of "world policy" in 1897, a proclamation given substance by the acquisition of Kiao-Chow, the Kaiser's 1898 Damascus speech, and Tirpitz's 1898 Naval Law, which laid the foundations for a battle fleet; it also reflected the growing influence of colonial and ultra-nationalist advocates of a "greater Germany" within German public opinion. In 1900 Goltz himself would accept the presidency of the German-Asiatic Society, a newly established group that aimed to promote German commerce and influence throughout Asia.[9] Nor was there anything unusual about Goltz's emerging anglophobia, which was shared by many of the colonial and ultra-nationalist groups, and which had been growing in public opinion at large ever since the furore provoked by the kaiser's "Kruger telegram" of January 1896.[10] More striking, and extreme, was Goltz's conviction that the

British would inaugurate the new era of overseas conflict, through a policy of aggression directed towards world conquest. Goltz saw two motives behind this new policy of aggression. The first was Britain's realization that its established world position was threatened by the emergence of commercial and naval rivals, including the US, Japan and, above all, Germany, and that it must take steps to knock out at least some of them before they grew too powerful. The second was Britain's recognition that it could not maintain its rule in India indefinitely, and that it must find a substitute to sustain it in the longer term:

> Since my years of wandering in the Orient I have maintained certain relations with important Englishmen, whose energy and determination I must admire. Nearly twenty years ago a senior military man, who had long served in India, expressed himself quite openly to me: "One day we will lose this country, not through Russia, but through the Indians themselves. They are beginning to outgrow dictation, and a people of 300 millions is not to be forcibly held down by a few hundred thousand. Then we require a substitute, and this substitute lies for us in Africa".[11]

It was in this light that Goltz interpreted Britain's decision to provoke a war with the two Boer republics. In September 1899, shortly before the outbreak of war, he warned his chief of staff, Colonel von Mudra:

> Whoever wishes, can learn what is to be expected from England from the fate of the Transvaal. Every concession from the Dutch republics is answered with new demands from England, which precisely *wants* war, in order to strangle the two free states, before they become strong . . . North America covers her rear, there is nothing to fear from Russia in view of the Tsar's weakness; otherwise the world is peaceful – so the moment is favourable. England will use it, to set out to plunder. In the end, one can scarcely criticise her and she pursues a powerful egotistical policy. A substitute for India, whose loss is a question of time, is for the British Empire a condition of existence – this question is even now, with considerable foresight, to be resolved . . . Fashoda has clearly and unmistakably shown that in the end they have their eyes on the whole of Africa . . . Of course, Caprivi's wise foresight has taken care that our colonies should not irritate England, but a dispute over them can offer the longed-for opportunity to annihilate Germany's blossoming trade and her sea-power, before both become dangerous.[12]

He made the same point to Pertev:

The world situation has changed considerably in the last years. Earlier all interest turned on the expected future war between France and Germany, that is between the Russo–French and Triple Alliances. Now North America has unexpectedly appeared on the stage, and cunning England has seized the opportunity to immediately come to an understanding with that new world power, and so protect her back and set out now to rob. Without any right she presently attacks the two small South African colonies, in order first to secure dominance in South Africa, but later to place the whole of Africa in her power. This conquest will allegedly form a substitute for India, should the latter ever be lost. As a secondary matter, the remaining Portuguese colonial possessions, and later the Dutch and the German, will come into question. This new policy of robbery and conquest must lead to a world war on the seas and the coasts.[13]

III

War between Germany and Britain would be inevitable sooner or later, and the British would prove to be a formidable opponent, although not an insuperable one. Even before the outbreak of the Boer War, Goltz had begun considering Germany's means of offence against Britain, and come up with two ideas: a direct invasion of the British isles, to be launched from the coast of Holland, and diversionary attacks by the Turkish army on Britain's colonial possessions in Egypt and India. In principle, he acknowledged that both were long-term projects, which would require lengthy and careful preparation; but under pressure of the events of the Boer War, and perhaps, too, of his fear that the British might strike first, he soon came to speak of them as immediate possibilities.

An invasion of the British isles would require Germany to achieve naval supremacy in the North Sea, at least for long enough to cover the initial landing of troops. Goltz was an enthusiastic supporter of Tirpitz's proposals for an expansion of the German navy, and in his capacity as inspector of the corps of engineers and pioneers, actively set out to develop links between the pioneers and the navy, and also introduced landing exercises.[14] He accepted that much remained to be done to prepare Germany for a "general struggle over international trade interests and the mastery of the seas", telling Mudra that "even we – at least I with my 56 years – will only manage to inaugurate the preparation".[15] A Turkish invasion of Egypt or India would similarly require long preparation. For one thing, Goltz knew that the reigning Sultan, whom he privately dismissed as a pacifist, would never entertain such an idea. For another, despite his profound admiration for the martial abilities of the Turkish people, he took a cautious view of the short-term worth of the

Turkish army. Even in the aftermath of the Turks' victory over Greece in May 1897, he warned that their army was far less fit for offensive operations than for simple defence.[16] A year later, the Turks decided to raise a supplementary reserve of 666 battalions, which would potentially double their army's wartime strength. Goltz's hopes rose, but he remained careful to express them as future possibilities only:

> Everything will depend upon Turkey's being able to withstand the first impact at the beginning of the next major war on her own. If she manages this, and disposes of 1373 battalions, she will find allies. Why should there not even come a time in the more distant future, when as allies we attack the English in Egypt and India?[17]

With the impending outbreak of the Boer War, Goltz's tone grew more urgent. In September 1899 he complained to Mudra:

> Had we positive goals in policy and not simply a negative "paix à outrance", the Turks would today be at the point where – led by German officers – they could occupy Egypt and march in the Persian Gulf against the frontiers of India, and we should have to be prepared and ready, in league with Holland, and from her coasts, to cross over at the favourable moment to Albion's shores, like William the Conqueror and [William] III of Orange.[18]

There followed a lengthy series of letters to Pertev, in which Goltz not only outlined his views on the inevitability of a world war on the seas and coasts, and the Turkish army's ability to strike "a mortal blow" against the British Empire in such a conflict, by threatening the Suez Canal, but also asked for detailed information on possible invasion routes across the Sinai peninsula, and across southern Persia to the frontiers of India.[19] Initially, Goltz emphasized that these were long-term plans, to be implemented by the "coming generation", but as the extent of the early British reverses in South Africa became apparent, he became less cautious. In November 1899, he suggested to Pertev that a rumoured Russian advance on Afghanistan might serve as the trigger for a world war in which the Ottoman Empire could play a crucial role, and in February 1900 he appeared to hint at the desirability of unilateral Turkish action:

> In view of the serious dimensions which the South African war has assumed for England, the situation for the Ottoman Empire becomes more and more auspicious. In my view, it could, by threatening Egypt, at the very least compel the retrocession of Cyprus without great effort, and this would be a moral success of great significance.[20]

He added, "I believe that we are indeed no longer too distant from a conflict at sea, particularly with England". As late as July 1900 he returned to the theme, suggesting that the "great overseas war" which he had predicted might yet be provoked by complications in China.[21] Thereafter he appears to have let the matter drop. Quite why is unclear, but with British forces in occupation of the capitals of the Orange Free State and the Transvaal, and the Boers reduced to a guerrilla resistance, he may well have felt that there was no longer any prospect that the South African conflict might set off a world war.

IV

Such were the ideas that Goltz expounded to his intimates. His attempts to raise them officially met with no success. In subsequent years he was often to recall, with some bitterness, a meeting at the palace in Berlin at which the naval representatives scouted any notion of challenging the British fleet, and at which his own suggestion that the Turks be encouraged to invade India was greeted with open laughter, and looks that suggested that he had taken leave of his senses.[22] The fact was that Goltz's ideas were not entirely new, although how far he understood this is unclear. Since 1896, when the furore created by the kaiser's "Kruger telegram" had first conjured up the spectre of an Anglo–German war, the naval and army staffs had been examining Germany's means of offence and defence against Britain, and drawn generally pessimistic conclusions. *Inter alia*, they had considered the notion of an invasion of the British isles, on the assumptions that the navy might secure a temporary supremacy over the British home fleet before the latter could be reinforced from around the globe, and that the Dutch ports might perhaps be available for embarkation. Both Schlieffen and Tirpitz had concluded that the whole enterprise was too hazardous to be considered realistic. Even the idea of a diversionary attack on British India had been raised in September 1898 by Vice-Admiral Knorr, Commanding Admiral of the navy, though he had envisaged the Russians, rather than the Turks, as its perpetrators. Tirpitz, however, could see no realistic prospect of such an attack, the more so as Russia was pre-occupied in the Far East.[23]

More broadly, Germany's political leaders did not share Goltz's alarmist view of the international situation. Britain was indeed regarded as a potential rival and obstacle to Germany's ambitious plans of "world policy" and overseas expansion; but Britain's decision to launch the Boer War was not seen as heralding a campaign of "world conquest". War with Britain was regarded as a possibility, but one to be avoided, at least until such time, a decade hence, when the German fleet might be strong enough to match the Royal Navy. Even then, the hope was that Germany's new naval strength would furnish her with diplomatic leverage, forcing Britain to recognize her "equal status",

from obstructing her in matters of "world policy". Pending the
n of Germany's naval programme, official policy was to avoid
ritain offence, partly out of fear that the British might otherwise be
ed to launch a pre-emptive strike against the fledgling German navy, but
y, too, in the hope that Britain's difficulties in South Africa and elsewhere
ght enable Germany to extract from it colonial concessions that, regardless
of their intrinsic value, would none the less assist the principal domestic aim
of the new "world policy"; namely, the raising of the prestige of the monarchy
and government, and the consolidation of Germany's conservative political
regime. Already, in August 1898, an Anglo–German agreement had envisaged
a possible partition of the Portuguese colonial empire, and in November 1899
the British were similarly induced to resolve a long-standing dispute over
Samoa.[24]

Yet if the Chancellor, Bülow, was prepared to wash his hands of the two
Boer republics, he had to cope with a press and public opinion, led by the
colonial enthusiasts and the pan-Germans, which was violently anti-British
and pro-Boer, and which was further outraged by such episodes as the British
seizure of German merchantmen off the South African coast. Bülow even
feared that the tone of the press might provoke the British to war. Here,
however, the government faced a further difficulty, for the British bogey was
needed to induce the Reichstag to vote through a new Navy Bill, submitted in
January 1900, which envisaged a virtual doubling of the size of the German
battle-fleet. As a result, the government felt obliged to indulge and even encourage a measure of public anglophobia, at least until the Navy Bill was secured in June 1900.[25]

Goltz himself intervened in the public debate with an article, "Sea Power
and Land Warfare", which expressly sought to persuade the Reichstag deputies to accept the government's new Navy Bill.[26] Conventionally enough, the
article cited Captain Mahan on the importance of sea power, and stressed
Germany's growing reliance on overseas trade and, in particular, on food
imports to sustain its growing population. It also reiterated Goltz's view that
future wars between nationally self-conscious and united peoples would be
struggles for existence, and, as such, likely to be protracted: "in future, the
victor in wars between civilised states will be the one which can support the
state of war longest". In a war between Germany and the Franco–Russian
Alliance, for example, the German army would be unlikely to overthrow even
one of its opponents with only half its forces. The state of war could consequently last a long time, and success would depend on Germany's ability to
hold out longer than France or Russia, which meant that it must keep its sea-
routes open, "for dearth would compel us to peace, once our imports were
entirely cut off". Further, naval supremacy would be essential to ward off the
threat of enemy landings, which, while not in themselves decisive in strictly
military terms, could have a disastrous effect on civilian morale: "in war,
much depends upon the masses' firm belief in victory". It followed that in the

case of a war against France and Russia, Germany would require a fleet "which is at least somewhat superior to each of those two opponents".

The main thrust of the article, however, lay in its explicit identification of Britain as Germany's inevitable enemy. The British, Goltz explained, had been the first to recognize the new situation created by the growth of imperialist competition overseas and heralded by the Sino–Japanese and Spanish–American wars. They had reached an understanding with the US, and promptly launched their "shameful aggression" against Transvaal and the Orange Free State, thereby setting in train their "long since secretly desired policy of world conquest". It was true that Germany had as yet few overseas interests that might bring it into collision with Britain, but this, Goltz argued, was to miss the point: already, the rapid growth of Germany's overseas trade was leading British opinion to identify Germany as a mortal threat:

> We should not conceal from ourselves that the opinion of broad sections of the British people frankly looks to a struggle of annihilation against Germany . . . In Germany's independence there is seen a kind of unjustified rebellion against British dominance . . . It is perceived as . . . unjustified presumptuousness, that in the rapidly advancing upswing of our maritime development we increasingly become worrying rivals. It is considered high time to impart a lesson to all continental rebels against England's supremacy – in the first place, to Germany.

Such, Goltz insisted, were the views of "the whole middle class" in Britain, which foresaw that "if England loses its absolute superiority in trade on the world seas, the collapse of its proud rule is only a question of time, for the natural strengths of the motherland are too few, to be able to maintain it over time".

It was, Goltz continued, essential that German opinion rid itself of its belief that Britain was invincible. Intelligent diplomacy could furnish weapons against the British: the Russians should be encouraged to continue their advance in Asia towards the frontiers of India, while "our friend Turkey stands on England's main communications route to India, which leads through the Suez Canal". Most important, Britain's naval supremacy was not all that it seemed. Crude statistics might endow Britain with a crushing superiority in numbers of warships, and even after the completion of the new German naval programme it would still enjoy a marked quantitative advantage, which it would doubtless seek to increase still further in order to ward off the menace of German competition. The crucial point, however, was that Britain's world-wide interests obliged it to scatter its naval forces across the globe, with squadrons in the Mediterranean, East Asia, India, Australia, the Red Sea, South Africa, the West Indies and the Pacific, as well as in home waters. In the event of a direct military threat to the British isles, the recall of these various squadrons would require time, and not all the foreign stations could be stripped, for the security of the empire would have to be maintained, and a bold opponent would deliberately act at a moment when portions of the British fleet were tied down by colonial disturbances, as in the present Boer War. At the start of a war that directly threatened the British isles, therefore, only the British home squadron would come into account. Germany, in contrast, could concentrate its entire fleet in European waters. The German fleet, if the proposed new naval programme were implemented, would increase to 34 ships of the line and 32 cruisers, and would not find in the British Home Fleet, with its 43 battleships and 35 cruisers, an insuperable opponent, particularly if the German navy could achieve qualitative superiority in gunnery and speed of mobilization.

By implication, Goltz was envisaging an offensive war against Britain, in which Germany's chances of victory would depend on surprise and the ability to strike first. He also alluded plainly enough to the possibility of invading the British isles:

> This notion [of landings on the English coasts] is unjustly consigned to the realm of fantastic self-deception. The route from the continent over there is short enough to be overcome, if the excellence of his fleet and the boldness of his action enables an enterprising Admiral to obtain predominance for a time in the northern seas. It would take us too far, to follow this idea in more detail; it suffices to mention it and to point to the extensive coastline of the United Kingdom.

V

The political lessons of the Anglo–Boer conflict were therefore considerable; Goltz held its military lessons to be of lesser significance. From the start, it had been evident that the British would enjoy an overwhelming preponderance in resources, and notwithstanding the Boers' initial successes in the field, and their eventual resort to guerilla methods, the outcome of the struggle was never in much doubt. With hindsight, Goltz argued that the Boers had had but two slender chances of success: first, if they had opened the campaign on the offensive, rather than the defensive, and driven the British from the whole of South Africa before they had time to reinforce from overseas; and secondly, if their resistance had gone so far as to force the British government to confront the domestic political risks of an attempt to introduce mass conscription. Neither case had obtained, and the Boers' decision to abandon the struggle in May 1902 had been prompted not by fatigue or exhaustion, but by the British policy of placing prisoners beyond rescue abroad, and by the ruthless British treatment of the fighters' families, which threatened "to decimate the race". Capitulation had been an act of wisdom, not weakness.[27]

From the narrower viewpoint of military technique and organization, Goltz believed, the war had little to teach, at least to the Germany army.[28] Its lessons, whether strategic or tactical, were either not new, or else irrelevant to German conditions. As early as February 1900, in the first flush of his enthusiasm following the initial British reverses, he had warned:

> for us, conclusions are to be drawn from the example of the Boer war only with great caution. It no doubt teaches us with greater certainty that the strength of capable troops in defence has undergone a quite extraordinary increase due to the new small-calibre rifle, and that a lesser force armed with it need not fear attack by a considerably superior number. The advantages of dispersed combat in thin firing lines, accompanied by skilful exploitation of terrain, have recently emerged. But these phenomena are not unexpected by us; we were already convinced of their importance before the war. In respect of the conduct of battles on a large scale, military organisation and troop training the lessons of the South African war tell us but little.[29]

Nor, he emphasized, did the Boers' successes in defeating regular British troops with a citizen army offer any ammunition to advocates of a militia system in Germany – a clear enough allusion to the Social Democrats, one of whose leaders, August Bebel, had in 1898 published a pamphlet that adroitly used arguments drawn from Goltz's own *Leon Gambetta and His Armies* to support the idea of a "people's army".[30] Goltz warned that those who believed that "in Germany, too, a levy of the masses could be a match for the opponents to be expected on its frontiers", forgot that "the conditions of life, that circumstances in general are quite different with us, and that we may absolutely not compare ourselves with either Boers or Turks".[31]

Two and a half years later, following the Boers' final capitulation, his views were substantially unchanged. The Boers' protracted resistance had been a salutary reminder that "number in war is not of such absolutely decisive significance as has been asserted in recent times. The 'rage des nombres' needs a damper". Otherwise, the war had demonstrated that artillery superiority alone could not deliver victory on the battlefield, that the strength of infantry in defence permitted a defender to occupy extended positions with small forces, and that the fire-power of modern weapons could render it difficult if not impossible for an attacker to advance frontally over open terrain. But these were old lessons, which had already been demonstrated in the Franco–Prussian war of 1870–71 and the Russo–Ottoman war of 1877–78, although the South African campaign had made them fresher and more urgent. The one genuine innovation had been the Boers' extensive use of mounted infantry during the second, guerrilla phase of their struggle. Although effective, Goltz doubted that this method could be employed in a European war, except, perhaps, a protracted campaign in Russia:

The sharp resistance of small, easily moved units against a large organised army, which has overrun the country and made itself master of the main lines of communications, demands our highest respect. In European wars, too, such methods may at times be used with profit, where it is a matter of disrupting the supplies and disturbing the garrisons on the base lines. But the conditions for employing it in the grand style are lacking - namely, great space, an uninhabited land with good hiding-places for those who know the country and an opponent who is in general but little mobile. But nor do we wish to spurn the method which, properly applied, can offer good service and also play a role in wars in the East, should they be of long duration.[32]

The true lessons of the Boers' struggle concerned war's moral dimension. The Boers had taken up arms against the world's most powerful empire, in sober consciousness of the risks, and done so in defence of ideal, not material goods: freedom, patriotism, and an outraged sense of justice. They had been a true nation in arms, waging a "struggle for existence". Their citizen army had been formed by volunteers aged from 14 to 70, placing three generations in the field, and had enjoyed the firmest support from the civilian population, despite all privations: "men and women of all living generations rose up with a unanimity which offers us the finest example". The people had responded with exemplary discipline to their government's decision for war, and with equal discipline to its eventual decision to lay down its arms. They had also thrown up outstanding leaders, men of the stamp of Botha, De Wet and De La Rey, who had not only been bold and skilful commanders, but had also known how to inspire and keep alive the spirit of resistance in the face of adversity.[33]

These moral achievements, Goltz argued, sprang from a combination of ideal and material circumstances that had formed the Boers' national character:

> This calls for dour, decisive men, who reckon as calmly with the possibility of defeat as with that of victory. Every nation could count itself fortunate to have them at the head. It is sufficiently known what strength the Boers found in their faith in God. It lifted them above the perplexing doubt which the superior numbers of the enemy would otherwise have provoked in their mind. To the living generation in Europe this irrefutable proof of the *practical* significance of ideal goods such as faith, freedom and fatherland can only be of use and benefit.
>
> No less evident was the value of a simple, hard way of life, which is passed in an almost uninterrupted struggle with tribulations and dangers. Only through such a school can there be trained men who

wage a desperate struggle for years, and whose leaders in the field in the end successfully might forbid them to sleep under a roof. Our great European cities do not produce such natures.[34]

It was the Boers' moral achievements that offered a necessary lesson and example to the Germans:

> They remind us yet again to sedulously foster and elevate our own, among which discipline and sense of duty are surely the most important . . . It is also essential for us to maintain the martial spirit in the people. These days it is exposed to a hard test, in a period of long tranquillity and material expansion. The all too frequent promotion of peace, and the necessity to preserve it, can easily lead war to appear something reprehensible in itself, as a crime between peoples, and feeling turns away from it. One forgets, that war too has its right, that it is inseparable from the dignity of a people, for whose preservation it is a good deed and a virtue. It is not easy to keep this conviction alive among highly civilised peoples.[35]

The Germans must be prepared for the coming struggle for existence. There could be no question, Goltz conceded, of regressing to a more primitive state of civilization for the sake of fostering martial virtues, but it was essential to counter the "softening influence of our higher civilisation". This must be reflected in the whole upbringing of male youth, but especially in the army, where conscripts must be accustomed to great efforts and to dangers, without excessive concern for accidents:

> Only the general adoption of such principles permits the formation of sufficient number of strong characters, whom we need in a future war, if we are not to lack capable leaders. For what is pending for us is no short, glorious national war waged with quantitative or qualitative superiority, as we experienced in 1866 and 1870, but a life and death struggle against stronger enemies, such as the Boers of South Africa have maintained for years. It teaches us that the *right* men step into the foreground only later in the course of the war, not right at the beginning. De Wet, Botha, De La Rey, Beyers and yet others were true soldiers through and through who still remained firm when hope of victory among the majority had long since vanished. They would too have been the only ones who might have saved country and freedom, had this lain at all within human power. Such unshakeable steadfastness, as these men possessed, will perhaps be most necessary to us in a future war. In 1870/71 war-weariness began to be more dangerous for us in the winter campaign than the enemy.[36]

There were also moral lessons to be learned from the British, who possessed two strengths that Germany at present lacked: namely, a far-sighted and ruthless political leadership, and a people with a strong sense of national solidarity. British statesmen had shown themselves capable of "a decisive policy directed towards great positive goals, which does not let itself be satisfied by praise and the maintenance of the status quo", and in launching the war against the Boer republics, they had sensed the right moment to act:

> The American–Spanish war was cleverly used by them in order to place themselves in good relations with the American cousins, which secured them against disturbance by them. The war-shyness of continental Europe, in which the great powers maintain the balance through mutual mistrust, lay clearly before their eyes. The oriental disturbances of the nineties had clearly shown how great states, even when they are allegedly *united*, can mutually paralyse one another. From Russia, which most likely could have uttered a decisive veto, there was nothing to fear, given its ruler's love of peace. Such a moment would perhaps not return in a century, and Chamberlain and co were not only sharp-sighted enough to recognise it, but they also possessed the decisiveness to exploit it ruthlessly. Morally, this was perhaps not very prettily, certainly not very magnanimously done, but from the statesman's point of view effective.
>
> The same men also stayed firm when disappointments came, when the hoped-for easy victory failed to materialise. That was their merit.[37]

Those same statesmen had also been able to rely upon determined popular support:

> It was the merit of the English people that in its great majority, despite the manifest failings of the army and its leadership, it stood unanimously by both. Criticism of military developments was for a time really open and sharp, but so was the decision to make good the losses and employ all means to lead the campaign of conquest, once begun, to its end, whatever the cost.
>
> This self-confident, energetic patriotism or national pride can – it would be blindness to deny it – serve us as an example no less than the great human and soldierly virtues of the Boers, which we so rightly admire.[38]

This admiration, however, was balanced by a certain contempt for the British army, rooted in Goltz's conviction that armies of paid volunteers must lack the moral strength of conscript armies imbued with patriotic ideals. "England's power rests essentially on her brutal ruthlessness towards the weaker party", he had informed Pertev at the start of the war, "inwardly she is hollow, like every power which still relies upon the recruitment of volunteer troops".[39] Given that the common British soldier was recruited for the most part from among "the lowest class of the population in the great cities, in so far as it cannot find a better accommodation", and commanded by amateurish officers, the early defeats that the British had suffered at the hands of hardened and patriotic Boer farmers were hardly surprising.[40] None the less, he foresaw that "in all probability England will emerge from this war a reformed power, and in particular fundamentally improve the constitution of her defences".[41]

VI

The Turks, too, could usefully draw lessons from the South African conflict, although they were the obverse of those that Goltz wished to impress upon the Germans. The Turks had no need of ethical lessons, for they, too, were the products of a traditional, patriarchal, rural way of life, which engendered in them moral and fighting qualities identical to those of the Boers. In early 1900 Goltz cited a correspondent from Johannesburg: "The similarity which the people here bear to the Turks is really astounding – the nation as well as the leaders". He added that Turkish military history could show examples enough of successful defences against overwhelming numbers to stand beside the Boers' victories at the Modder and Tugela rivers.[42] Rather, the lessons for the Turks concerned military technique. Writing to Pertev in February 1900, Goltz declared:

> The lessons of the Boer war are really worth taking to heart and even of importance for you in Turkey. First of all the Mauser rifle proves itself excellently. Then it is shown how much a brave and prudent infantry can achieve in defence. Thus far the Boers have been in a great minority on every occasion in all their victorious battles against the English. Their strength has as yet never exceeded a quarter to a third of the English. With a few thousand men they have understood how to maintain battle positions 8–10 km long against all attacks, and in addition to seriously threaten the flanks of the attacking English through mobile units placed forwards on the sides. This might also be shown to advantage in a new Turkish war against a superior power, e.g. Russia. The terrain in Natal seems in many parts to be quite similar to that in Turkey; this creates the possibility of using similar tactics. It will however require you to successfully ensure that the Turkish infantry can be trained as capable, reliable marksmen.[43]

Marksmanship, in which the Boers excelled, was the Turks' weakness:

> The Turk is in general a good shot when hunting, but not in war. Only particular tribes, like the Albanians, the Kurds and Laz, know the handling and use of modern military firearms really well, have also a sense of their ballistic capabilities and can match trained infantry in battle; but they are exceptions.[44]

For the Turks, too, supplementary militia-type forces were entirely appropriate, for as with the Boers, their innate fighting qualities would ensure that such semi-regular formations were effective. As noted, in 1898 Goltz had responded enthusiastically to the news that the Ottoman army had decided to raise a supplementary reserve of 666 battalions, which would represent "a final contingent for the case of the battle of decision against a superior power, resembling to some extent France's 'suprême effort' in the period of Gambetta's rule". The battalions would be formed at mobilization from among men left over after other reserve units had been made up, in good part men hitherto excused from military service, and would receive little formal training and a motley crew of officers. Goltz, however, did "not doubt for a moment that much may be achieved with these troops, if it is a question of defending the soil of the fatherland". Similar scratch formations, indifferently equipped and armed, and lacking almost any training, had formed a large part of the army that had resisted the Russians so brilliantly at Plevna in 1877. The Turks' moral qualities, like those of the Boers, had made up for their deficiencies in material and training, and could be counted on to do so again.[45]

VII

Goltz's interest in the Boer War had sprung chiefly from his belief that it might serve as the trigger for a wider conflict that would pit Germany against Britain. As that belief faded, his interest in the war appears to have diminished: his surviving correspondence contains few references to the war after July 1900, and not until after its conclusion in 1902 did he again publish on the subject. His admiration for the Boers, and the moral example they had set, remained undimmed. In October 1902 he made a point of seeking out the defeated Boer generals Botha, De Wet and De La Rey when they visited Berlin. The kaiser, concerned for British sensibilities, declined to receive them.[46] Thereafter Goltz showed no further interest in South African affairs. Nonetheless, the Boer War had marked an important stage in the evolution of his ideas about world politics. His belief that the destinies of the world would increasingly be shaped outside Europe remained, and was to be reinforced by the Russo–Japanese war of 1904–5. So did his belief in the inevitability of a future "struggle for existence" between Germany and Britain; the struggle, he held, had merely been postponed, and not least because of the blindness of Germany's political leaders to the British danger. Finally, right up until his own death on active service as commander of the Ottoman 6th army in Mesopotamia in 1916, he held that the British could be fought effectively overseas by Turkish armies advancing on Egypt and India.[47]

Notes

1. For Goltz's life, career and ideas see Friedrich von der Goltz and Wolfgang Foerster, *Generalfeldmarschall Colmar Freiherr von der Goltz: Denkwürdigkeiten* (Berlin, 1929); Bernhard v. Schmiterlöw, *Aus dem Leben des Generalfeldmarschalls Freiherr v. d. Goltz Pascha: Nach Briefen an seinen Freund* (Berlin, 1926); Pertev Demirhan, *Generalfeldmarschall Colmar Freiherr von der Goltz: Das Lebensbild eines grossen Soldaten* (Göttingen, 1960); Hermann Teske, *von der Goltz, ein Kämpfer für den militärischen Fortschritt* (Göttingen, 1957); F. A. K. Yasamee, "Colmar Freiherr von der Goltz and the Rebirth of the Ottoman Empire", *Diplomacy and Statecraft* 9(2), July, 91–128 (1998).
2. Bernd F. Schulte, *Die deutsche Armee 1900–1914: Zwischen Beharren und Verändern* (Düsseldorf, 1977), p. 17.
3. His formal confirmation in these posts was even more recent, in May 1899.
4. Colmar Freiherr von der Goltz, *Léon Gambetta und seine Armeen* (Berlin, 1877); Colmar Freiherr von der Goltz, *Das Volk in Waffen*, (Berlin, 1883).
5. This point has been well made by Stig Förster, "Der deutsche Generalstab und die Illusion des kurzen Krieges 1871–1914. Metakritik eines Mythos", in *Lange und jurze Wege in den Ersten Weltkrieg: Vier Augsburger Beiträge zur Kriegsursachenforschung*, J. Burkhardt, J. Becker, S. Förster and G. Kronenbitter (Munich, 1996).
6. C. Freiherr von der Goltz, "Bilder aus der türkischen Armee VII", *Militair-Wochenblatt* 70, 7 August, 1907–12 (1897).
7. C. Freiherr von der Goltz, "Seemacht und Landkrieg", *Deutsche Rundschau* 102, January–March, 335–52 (1900).
8. Bundesarchiv-Militärarchiv Freiburg, Nachlass Colmar v. d. Goltz, NL Goltz 8, Goltz to Pertev, 14 May 1898.
9. Yasamee, "Colmar Freiherr von der Goltz".
10. Paul M. Kennedy, *The Rise of the Anglo-German Antagonism 1860–1914* (London, 1982), chs 12–13; cf., Pauline Relyea Anderson, *The Background of Anti-English Feeling in Germany, 1890–1902* (Washington, 1939); Roger Chickering, *We Men Who Feel Most German: A Cultural Study of the Pan-German League* (London, 1984).
11. C. Freiherr von der Goltz, "Was können wir aus dem Burenkrieg lernen?", *Deutsche Revue* 27(iii), August, 129–36 (1902).
12. Goltz and Foerster, *Generalfeldmarschall Colmar Freiherr von der Goltz*, pp. 220–21. It may be noted that Goltz's daughter and son-in-law were resident in Johannesburg at this time; see NL Goltz 8, Goltz to Pertev, 19 February 1900.
13. NL Goltz 8, Goltz to Pertev, 8 October 1899.
14. Goltz and Foerster, *Generalfeldmarschall Colmar Freiherr von der Goltz*, pp. 180–81, 214; NL Goltz 34, Mudra to Goltz, 22 September 1899; Bundesarchiv-Militärarchiv, Nachlass Bruno v. Mudra, NL Mudra N80-1, Goltz to Mudra, 24 September 1899, and 27 September 1899.
15. *Ibid.*, p. 221.
16. C. Freiherr von der Goltz, "Der thessalische Krieg und die türkische Armee", *Deutsche Rundschau* 24, June, 346–69 (1898); Goltz, "Bilder aus der türkischen Armee VII".
17. NL Goltz 8, Goltz to Pertev, 28 August 1898 and 3 June 1899.
18. Goltz and Foerster, *Generalfeldmarschall Colmar Freiherr von der Goltz*, p. 221.

19. Yasamee, *Colmar Freiherr von der Goltz*.
20. NL Goltz 8, Goltz to Pertev, 18 February 1900.
21. *Ibid.*, Goltz to Pertev, 5 July 1900.
22. The date of this meeting has not been traced, but it evidently took place before October 1899; see Goltz and Foerster, *Generalfeldmarschall Colmar Freiherr von der Goltz*, pp. 269, 328–9; Demirhan, *Generalfeldmarschall Colmar Freiherr von der Goltz*, p. 52; NL Mudra N80-1, Goltz to Mudra, 3 September 1908.
23. Paul M. Kennedy, "The development of German naval operations plans against England, 1896–1914", *English Historical Review* **89**, 48–76 (1974); Ivo Nikolai Lambi, *The Navy and German Power Politics, 1862–1914* (Boston, 1984), pp. 118–29.
24. Paul M. Kennedy, "German World Policy and the Alliance Negotiations with England, 1897–1900", *Journal of Modern History* **45**, 605–25 (1973); Kennedy, *The Rise of the Anglo–German Antagonism*, pp. 234ff.; Harald Rosenbach, *Das deutsche Reich, Grossbritannien und der Transvaal (1896–1902): Anfänge deutsch-britischer Entfremdung* (Göttingen, 1993), especially ch. 6.
25. Rosenbach, *Das deutsche Reich*, pp. 222ff.; Kennedy, *The Rise of the Anglo–German Antagonism*, pp. 239–40; Volker R. Berghahn, *Der Tirpitz-Plan: Genesis und Verfall einer innenpolitischen Krisenstrategie unter Wilhelm II* (Düsseldorf, 1971), pp. 205–48; Eckart Kehr, *Battleship Building and Party Politics in Germany 1894–1901* (Chicago, 1973), pp. 177–219.
26. Goltz, "Seemacht und Landkrieg".
27. Goltz, "Was können wir aus dem Burenkrieg lernen?"; Goltz, 'Seemacht und Landkrieg"; Freiherr von der Goltz, "Moralisches Heimweh", *Deutsche Revue* **28**(i), January, 1–6 (1903); Goltz and Foerster, *Generalfeldmarschall Colmar Freiherr von der Goltz*, p. 249.
28. The surviving Goltz papers contain a draft memorandum or article concerning the lessons that the Boer War might have for a future European war. The draft is incomplete and unsigned, and it is not certain that Goltz was the author. Its arguments are similar to those in Goltz's published articles on the subject; NL Goltz 2, "Was ist aus den Kämpfen in Südafrika für einen europäischen Krieg zu lernen".
29. C. Freiherr von der Goltz, "Türkische Armeereformen und der Burenkrieg", *Militär-Wochenblatt* **13**, 3 February, 313–20 (1900).
30. Martin Kitchen, *The German Officer Corps 1890–1914* (Oxford, 1968), p. 144.
31. Goltz, "Türkische Armeereformen und der Burenkrieg".
32. Goltz, "Was können wir aus dem Burenkriege lernen?"
33. *Ibid.*; Goltz, "Moralisches Heimweh"; Goltz and Foerster, *Generalfeldmarschall Colmar Freiherr von der Goltz*, p. 249.
34. Goltz, "Was können wir aus dem Burenkrieg lernen?"
35. Goltz, "Türkische Armeereformen und der Burenkrieg".
36. Goltz, "Was können wir aus dem Burenkrieg lernen?"
37. *Ibid.*
38. *Ibid.*
39. NL Goltz 8, Goltz to Pertev, 8 October 1899.
40. Goltz, "Türkische Armeereformen und der Burenkrieg".
41. Goltz, "Seemacht und Landkrieg".
42. Goltz, "Türkische Armeereformen und der Burenkrieg".
43. NL Goltz 8, Goltz to Pertev, 18 February 1900.
44. Goltz, "Türkische Armeereformen und der Burenkrieg".
45. *Ibid.*
46. For this episode see Goltz and Foerster, *Generalfeldmarschall Colmar Freiherr von der Goltz*, p. 249; cf., Rosenbach, *Das deutsche Reich*, pp. 298ff.; Anderson, *The Background of Anti-English Feeling*, pp. 340–42.
47. Yasamee, "Colmar Freiherr von der Goltz".

Index

Undergraduate Lending Library WITHDRAWN